TACTICAL ESPIONAGE ACTION

METAL GEAR SOLID 2
SUBSTANCE
TABLE OF CONTENTS

MW00783288

Solid Tactics		2
Weapons		14
Items and Equipment		16
Mission Analysis		18
Part 1:	**Tanker**	18
	Aft Deck	18
	Deck-A-	21
	Deck-B-	24
	Deck-C-	25
	Deck-D-	26
	Deck-E, The Bridge	28
	Navigational Deck-	29
	Deck-E, The Bridge	30
	Deck-D-	30
	Deck-C-	31
	Deck-B-	31
	Deck-A-	32
	Engine Room -	32
	Deck-2, Port	36
	Deck-2, Starboard	38
	Cargo Holds 1,2, and 3	39
Part 2:	**Plant-**	44
	Mission 01: Reconaissance	45
	Mission 02: Bomb Disposal	53
	Mission 03: Hostage Situation	72
	Mission 04: The Crossing	83
	Mission 05: Presidential Rescue	90
	Mission 06: The Child Genius	92
	Mission 07: Deliver the Disk-	99
	Mission 08: Arsenal Gear -	101
	Mission 09: Sons of Liberty	108
Missions Basics		109
	Sneaking	
	Sneaking-	114
	Eliminate All -	120
	Weapon Mode -	127
	Handgun-	127
	Assault Rifle-	129
	C4/Claymore	132
	Grenade -	134
	PSG1	136
	Stinger -	138
	Nikita	140
	HF Blade & No Weapon	143
	First Person Mode-	145
	Variety Mode-	148
	Streaking Mode-	153
ALTERNATIVE Missions		154
	Bomb Disposal	154
	Eliminate-	160
	Hold Up	164
	Photograph	168
SNAKE Tales		173
Secrets and Bonuses-		176
Dog **Tag** Checklist-		179
CHARACTERS		183

SOLID TACTICS

Any top-level operative must understand the basics of infiltration, as well as more advanced survival tactics. This briefing is designed to unify the methods and terminology of field agents at various levels.

BASIC CONTROLS (DEFAULT SCHEME)

CONTROL	FUNCTION
Left stick/D-pad	Movement/First Person View control/Menu choice
Press left stick	Toggle First Person View
Right stick	Adjust camera in Corner View/Blade attacks
BACK	Codec menu
START	Pause game/Big shell map
⬤	Toggle crouch position or standing position/Roll
⬤	Punch/Knock on wall/Swim
⬤	Use weapon/Throw or choke enemy
⬤	Action button (various uses)
⬤	Vent peek inside a locker
R	Weapon menu—Tap to equip or unequip last weapon
L	Item menu—Tap to equip or unequip last item

Controller Flexibility

At various times and during the mission, the operative's controller buttons will take on different functions, depending on the type of environment the agent must infiltrate, what items are being used, and which weapon is equipped. For details on weapon- and item-specific controls, please turn to the appropriate chapters.

DIFFICULTY LEVEL

When beginning a game of *Metal Gear Solid 2*, there are four choices of difficulty level. After the game has been "cleared," Extreme or European Extreme Difficulties become available.

Very Easy

This mode is the choice for players who are unfamiliar with the action genre. The fewest number of enemies are present, patrolling guards move and turn more slowly, and the various alert modes last for much shorter periods of time. Your character can carry vast quantities of items and ammunition. During the "Plant" chapter, all maps for the Big Shell are downloaded from the first local network Node. There is no need to download the map for every level. Boss enemies take greater damage from the player's attacks, and your character receives less damage from enemies.

Easy

This mode is designed for players familiar with action games who just haven't played Konami's *Metal Gear* series games before. Compared to Very Easy mode, a few more enemies are present. Slightly fewer items and quantities of ammunition can be carried. During the "Plant" chapter, each level's map has to be downloaded from the local network Node. Boss enemies are slightly tougher.

Normal

This is the mode at which *Metal Gear Solid 2* is meant to be played. Designed for veterans of the *Metal Gear* series of games. Virtually each small area has an enemy on patrol. Boss enemies are at their regular strengths and weaknesses. New items can be unlocked by completing a game in Normal difficulty.

Hard

For players who have cleared the full game, are familiar with the layout and patrols of each area, and are looking for more of a challenge. More enemies are encountered, areas are patrolled more quickly, and patrol routes are less predictable. Enemies have a wider and longer cone of vision.

Extreme

Becomes available after any other difficulty level is cleared. Most areas have too many enemies to sneak past. Your character can carry only one of each item and one clip of ammunition for each weapon. For die-hard gamers who aren't frustrated easily.

Game Over When Discovered

On Hard and Extreme difficulty levels, there is an extra option to end the game whenever your character is discovered. Since death is nearly inevitable if detected in either of these modes, you can avoid the hassle of attempting to fight your way clear.

MOVEMENT

Like many other buttons, the character movement control is pressure-sensitive. The operative must have a steady hand and a gentle touch when necessary. By pressing the Left Stick or Digital Pad in any direction, the character moves in that direction. When the Left Stick is pressed to its extent of motion, the character will run. Pressing the Left Stick just slightly in the desired direction causes the character to "sneak."

"Sneaking"

The object of *Metal Gear Solid 2* is to infiltrate deep into enemy territory, unseen and undetected. If the character runs over iron gratings, down stairs, or across other areas where his footsteps can be heard, the sound may alert guards to the intruder's presence. To pass unheard, use the "sneak" method to move over gratings and other tricky areas by pressing the Left Analog Stick very lightly. Another way to move across gratings and other hazardous floor areas quietly is by crouching and crawling across them.

will think twice about their nuclear strategy

Crouching

While standing still, press  and the character will crouch. This position is useful for hiding behind low crates and other waist-high obstacles, to hide from enemy patrols, or to see better around corners or behind boxes. From this position, use the movement control to enter crawling position.

Crawling

When the character is crouching, press the movement control in any direction to make the character flatten out on the ground. The character will crawl across the ground on his stomach in the direction you press. To turn the character, rotate the Left Stick in a new direction. Crawling is useful for entering vents, moving under obstructions, and for silently crossing floor areas where the character might make noise. Press ⭘ to make the charcter stand upright.

Rolling

While moving across an area, press ⭘ and the character will initiate a roll. Each character's roll move is different. Solid Snake dives across the ground and performs a somersault. Raiden leaps foot over foot in a sort of torso-axial flip. Executed precisely, a roll may be used to dive from one corner across an open space to another corner without being seen. A roll can also knock an enemy down. But, if the enemy has already spotted the intruder, there is a better chance that the soldier will kick the character to defend against this form of attack. Raiden's torso-axial flip can also be used to jump over short gaps and to leap quickly down flights of stairs.

Swimming

When the character dives into water, the control scheme shifts to swimming mode. After the character dives or walks into the water, he will surface and tread water. While the character is on the surface, press the movement control to make him stroke across the water in the direction you desire. Press ⭘ , and the character will dive underwater.

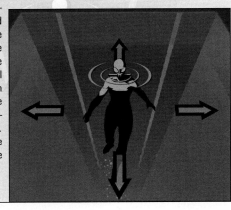

When underwater, press ⭘ to swim forward. While stroking through the water, press the movement control upward to make the character swim toward the surface. Press down to make the character swim deeper, and press left or right to make the character turn. Use the Right Stick to make the character perform hard turns and flips underwater. Press left or right on the Right Stick, and the character will turn 90° left or right. Press downward on the Right Stick, and the character will flip under himself to do a 180° turn.

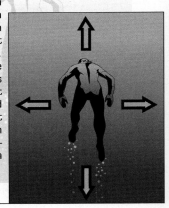

O2 Gauge

While underwater, the character's **O2 Gauge** will be displayed. The O2 Gauge is a reading of how much oxygen is left in the character's lungs. While underwater, the O2 Gauge decreases. If the character's Life Meter is not full, the O2 Gauge will decrease more rapidly. When the O2 Gauge drops to zero, the character's life will begin to decrease. At the beginning of the "Plant" chapter, Raiden is equipped with a deep-sea diving mask that elongates the O2 Gauge. When the mask is removed, the O2 Gauge will be reduced to the normal level 1 length. The O2 Gauge can be lengthened and increased in level by swimming often and exercising underwater. While swimming underwater, press the Action button (🔘) to make the O2 Gauge last longer. The more you press the Action button whenever you are underwater, the more likely that the O2 Gauge will be lengthened or "leveled up."

Quick Turns Underwater

Aside from using the Right Stick to make quick turns underwater, you can also make quick turns by entering First Person View mode. Rotate the First Person View to the new direction of travel, and when you release the Right trigger button, your character will be facing that direction and ready to swim that way.

HIDING

Since *Metal Gear Solid 2* emphasizes the need to move through areas undetected, hiding from enemies is a major factor in game play. The character can hide behind any object or environmental feature that the enemy cannot see through. This includes walls, crates, and boxes. Characters can even hide from enemies by hanging under railings as guards pass on the platform overhead. Hiding well is a skill for any player to develop in order to master the game.

Pressing Against a Wall

Enemies cannot see through walls and boxes, so if you stand just around the corner from a guard, he cannot see you. However, there is a more advantageous way to hide. Move toward any wall, and the character will turn and press his back against it. While his back is pressed against a wall near a corner, the camera angles out in front of the character. From this angle, the player is capable of seeing the area and any guards around the corner from the character. A guard is not likely to spot a character hiding behind a corner or behind a crate when his back is pressed up against it.

While the character's back is pressed against a flat surface, press ⬤ to crouch. This enables the character to hide behind low, waist-high objects, such as low walls and boxes.

Side-Stepping

When the character's back is pressed against a surface, he can "side-step" left or right along the surface by angling the Movement control slightly left or right. The side-step can also be achieved by pressing the Right or Left trigger button the while pressed up against a wall.

The side-step is an extremely useful action. The player can use the side-step to move the character closer to the next corner, to angle-out the camera in order to see the next area. The side-step move can also be used to cross extremely thin ledges. While pressed up against a surface, press ⬤ to crouch. The character can "crouch-step" to the left or right in the same fashion as side-stepping.

Corner View & Peeking

While the character's back is pressed up against a wall near a corner, the player can see the area around the corner. To get a better view of the area beyond the corner, press either trigger button while in Corner View in order to "peek" around the corner. The character will lean out and look at the area around the corner. While in this position, move the Right Stick to adjust the camera angle. Peeking is extremely useful when the player has opted not to use the Radar. But be cautious, because if an enemy spots your character peeking, they might sound an alarm and radio for help.

Knocking on Walls

Sometimes it is possible to "bait" an enemy into leaving his regular patrol route and moving into a more desirable position by creating a noise. To create a noise by "knocking," press the character's back against a wall or a flat surface. Then press ⬤ to knock. When the enemy is in a range equal to twice the length of his cone of vision, he will hear the knock and will move to investigate.

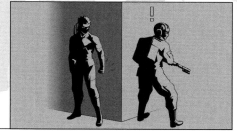

Hiding in Lockers

If the character has been spotted, and the guard is moving in to investigate, you must quickly find a place to hide your character from view. One of the best hiding spots is inside a locker. To open a locker, face it and press the Action button (). To hide in a locker, move inside and the character will shut the door behind him. While hiding in a locker, the camera switches to "Intrusion Mode." In this forced First Person View, the character can see through the vents in the top of the locker. Press the Right trigger button, and the character will peek through the vents more closely. But don't press the button too hard, or your character will bang his head against the door! During a "clearing," which is detailed later in this chapter, it is unwise to peek through the vents to see what soldiers are doing outside. If one of the guards happens to shine a light through the vents, he will spot you in the locker! The character can crouch inside a locker by pressing  . This is a safe way to hide in a locker and not get spotted through the vents.

Also, useful items are sometimes stowed in lockers. Some lockers are locked, but they can be broken into by punching the locker. If the door falls inward, then there is no item hidden in the locked compartment. But if the door falls outward, then you have most likely found a secret item! However, avoid falling locker doors.

CAMERA BASICS

Controlling the camera angle is important in *Metal Gear Solid 2*. The regular view in the game is a top-down, overhead view. Very little in front of or behind the character is visible in this angle, so it's good to learn some basic camera-using techniques. Move from corner to corner, hiding and using Corner View to scope out the next area before moving on. Unless you know for certain that you have a clear run at the next section of an area, try to stay out of the top-down view as much as possible.

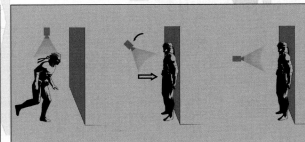

Move to a wall or flat-surfaced object and press the character's back against it in order to angle-out the camera for a better view. Use this function not only to hide, but to study the layout of areas and memorize the patrol patterns and timing of guards. Also, make regular use of the First Person View mode to see an entire area from the character's perspective.

First Person View

Press the Left Stick to enter First Person View. The camera angle shifts to the character's perspective, so that you are seeing through his eyes. First Person View is a much more flexible control option in *Metal Gear Solid 2*. While in First Person View, you can press  to crouch. Press the Left and Right trigger to strafe a step left or right. The strafe can be used to peek very quickly around corners and to dodge enemy fire. The character will stand on his tiptoes if you press both trigger buttons while in First Person, allowing you to see and aim over high obstacles.

Your character can fight in First Person View if you press the Attack () button. Entering First Person prevents the character from moving, so it is usually better to stay in Third Person perspective when dealing with a boss, an attack team, or other enemies. But First Person is excellent for aiming shots at unsuspecting guards, because the point of impact on a target determines what kind of damage you'll inflict on an enemy. First Person is essential for aiming tranquilizer darts at guards, because a tranquilizer fired at the head will put a guard to sleep instantly.

Intrusion Mode

When the character crawls into a vent or hides inside a locker, the camera view automatically shifts to "Intrusion Mode." This is a sort of forced First Person View. If Radar Type 2 is in use, the Soliton Radar display will disappear when the character crawls into a vent or hides in a locker. For this reason, it is easier to use Radar Type 1 so that the Soliton display does not disappear while you are hiding in lockers and crawling through vents. You don't want to crawl out of a vent while a soldier is watching!

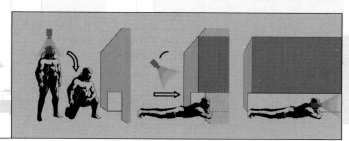

ACTION BUTTON COMMANDS

The Action button (⊙) has various functions, depending on what the character is facing. The Action button also gains temporary functions during certain events in the course of the mission.

Opening Doors

One of the first functions of the Action button to be explained in the game is opening watertight doors on the Tanker. When facing a watertight door, press ⊙ and the character will start to turn the handle on the door. Tap the Action button rapidly to open the door more quickly. If enemies have spotted the character, they will shoot him each time he tries to open a watertight door.

Calling Elevators

Face the call button beside an elevator and press ⊙ to summon it. An elevator may take some time to arrive at your level. To make the elevator come more quickly, press the Action button twice in a row.

Climbing Ladders

Face a ladder and press ⊙ . The character will climb onto the ladder. Then press the Movement control up or down to ascend or descend the ladder. If you reach a level and want to get off, stop and press the Movement control left or right to step off the ladder.

Climbing Onto Obstacles

The character can climb onto any waist-high surface by pressing the Action button. Use this to hop over obstacles in order to reach areas that you otherwise could not access.

Hanging From a Railing

As you face a railing on the edge of a platform or walkway, press ⊙ . The character will hop over the rail and hang from the edge on the other side. While the character hangs, he can shimmy along the rail left or right by pressing the Movement control. Press ⊙ to hop back over the rail onto the platform, or press ⊙ to drop from the rail to the level below.

Grip Gauge

While the character hangs from a rail, the Grip Gauge is displayed. The Grip Gauge will gradually decrease as the character hangs. If the character's Life Meter is not full, the Grip Gauge decreases more rapidly. If the character is still hanging from the rail when the Grip Gauge reaches zero, the character falls. If that happens, hopefully there is a platform not far below to break your fall.

The Grip Gauge is lengthened just slightly after each successful hang. In order to increase the level of the Grip Gauge, the character must "work out." As you hang from an edge, press both trigger buttons together to do chin-ups. After doing a certain amount of chin-ups, the Grip Gauge's level will increase—pretty cool! A leveled-up Grip Gauge can come in handy in several areas, including the Tanker's Engine Room and Cargo Holds.

Using a Node

During the "Plant" chapter, Raiden must download the map of each level from the local area network Node. He will not be able to use his Soliton Radar to survey the area or scout patrol positions until the map is downloaded. To use a Node, face it or press Raiden's back against it and press the Action button ().

Nodes can also be used at any time to access the Options menu in order to change the game settings.

Guiding Emma

During a certain time late in the game, Raiden must lead a drugged and weary Emma Emmerich through the Shell 2 Core. In order to lead Emma, press and hold 🔘 until she takes Raiden's hand. Then lead Emma through the enemy territory using the Movement control, keeping your finger firmly pressed on 🔘 .

While Emma accompanies Raiden, she is his "life partner." Her Life Meter appears on screen and if she dies, then the game ends. If Emma's Life Meter is low, let go of her and let her sit down for a while. Her Life Meter will gradually recuperate while she is seated.

Stubborn Emma

Sometimes Emma will refuse to cross an area. Will you spend time removing the obstacle, or should you just punch Emma until she falls unconscious and drag her?

ATTACKING

Infiltration and espionage are not the only tools at an agent's disposal. Wetworks are not recommended, but sometimes yours is a dirty job.

Using a Weapon

In order to equip any weapon located in your weapons inventory, hold the Right trigger button and use the Left Stick to scroll through the armaments you've acquired. To fire, throw, or place the weapon (depending on its intended use), press and release the Attack button (🔘). The effect of each weapon

When the Attack button is pressed, the character turns to face the nearest target. The shot is not aimed at any specific body part, but at the enemy as a whole. To aim a shot at an enemy's specific body part using a handgun, go into First Person Mode and hold 🔘 . The character will auto-face the enemy and aim at his midsection. From there, adjust your aim with the Left Stick or Digital Pad. When you release the button, the weapon will fire. Shots to an enemy's hands or shoulders will disable their arms and can prevent them from firing. Shots to the legs will prevent a guard from chasing you. Shots to the neck or head will kill instantly. If you are using a tranquilizer weapon, the drug will take effect more swiftly if you fire a shot at the enemy's head. If you shoot out the radio on an enemy's belt, he will not be able to radio for help or arouse suspicion.

For weapon-specific instructions and tips, refer to the Weapons chapter.

Throwing

When a character does not have a weapon equipped, he can grab and throw an enemy. If the enemy hits a wall or other object head-first, he could be knocked unconscious. To throw an enemy, run at the opponent barehanded and hit  at the proper instant. Enemies that are knocked out will be unconscious for only a short time, but you might be able to shake their Dog Tags out of them.

Choking

Without a weapon equipped, the character can grab an enemy in a headlock and choke him until he passes out. To execute this, sneak up behind a stationary enemy as close as possible without touching him. Stop just behind the vulnerable guard. Then press and hold the Attack button (), and the character will grab the enemy in a chokehold.

After grabbing an enemy in a stranglehold, tap the Attack button rapidly, and your character will snap the enemy's neck.

After an enemy has been in a headlock for some time, he will pass out and slip out of your character's grip. Stars swirling around the enemy's head indicate that he is temporarily unconscious. The enemy can be disposed of, hidden, or "shaken down" for useful items and possibly even his Dog Tags.

With an enemy in a headlock, you can drag him with you some distance. If an enemy begins to struggle in your character's grip, tap once or twice and then resume holding the button to choke him back into submission.

The Human Shield

A difficult maneuver to pull off, it is possible to grab an enemy and use him as a human shield against other enemies. When facing an attack team, if you can grab one of them and drag him away, the other soldiers will hesitate to fire.

Dragging

Once an enemy has been knocked out or tranquilized, you should drag the body out of sight and hide it in a safe location. If another enemy sees a guard's dead body, he will immediately call in an attack team and the area will be thoroughly searched. If an enemy finds a guard who has been knocked out or tranquilized, he will kick that enemy to wake him up. This is why tranquilizing an enemy is much safer than killing him.

To drag an unconscious or dead enemy, stand at his head or feet and press  . Without a weapon equipped, your character will pick up the guard and drag him wherever you wish using the Movement control.

Disposal Gates

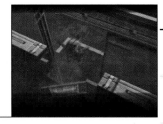

Drag an unconscious or dead enemy to a disposal gate or a hole in the floor, and your character will toss the body into the waters below. Disposal gates are located on either side of the Tanker's Aft Deck, and in Strut D of the Big Shell. There are other locations where you can dispose of bodies by similar means.

"Shaking Down" Enemies

After rendering an enemy unconscious or dead, it is possible to "shake" useful items out of the enemy's body. Stand at the head or feet of a prone enemy and pick him up by pressing 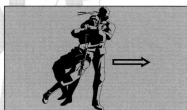 . Keep picking him up and dropping him until an item comes loose. If you aren't having any luck, move to the other side of the body and pick him up from there. Enemies that are unconscious are easier to shake down than enemies that are dead.

Hiding Bodies

As mentioned previously, it is very important to hide unconscious bodies. If another guard spots an unconscious soldier, he will kick him awake, and you will be forced to start over with whatever strategy you were about to attempt. This could lead to some compromising situations. However, if a guard finds a *dead* body, he will immediately call in backup support. An attack team will begin searching the area for your character. Also, if you execute a guard in a highly-traveled area, his blood will cover the floor. If another guard spots a bloodstain, he will also call in an attack team.

The best method is to tranquilize guards and quickly drag them to out of the way locations. Hide them behind low walls or obstructions where they won't be seen. If you're going to remain in an area for a while and absolutely must kill a guard, do it someplace where the mess won't be seen.

The best place to hide a guard is inside a locker. Drag a guard into an open locker, and your character will stand the body inside the compartment and close the door. Guards that are hidden in lockers will be less likely to wake up as quickly as they normally would.

Punching and Kicking

To execute punches and kicks, press ●. Your character will perform a combination of two punches followed by one or two kicks, depending on how many times and how rapidly you press the button. The best time to use punches and kicks against an enemy is when he has spotted you at extremely close range. If you can knock the guard out before he gets a chance to call for help, the Alert will be canceled and you'll still be safe.

Jump-Out Shot

The Jump-Out Shot is an exciting new feature in *Metal Gear Solid 2*. While standing at a corner with your back pressed against a wall or flat surface, press the Attack button (●), and your character will step around the corner and aim his gun at the closest enemy. If the enemy is standing with his back to the corner, the Jump-Out Shot will allow you to get the drop on the guard and possibly hold him up for his Dog Tags or other useful items.

The Jump-Out Shot works wonders in tense combat situations when your character is outnumbered. Hide around the corner from an attack team, then jump out and fire. When your character has finished the attack, he will step back behind the safety of the corner. Any time you find yourself unable to escape from an attack team, this is the tactic to use.

The Jump-Out Shot also works from a crouch position behind a wall. A variation allows you to throw grenades from the safety of the corner, without risking exposure.

Throwing Grenades from Corners

This is a great way to throw grenades without risking exposure to enemy fire. With the character's back pressed against a wall or object, equip grenades and press the trigger buttons to peek around the corner. The character will shift the grenade to the appropriate hand. Then press and hold ● before releasing it. The longer you hold the button, the farther your character will throw the grenade. Don't hold it forever though, or your character might blow off his own hand!

Blade Attacks

Late in the game, Raiden acquires a High Frequency Blade. Press the Attack button (●) to switch between Edged style (red) and Blunt style (blue). In Edged style, hits with the Blade will kill an enemy or reduce a boss's Life Meter. Hits with the Blunt Blade will knock out an enemy or reduce a boss's purple Stun Gauge. Both styles are important. Press ●, and Raiden will defend with the sword, auto-face the enemy, and even deflect bullets just like the Cyborg Ninja!

Controlling the Blade takes a certain amount of self-control. The weapon is controlled with the Right Stick. Pressing the stick up and down causes Raiden to perform uppercuts and chops. These are most effective when an enemy is attempting to defend his midsection. Don't panic and wildly press the Right Stick in every direction. Calmly think about what you are doing and press the stick, measuring each slash and the damage it does to your foe.

Pressing the Right Stick left and right commands Raiden to swing the sword back and forth. These attacks are most effective when an enemy seems to be defending or attacking from up high or down low.

Rotate the Right Stick 360°, and Raiden will perform a spin-slash. This move damages enemies in all directions, and is most effective when Raiden is surrounded.

To thrust forward with the sword, press down on the Right Stick as you would a button so that it clicks. Raiden will step out and jab the sword into his enemy. This is an excellent attack for cutting enemies from just outside their range. However, it does little damage and is more effective when combined with a series of slashes and chops.

Attack Block Extreme

The most important tip to remember about the High Frequency Blade is to keep your finger on the ⊙ button whenever you are not attacking. Always be ready to deflect attacks and bullets. You can also move while defending, so use this to get in close to an enemy before hacking him up!

Bleeding

When your character's Life Meter has been reduced to one fourth or less, the meter will turn reddish orange. This indicates that your character is suffering severe blood loss. The Life Meter will gradually decrease on its own until it runs dry. At that point, the next hit that your character takes will kill him. The worst part is that while he is bleeding, your character will drip blood on the floor everywhere he goes. As you try to avoid enemies, the trail of blood will lead the terrorists to your character's location. You can stop bleeding by applying a Bandage, but you will not recover health unless you use a Ration.

Another way for Raiden to stop his bleeding and recover a small amount of health is to lay flat on the floor for a time. Remaining still, the nanomachines in Raiden's blood will coagulate the blood around his wound and repair damaged tissue.

Using Rations

Rations will restore some amount of health, returning the Life Meter to its full length. To use Rations, press the Left trigger button and select them in the Left Item Menu. Press ⊙ while the menu is open to use a Ration.

During boss fights, it is wise to equip the Rations in the left item menu and keep them handy. With the Rations equipped, a Ration will be used automatically if your character's life is reduced to zero.

MENU BASICS

Your inventory menus are controlled with the Left and Right trigger buttons. The menu on the left is the Item Menu where key cards, Rations, electronic sensors and other useful equipment is stored. Hold the Left trigger button and scroll through the items with the Movement control. When you select an item, it remains in the lower-left corner of the screen to show that it is in use. To unequip the item, tap the Left trigger button. Press the Left trigger button again to equip the last item again quickly.

The right Weapons Menu is controlled with the Right trigger button. This menu features items that are visibly equipped in your character's hands, so not all of them are weapons. To equip a weapon, hold the Right trigger button and scroll through the items with the Movement control. When the item is equipped, the icon remains displayed in the lower-right corner of the screen. To unequip a weapon, tap the Right trigger button. Quickly tap the button again to equip the last weapon once more.

In the Options menu, the inventory can be made to group items by type or to display each item in its own slot, similar to the menu setup of the last *Metal Gear Solid* game.

RADAR BASICS

Beginning a game of *Metal Gear Solid 2*, the player is offered three Radar options. Two of the oprions determine if the Soliton Radar is displayed during Intrusion Mode or not, and there is also the option to navigate without any Radar display whatsoever. Navigating without the aid of the Soliton Radar is recommended only for expert players who have memorixed the locations in the game.

Type 1 Radar

The Soliton Radar functions exactly like it did in the previous game. Your character's position and the positions of enemies are tracked in the Radar display in the upper-right corner of the screen. The radar stays on when your character is inside a locker or a vent. This is the easiest and most advantageous type of Radar to use.

Type 2 Radar

The Radar is invisible when your character is inside a locker or a vent. The display may also disappear during Caution Mode in certain areas of the game.

Electronic Jamming

The Radar will not display when electronic interference is present. Interference can be caused by equipment or high voltage electricity in the area. The detonation of a Chaff Grenade also causes Jamming. While Jamming is in effect, your character also cannot use remote control missiles, lock-on Stinger missiles, or C4 with a remote detonator. But the electronic interference also invalidates the enemy's equipment. Guards cannot radio for help, surveillance cameras cannot function, and guided missiles cannot be targeted at your character.

ALERT MODES

The *Metal Gear Solid 2* instruction manual discusses the various Alert Modes in detail. Knowing the situation of each mode is essential to survival.

An "Investigation"

In certain areas, one of the guards is required to radio in a status report every few minutes. If the guard does not radio in, an investigation is ordered. During an investigation, other guards in the area will search for the guard who is missing. If no other guards are in the area to carry out the search, then additional guards may be dispatched to the area to find out what is going on.

An investigation can be avoided by leaving an area just before the commander finishes giving the order to investigate. This will cancel out the investigation. Then you can return to the area immediately and have a few more minutes to finish your business before the next demand for a status report comes over the radio.

A "Clearing"

When a guard has spotted your character, it's time to hide. If your character hides in the same area where the guard spotted him, then an attack team is called in to search the area. The room-to-room search that takes place is called a "clearing." While a clearing is in effect, the player will notice the movement of the attack team is displayed in the window where the Soliton Radar is normally shown.

During a clearing, guards may also search in lockers and other areas that can conceal your presence if they believe that is where you are hiding. If your character is hiding in a locker, it is always safer to crouch inside just in case the guard looks through the vents.

Cancelling an Alarm

When your character is spotted, there are still ways to cancel an alarm before it occurs. When the guard is using the radio to call for assistance, use First Person View to aim at and shoot the device in is hand. If the guard gets to say a few words before the radio shorts out, an investigation team will be sent. But if you can tranquilize the guard and escape to the next area before the team is dispatched, the investigation will never take place. Then you can return to the area immediately and continue your business.

If the game enters Alert Mode, where guards have spotted your character and are attacking, you can cancel this mode by escaping through a door to another area. The alarm status will be downgraded to Evasion Mode, and the game enters Caution Mode soon thereafter. If you move from one area to the next while Caution Mode is in effect, the alarm will be ineffective in the next area.

DOG TAGS

Most of the guards that patrol areas of the game are carrying a set of Dog Tags, which can be taken from them by force. Collecting every Dog Tag in the game is a key element to unlocking secret items for use in your next game. To see if a guard is wearing Dog Tags, tranquilize or knock out the soldier and use the Thermal Goggles to view his neck area. The Camera and Digital Camera will show that you have already collected Dog Tags from a solider. More on this feature is discussed in the Items and Equipment chapter.

Capturing a Guard

The surest way to collect a guard's Dog Tags is to capture the guard by getting the drop on him from behind. If the player can determine a way to sneak up on the guard from behind and aim a handgun at the enemy, your character will yell "FREEZE!" and the guard will raise his hands in surrender. Once a guard is captured, gently release the Attack button and move directly in front of him. From this position, you can threaten an enemy and make him offer up the tags.

Coercing Dog Tags From an Enemy

After you have captured an enemy, and no other sentries are nearby, move directly in front of the arrested soldier and press Attack to aim the handgun at him again. Then enter First Person View and aim the weapon at the guard's head or crotch area. The guard will beg for mercy and should soon shake out his Dog Tags. Then shoot the guard and collect the tags.

Some guards will resist capture, taunting your character. These soldiers must be threatened by firing a loud warning shot at their feet or past their head. Equipping a heavy artillery weapon, such as the Stinger, the Nikita or the RGB6 will cause any guard to offer up the tags immediately, without having to aim at his body parts. If the guard does not respond to warning shots, or if the SOCOM pistol has been equipped with a suppressor, shoot one of the guard's hands or legs. Then he'll beg for mercy and offer his tags.

If you do not have strong enough firepower to threaten a guard, tranquilize him and try again later. If you stand in front of a taunting guard for too long, a twinkle appears in the soldier's eyes and he will attempt to overthrow your character!

Knocking Out a Guard

Another way to acquire Dog Tags from a guard is by knocking him unconscious. An enemy sentry can be knocked out by punching and kicking him, by throwing him, or by choking him until he passes out. A guard is shown to be knocked out when small stars circle around the guard's head. Being knocked out lasts for a much shorter time than tranquilized sleep. While the guard is unconscious, you can shake down his body for useful items. With some luck, the guard's Dog Tags will be dropped. This method is more risky than using the capture approach, and the chances of shaking out the guard's tags are slim.

Dog Tags and Difficulty Modes

Depending on which Difficulty Mode you select, there are fewer or more guards patrolling the various areas. This means that there are *fewer* Dog Tags to collect in easier modes and *more* tags to collect in harder modes! After completing the full game, use the Dog Tag Viewer to see which tags have been collected and which remain to be taken. Highlight any empty space to see which area the missing guard is patrolling. Also, you can use the Dog Tag Viewer in advance to see where new guards will be posted in Hard Mode and Extreme Mode.

Item-Specific Tips

You will find that this guide is generally crammed from cover to cover with helpful tips and fun strategies to try in *Metal Gear Solid 2*. For some interesting tips on various uses of items and weapons, some of which you may not have considered, read the Weapons chapter and the Items and Equipment chapter.

WEAPONS

Infiltrating enemy territory requires an unarmed insertion. All weapons must be acquired OSP (On-Site Procurement). Each weapon has a different use and attack method, and so the Attack button ( ) functions differently for each item. Also, some weapons have alternative uses that you might not have considered

M9 Tranquilizer Gun

An M92F customized to fire tranquilizer darts, equipped with a suppressor and laser sighting. Press to aim, release button to fire. Releasing the Attack button slowly will cause the character to lower the weapon without firing. Shots to the head or heart knock out the subject quickly, while shots to the feet or hands knock out the subject more slowly. Can also be used to shoot out lights.

USP Pistol

A Russian 9mm handgun with laser sighting and a flashlight mounted under the barrel. Not usable with a suppressor, so noise is a factor. Press to aim, release button to fire. Releasing the Attack button slowly will cause the character to lower the weapon without firing. In dark sections, the flashlight will come on when the weapon is aimed. The light may alert nearby patrols. In combat situations, the light may temporarily blind enemy soldiers at close range. Can be used to destroy electronic equipment, such as surveillance cameras and C4 control boxes.

SOCOM Pistol

A lightweight handgun perfect for infiltration ops, with laser sighting. A suppressor can be attached to muffle gunshot noise. Press to aim weapon, release button to fire. Releasing the Attack button slowly will cause the character to lower the weapon without firing. Can be used to destroy cameras and C4 control boxes. Target enemy hands to negate firing abilities, and shoot guards in the legs to prevent them from pursuing you.

M4 Semi-Automatic

A heavy machinegun for use during intense combat sections against large squadrons. Uses laser sighting. Press lightly to aim, press firmly to fire. Gun continues to fire as long as button is pressed, until clip magazine empties. Short bursts will destroy Cyphers and Gun Cameras. Continuous fire will destroy attack team riot shields. Character adjusts aim up or down to shoot high or low targets. You can also center target in First Person View, and the character will shoot the object.

AKS-74u Assault Rifle

A lightweight and versatile assault version of the standard AK-74, the favorite weapon of small armies around the world. Uses laser sighting, and can be equipped with a suppressor to muffle gunshot sounds. Press lightly to aim, press firmly to fire. Gun fires in 10-round bursts. Will destroy most objects and defenses, same as the M4. Required in order to pose as a terrorist with the Body Disguise Uniform (B.D.U.).

PSG-1 Sniper Rifle

A compact, long-range sniper weapon with zooming scope sighting and a standard crosshair aim. When equipped, character enters First Person View, looking through the scope. Press to zoom in, to zoom out. Aim can be steadied by ingesting Pentazemin and/or laying down on the ground. Press to fire. The noise cannot be muzzled, so attack from long range. Zooming in closer to your target helps insure a direct hit. Target specific body parts to disable their function, or target the head for a one-shot kill. Can also be used to eliminate C4 control boxes, surveillance equipment, Gun Cameras, and Cyphers. Use in conjunction with Thermal Goggles to spot Claymores, enemy soldiers, and other targets in dark areas.

PSG-1T Tranquilizer Rifle

A customized version of the PSG-1 modified to fire tranquilizer darts instead of standard rifle rounds. Equipped with a silencer to muzzle gunshot noise. Target the head or heart to put the subject to sleep more quickly. Can also be used to destroy lights. When equipped, character enters First Person View, looking through the scope. Press to zoom in, to zoom out. Aim can be steadied by ingesting Pentazemin. Press to fire.

Chaff Grenades

A silent, non-fragmenting, timed explosive that spreads a cloud of tiny metallic pieces, disrupting any electronic equipment in the area. Surveillance cameras, Gun Cameras, Cyphers, Gun Cyphers, enemy soldier radios, and mobile target lock-on tracking can be jammed by the use of a Chaff Grenade. However, the effect also negates usage of the Soliton Radar. Equip and press to throw. Hold the Attack button before releasing in order to increase the distance thrown. Can be thrown by peeking out from behind a corner.

Stun Grenades

Also known as a "flash-bang" grenade, this non-fragmenting, timed explosive creates a sudden bright light that temporarily knocks out all enemies in range of the flash. Use in order to cross areas unnoticed or escape persecution by attack teams. However, when sentries awake, they will radio for help. Equip and press to throw. Hold the Attack button before releasing to increase the distance thrown. Can be thrown from behind a corner by peeking out.

Grenades

Standard palm-held, timed fragmentation explosive. Instantly kills targets standing over the grenade, damages all ene-mies in range of the blast. Equip and press ⓦ to throw. Hold the Attack button before releasing in order to increase the distance thrown. Must be thrown in five seconds or less, or it will explode in the thrower's hand! Can be thrown by peeking out from behind a corner. Best used during heavy confrontations with small squads of enemy soldiers.

Empty Clip Magazine

An empty clip retained in the inventory. Can be thrown in order to create a small noise to distract an enemy. Use this to make soldiers leave their patrol routes. Equip and press ⓦ to throw. Hold the Attack button before releasing in order to increase the distance thrown. Can be thrown by peeking out from behind a corner.

Book

A magazine filled with naughty pictures and articles just for men. Equip in the hand and press ⓦ to open the book and set it on the ground. Any soldier who spots the Book open on the ground will get on his hands and knees to examine it for a while. When the guard's cone of vision disappears from the radar, you may sneak around the guard quietly. Use this to bait guards into compromising positions outside their normal patrol routes, so that your character can take them by surprise.

C4 Semtex Explosive Charge (Remote Detonator)

A small block of C4 Semtex explosive wired with a remote detonator. Press the ⓦ button, and the charac-ter will set the charge at his feet. Press the character's back against a surface to set the device on a wall or a crate. Move some feet away and press ⓦ to detonate. Can be used to set up elaborate traps for guards.

Claymore Directional Sensor Landmine

A landmine with a directional sensor that explodes when an upright target enters its forward field of vision. Equip, face direction of predicted enemy approach, and press ⓦ to set the Claymore on the ground. Use the Mine Detector or the Thermal Goggles to detect the presence of Claymores in an area. Obtain or circumnavigate Claymores by crawling across them.

RGB6 Grenade Launcher

A heavy six-shot revolving barrel grenade launcher. Lobs a grenade in a long arc. Hold ⓦ to aim the weapon, release the button to fire. Use First Person View and raise the weapon to compensate for the arcing trajec-tory of the projectile. The grenade's detonation damages all enemies in range, kills enemies that are struck directly. Due to weight, character cannot move while firing the RGB6.

Nikita Remote Control Rocket Launcher

A long-range launcher that fires a remote control fuel-propelled rocket. Press ⓦ to aim, and press the Left stick to aim in First Person View. Release Attack button to fire. When launched, the view shifts automatically to first person targeting. Guide the missile with the Movement control, turning it left or right. Changing the rocket's direction causes it to slow down. The rocket has a limited amount of fuel to propel it, and will detonate when the fuel runs out. Use the Nikita to seek out and destroy electronic and living targets in connecting corridors. Guide rockets through vents to destroy objectives.

Stinger Surface-to-Air Missile Launcher

A surface-to-air, electronically targeted guided missile launcher. When equipped, character automatically enters First Person View and looks through the tracking scope. Press the White button, and the character will hold the Stinger away from his eye, increasing peripheral vision. The Stinger uses a computerized tracking system, calculates viable tar-get points, and marks them in the scope with small squares. The Stinger locks on to a target when the center "M" crosshair meets with a calculated targeting square. The target will turn red when a lock is acquired, and the system emits a high-pitched beeping. Press ⓦ to fire the missile. The Stinger will lock on to aircraft, electronic surveillance equipment, and live targets, as well.

Directional Microphone

A handheld, long range sound amplification system. Can be used to penetrate walls and soundproof barriers in order to listen in on conversations from far away. Must be used to listen for a certain heartbeat during the hostage search event. When equipped, the character automatically inserts the earphone and enters First Person View. Use the Movement control to target sound source. When subtitles are turned on, the caption lettering size will increase or decrease in relation to the volume and distance of the sound. Can be used to listen to secret conversations in impenetrable rooms.

Coolant

A can of nitrogen coolant, used to freeze and defuse active bombs. When equipped, the character auto-matically enters First Person View. Use the Movement control to target, then press and hold ⓦ to emit a continuous blast of cold vapor. The Coolant never runs out, but the blast will eventually lose power. The character will then shake up the can to reactivate it. When a bomb is defused, it will become covered with frost and its deto-nator will chime as it powers off. The Coolant can also be used to extinguish fires, drive away bugs, and to wake up uncon-scious enemy personnel.

ITEMS AND EQUIPMENT

003200 20069

In the field, specialized equipment is required to carry out surveillance operations and to sustain the operative during intense combat situations. Equip items by pressing the Right trigger button and scrolling through the inventory with the Movement control. Tap the Right trigger button to equip and unequip the last item used.

Rations

Consumable field food source that's high in protein and nutritional elements. Restores health. Press the Left trigger button and select Rations, press ⊙ with the inventory open to use. By leaving the Rations equipped, your character will use them automatically when his Life Meter is reduced to zero.

Bandage

A gauze compress lubricated with triple antibiotic ointment. Used to stop bleeding. When a character's Life Meter is red and decreasing, use a Bandage to turn the meter green again. Press the Left trigger button and select the Bandages, press ⊙ with the inventory open to use. No health is restored, but the operative will stop leaving a trail of blood everywhere he goes.

Pentazemin

An anti-depressant used to quell nervous tension and boost the immune system. Pentazemin can be used to steady your character's aim, to prevent sea sickness in outside areas during the "Tanker" episode, and to cure common colds by expunging harmful germs. Use in conjunction with the sniper rifles to become an expert marksman. Press the Left trigger button and select Pentazemin, then press ⊙ with the inventory open to use.

Medicine

A highly concentrated flu remedy and nasal decongestant that suppresses cold symptoms instantaneously. However, further exposure to cold and wetness will negate the effects of Medicine. Press the Left trigger button and select Medicine, press ⊙ with the inventory open to use.

PAN Security Card

A security card that allows the bearer to enter doors equipped with the PAN security system. Developed by engineer Hal Emmerich, the Personal Area Network system uses a person's body salts to transmit an electronic signal to a sensor built into the door. When the person bearing the card approaches, the door opens automatically. The doors are assigned levels so that access by personnel can be limited in terms of rank. Assuming you've acquired a PAN security card of sufficient level, you need only approach a secured door to open it.

MO Disk

An optical data disk containing a computer virus targeted at destroying "GW," the Artificial Intelligence of the new Arsenal Gear. The virus is modeled after the FOXDIE program, which was created by Dr. Naomi Hunter and targeted at various members of FOXHOUND, including Solid Snake.

B.D.U.

A Body Disguise Uniform that is identical to the unique uniforms worn by terrorist sentries in the Shell 1 Core. Equip in the right Item Menu to disguise your character as a terrorist while in the Shell 1 Core. Will not work in other areas of the Big Shell, because the uniform will not blend in with other guards. Must be used in conjunction with an AKS-74u in order to complete the disguise.

Body Armor

A lightweight Kevlar armor capable of deflecting a certain amount of shrapnel, cutting damage by half. When equipped in the right Item Menu, the tactical vest will appear on your character. However, the armor will deteriorate with use and becomes ineffective after sustaining constant damage. Use only in desperate situations when Rations have run out.

Cardboard Box

A cardboard box that your character can hide inside. Equip a box in the right Item Menu, and your character covers himself. Press the Movement control, and your character will move with the box on. Hold the White button and your character peeks through the handle hole in First Person View. There are six cardboard boxes in the game. Boxes must be used cleverly in conjunction with the area so as to blend in. If your character equips a box with a design that does not match the surrounding boxes or the purpose of the area, then guards will become suspicious and investigate. Cardboard Box 5 has such an attractive design that it may actually draw unwanted attention. Usage of Cardboard Boxes for hiding requires some forethought and strategy.

Scope

A long-range, lightweight set of zoom binoculars that can be used to scout great distances away. Equipping the Scope in the right Item Menu causes your character to enter First Person View as he looks through the electronic lens. Press ⊙ to zoom in and ⊙ to zoom out.

Camera

A long-range zoom lens surveillance device that can be used to scout areas far away and capture photographic evidence of enemy activities. The Camera can retain up to six photographs. The memory stick is wiped clean if the shots are uploaded to the local network Node or if the game is turned off. Press ⬤ to zoom in and ⬤ to zoom out. Press ⬤ to capture an image. Improving the composition of mission-critical shots will prompt exclamations of approval from your character. The Camera can also be used to determine which guards' Dog Tags have been collected. Look at the guard from a distance with the Camera and press the Action button (⬤). If the guard's name appears in blue above his head, it means you have already collected his Dog Tags.

Digital Camera

A portable digital camera with a long-range zoom lens that can capture photographs and record them to your memory card. Can also be used like a Scope to scout distant areas. Press ⬤ to zoom in and ⬤ to zoom out. Press ⬤ to capture a digital image. The photo save screen then appears, which allows you to save new photos or overwrite old ones. You can view your photos with the Photo Album feature, and each photo is rendered as an icon on the memory card menu. The Photo Viewer allows you to view photos, to adjust their color tones and to rename them. Press the Right trigger button to view a photo in full screen mode. The Digital Camera can also be used to determine which guards' Dog Tags have been collected. Use it to look at the guard from a distance and press the Action button (⬤). If the guard's name appears in blue above his head, it means you have already collected his Dog Tags. You can find the Digital Camera late in the game, but after you complete the game in Normal or greater difficulty, it will be in your inventory at the beginning of a replay game.

Thermal Goggles

A set of electronic thermal imaging goggles that can be strapped to your character's head. When equipped, the surroundings appear filtered through an infrared field. Electronic and living materials are displayed brightly as solid images. Thermal Goggles allow you to see in the dark, and to better see electronic devices that might otherwise hide in plain sight. Thermal Goggles can also be used in First Person View.

Night Vision Goggles

A headset with light-magnifying sensors to intensify the natural lighting of any area, allowing the individual to see clearly in utter darkness. When equipped, the entire area glows green. Guards and objects that lie in the dark are rendered with enormous clarity. Unfortunately, they are almost useless underwater. Night Vision Goggles can also be used in First Person View.

Anti-Personnel Sensor

A vibrating and sonic emission sensor that is tuned to filter out the sound of the user's heartbeat and focus on the cardiac rhythms of other nearby personnel. As enemy personnel approach, the AP Sensor will cause the controller to vibrate in warning. The vibration becomes stronger and faster as the subject approaches. For controllers without vibration technology, the device will emit a sonar beep that increases in frequency as an enemy approaches. Works automatically when your character is sealed inside a locker or crawling in a ventilation duct, but must be equipped in the right Item Menu to work otherwise. Cancels all other vibration functions when in use.

Sensor A

A bomb detection system designed and built by explosives expert Peter Stillman. The sensor detects the odors emitted by Semtex C4 bomb packages and displays them as a greenish vapor cloud on the character's Soliton Radar display. Keep this device equipped in the right Item Menu in order to narrow down the locations of C4 bombs set in the struts of the Big Shell.

Sensor B

A bomb detection system designed and built by explosives expert Peter Stillman. The sensor detects the electronic detonator signal of odorless Semtex C4 devices and beeps to indicate your character's proximity to the bomb. Equip this device in the right Item Menu when you're searching for special odorless bombs. When the frequency of the beeps increases, your character is moving closer to the explosive's location.

Mine Detector

An electronic radar enhancement system that detects the location of Claymore mines and indicates their position and direction of scanning on your character's Soliton Radar display. Keep the device equipped while moving through mined areas, and steer your character's movement around the cones of "vision" displayed on the screen. Use this device to locate and obtain Claymores.

SOCOM Suppressor

A silencer especially fitted for a SOCOM handgun. This item suppresses muzzle flash and quells gunshot noise. To attach, equip the SOCOM Suppressor in the right Item Menu and the SOCOM Pistol in the left Weapon Menu. The device will be permanently attached to the weapon. Allows the user to kill with stealth.

AKS-74u Suppressor

A silencer especially fitted for any AK series lightweight assault rifle. Suppresses muzzle flash and quiets gunshot noise. To attach, equip the AKS-74u Suppressor in the right Item Menu and the AKS-74u in the left Weapon Menu. The device will be permanently attached to the weapon. Allows the user to kill and destroy hovering Cypher devices with stealth.

Dog Tags

The number of Dog Tags that your character has stolen from guards is displayed beside this icon. Can be used in conjunction with the Dog Tag Viewer to determine how many Dog Tags remain to be obtained in the current Difficulty Mode.

"Solid Snake *did* die... Either he survived, or there are *two* of them."

-Secretary of Defense, Richard Ames

part MISSION ANALYSIS

TANKER

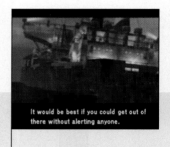

It would be best if you could get out of there without alerting anyone.

SOLID SNAKE (David Hayter)

U.S.S.
DISCOVERY, AFT DECK

Mission Analysis:
Normal Difficulty

The entire Mission Analysis describes Normal difficulty mode, and the guard patrol routes, enemy placements, and item locations correspond to that mode.

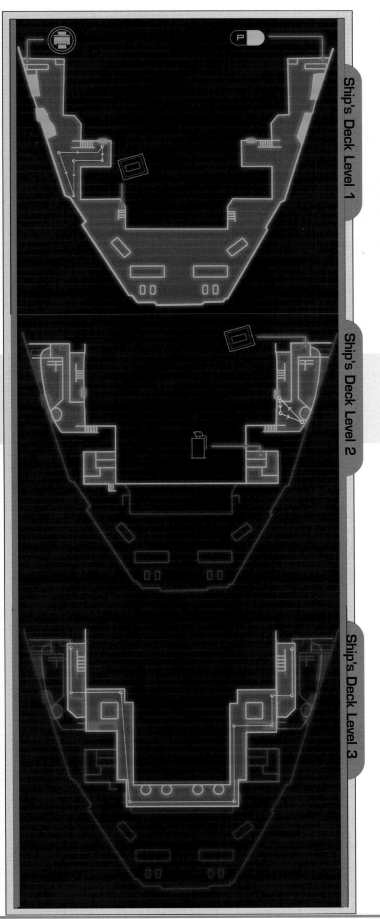

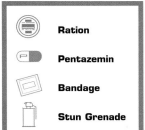

(icon)	**Ration**
(icon)	**Pentazemin**
(icon)	**Bandage**
(icon)	**Stun Grenade**

Patrol Paths

The maps in this guide are marked with guard and Cypher patrol patterns. Yellow lines represent these routes. Red dots indicate stopping points along the path. Arrows show the direction the guard travels, except in the many cases where the guard backtracks the same route in both directions

Snake is in contact by Codec with Hal Emmerich, a.k.a. Otacon. Otacon will explain several combat and control maneuvers that Snake can perform. Most of these are reviewed in the Solid Tactics chapter of this guide, and you should take all the time you need on the Aft Deck to get used to moving and controlling Snake.

This is Snake.
Do you read me, Otacon?

Otacon, how many men do you need
to take over a tanker of this size?

Ship Directions

While Snake is aboard the tanker, directions will be given in ship terminology. Therefore, as one faces the vessel from the back, the "port" side is to the left, and the "starboard" side is to the right.

I'm transmitting a photo.
Let's get an ID on him ASAP.

Use frequency 140.96 to let Otacon know that you want to save your game data.

Otacon acts as Snake's intelligence advisor on this mission. Call him to get several useful strategies for getting inside the ship, as well as surviving the entire game. If you want to know more about your equipment and weapons, use the Right and Left trigger buttons to equip Snake, and then call Otacon.

Starboard
Reconnaissance

Move to the starboard side and ascend the first set of steps. Press ● to get over the rectangular obstacle here, and collect the box of **Chaff Grenades**. Search the covered portion of the starboard lower deck, behind the disposal gate, to find a box of **Pentazemin Benzodiazepine Anti-Depressant** hidden in the small space behind a winch drum.

There is a door that leads to Deck-B on the second starboard level. Entering the ship through this door can greatly cut down on your game time, but you'll miss some items on Deck-A. Further back on starboard level 2, there is another small alcove where you can obtain a **Bandage**.

Flu Alert!

It's possible for Snake to catch a cold if he remains on the rainy Aft Deck for too long. If Snake sneezes in the presence of enemies, he might be discovered. Alleviate his symptoms by taking a Pentazemin. In addition to steadying nerves when aiming a sniper rifle, Pentazemin also adds a boost to the bloodstream. However, the effects may only be temporary depending on how long it takes you to administer the medicine after the first sneeze.

Port Side
Reconnaissance

Approaching from the rear portion of the Aft Deck, search under the first set of stairs for a **Bandage**. The door at the bottom of the stairs leads to Deck-A, and it is the preferred way of entering the ship. Continue back along the lower deck, past the disposal gate, to a small alcove at the rear, where Snake can obtain a **Ration**.

Aft Deck Tactics

1024013295001002148601 87
0147873705011

Cleaning Crew

When you knock out a guard, it is imperative to dispose of or hide his body. Otherwise, he might wake up and discover Snake, or other guards might be sent to investigate his lack of reports. Drag him to one of the gates on either side of the ship. Snake will open the gate and toss the enemy overboard. Don't forget to "shake down" the guards first for useful items!

Aft Deck Tactics

All of the guards on the rear outside portion of the ship are pretty easy to capture in order to collect their Dog Tags.

STRATEGY

Starboard Guard

This is one of the easiest Dog Tags to collect in the game. The soldier stands at the rail for a long time looking through his binoculars, and then he goes to check up the stairs nearby. While the soldier looks through the binoculars, move quietly up the stairs behind him by gently pressing the Left stick. When the guard turns to head for the door, run up behind him and press ⬤ to get the drop on him easily! Shake down the guard for more items, and then drag his body downstairs and dispose of him through the starboard-side gate.

STRATEGY

Port-Side Guard

With the other two guards neutralized, there's less risk of discovery while you tackle the fellow who patrols near the lower entrance to the ship on the port side. On the top deck, move to the port side, leap over the rail, and hang there. Shimmy over until Snake is positioned above the raised platform below, and then drop down. Hop over the rectangular object and stand near the rail. Watch the guard carefully. When he leaves the bottom of the stairs and heads to the left, leap over the rail, drop, and run up behind him.

Dog Tag Strategies

Tranquilizing guards and sneaking through the shadows require little strategy and allow you to speed through the game. The true challenge of the game is to arrest enemy sentries and force them to turn over their Dog Tags. The more Dog Tags collected, the more bonus items are unlocked for future use. For detailed information about Dog Tags and how to surprise guards from behind, please consult the "Solid Tactics" chapter of this guide.

STRATEGY

Top Deck Guard

Next, focus on capturing the guard who patrols the entire back portion of the upper deck. During his route, he moves to the starboard staircase and looks down. Wait at the bottom of the stairs, just out of sight, until he makes this check. As he heads back toward the rear of the ship, head upstairs and follow him until he stops. Press ⬤ to aim the M9 and capture the guard. Be sure to tranquilize him after you have the tags.

U.S.S. DISCOVERY, DECK-A

Deck-A Crew's Quarters Reconnaissance

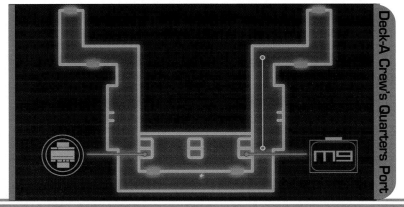

Deck-A Crew's Quarters Port

	Ration
M9	M9 Ammo

■ Try to open the sealed door at the end of the corridor, and Snake will accidentally pull off the handle!

Move to the right from the entrance and down the corridor until you reach the first automatic sliding door. The first locker on the far-left wall contains a **Ration**. There's a rather alluring pinup poster inside the door of the second locker on the far left. There are several weird things you can do with this if you're perverted enough...

The only other item is in the first locker on the far-left side of the room, a box of **M9 Bullets**. Use First Person View and you'll notice another pinup girl plastered on the inside of the door.

KONAMI EYES GIRLS

The poster girl in the black swimsuit is from KONAMI EYES, a Konami publication in Japan. There are some funny things to do with this poster. First, get inside the locker and close the door. Use the Left Stick to look down at the girl and press the White button. Snake makes a smooching sound and kisses the poster! Now leave the locker door open, stand directly in front of the poster and go into First Person View. Press SELECT and call Otacon. A funny Codec conversation happens. Also with the locker door open, press Snake's back up against it. With a weapon equipped, position Snake so that when he knocks on the door (⬤), he taps her chin. Tapping on the poster in this manner makes a funny sound! Also, equip the camera and take a picture so that the entire poster is captured in the shot. If Snake says "Gooooood," then you know it's the right shot. Otacon will appreciate it later, as well...

The second poster has all the Easter Eggs of the other pinup. Plus, you can cause something really funny to happen. Unequip Snake's weapon, press his back against the door, and position him so that his right hand is touching her leg. Press ⬤ to knock on the poster, and the pinup gets offended! Her reaction alerts the guard outside, and an attack squad will storm the locker room. Quickly get inside the locker and stay quiet to avoid detection. It's risky, but seeing the poster react to Snake's advances is quite amusing.

Deck-A Crew's Quarters Tactics

If the lone guard on this level is captured, he will refuse to hand over his Dog Tags. He won't be threatened by the M9, so you'll need to return here once you obtain the USP.

STRATEGY

Deck-A Crew's Quarters Guard

The guard's route changes depending on which door Snake uses to enter the area. If Snake enters from the port side exterior hatch, the guard patrols on the starboard side. If Snake enters from the sliding door on the starboard side, the guard patrols near the hatch on the port side. Either way, move to the lower corner of the corridor on the side the guard is patrolling. Press Snake's back against the corner to view the guard's movement while staying out of sight. The guard moves to the lower corner, near Snake's location, and then turns and heads upward. As soon as he turns, move up behind him and capture him. When the guard begins to taunt Snake, switch to the USP pistol and use First Person View to shoot him in the hand or leg. After the guard turns over his tags, dispose of him however you wish.

Locker Strategies

OTACON

While you're in the locker room, call Otacon several times. He provides Snake with valuable tactics regarding the lockers. Not only can Snake hide in the lockers, but he can also hide enemy bodies in them. In a firefight, Snake can use the locker door as a shield if it is far enough back from the door.

Deck-A
Crew's Lounge
Reconnaissance

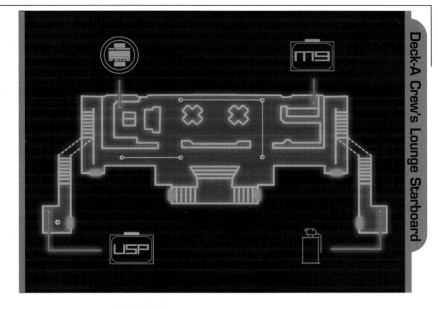

Ration	
M9	M9 Ammo
USP	USP Ammo
	Stun Grenade

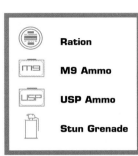

There's a descending stairway in the starboard corridor with a box of **Stun Grenades** at the bottom. The auto-sliding door leads to the Engine Room.

Use the methods outlined in the following Tactics section to put the guards to sleep. Then search behind the bar for **M9 Bullets**. There is a **Ration** among the couches in the Lounge area. Also, notice the scrolling image on the widescreen television on the port side wall—it's Metal Gear RAY, stowed in the tanker's hold! As you're staring at the screen in First Person View, call Otacon to have a discussion.

The corridor on the far side of the Lounge also has a descending stairway with a dozing guard at the bottom, who is swarmed by flies! There's a box of USP Bullets nearby, but you cannot obtain them until you have the USP pistol.

Lounging Around

141.12

OTACON

While you're standing outside the lounge in the starboard stairwell, contact Otacon, and he will point out the steam pipes in the ceiling. Shooting these in a crisis situation can distract guards just long enough for you to escape.

Deck-A Crew's Lounge Tactics

STRATEGY

Deck-A Crew's Lounge Guards (Both)

To capture Dog Tags in this area, Snake must deal with both guards simultaneously to avoid detection. Standing in the starboard corridor outside the lounge, use First Person View to aim at the most distant guard, but wait to shoot until he's at his farthest patrol point, near the port-side doorway. Then proceed into the lounge just a short distance so that Snake remains hidden from the bar area and pressed up against the wall. When the remaining guard emerges, all you have to do is step out from the wall and aim your gun to capture him. Once you have his tags, tranquilize him and hide his body behind the bar.

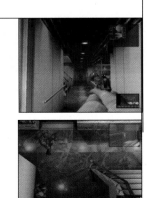

Now move to the port-side guard and start picking him up and dropping him to decrease his sleep time. Make sure to roll the guard onto his back if needed, and step back a little as he starts to revive. As soon as he's on his feet again, capture him before he starts to look around.

Stairwell Guard

The dozing, fly-infested guard at the bottom of the port-side stairs will rebel if you attempt to capture him with only the M9. We will provide tactics for this stubborn Russian at the proper time.

Ration

M9 M9 Ammo

USP USP Ammo

In the starboard corridor, move upward and Snake will spot the shadow of a guard around the corner.

The Shadow Knows

Be sure to look for guards' shadows around corners from now on. Concentrate on getting the two guards' Dog Tags now while the time is ripe. Things won't be so advantageous later.

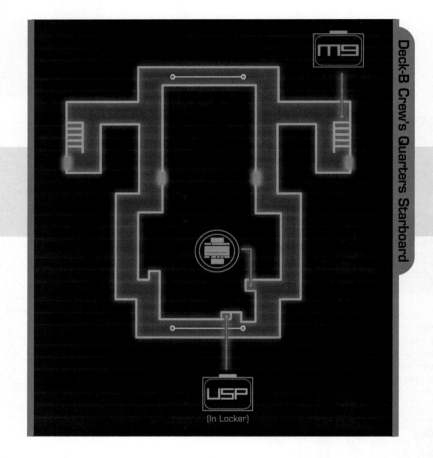

Deck-B Crew's Quarters Starboard

USP (In Locker)

Move left to the starboard stairwell. The lower watertight door leads back out to the Aft Deck, so this is the other possible entry point into the ship. There's a box of **M9 Bullets** hidden in the small niche under the stairs. There's a **Ration** in a tiny, dark alcove near the bottom corner.

In the rear portion of Deck-B, a lone guard patrols the corridor in front of a locker. There's a box of USP Bullets inside the locker.

Deck-B Crew's Quarters Tactics

STRATEGY

Forward Hallway Guard

If Snake moves forward in the corridor immediately upon entering, he'll notice this guard's shadow coming from around the corner. This guard is really easy to arrest. Use the radar rather than watching Snake onscreen, and swiftly but carefully  run around the corner to aim your weapon at the back of the guard's head. If you capture him before he begins to patrol his designated route, this guard is even easier to capture!

STRATEGY

Rear Hallway Guard

Move to the starboard side of his patrol route, near where that Ration is located in the nook. As the guard is walking toward the port side, move into the small alcove where the locker stands and press your back against the vented door.  When the guard stops in front of Snake's hiding spot, step out just a little and aim your weapon at him. With the guard arrested, move in front of him and get his tags. Tranquilize him and stuff him into the nearby locker.

U.S.S. DISCOVERY, DECK-C
Deck-C Crew's Quarters Reconnaissance

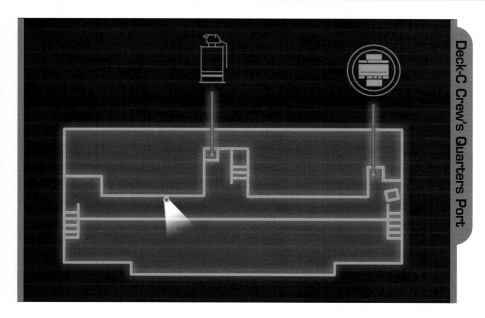

Deck-C Crew's Quarters Port

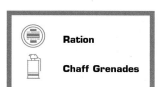

- ⊙ **Ration**
- ⛴ **Chaff Grenades**

Snake notices a surveillance camera mounted in the hallway. There is a locker containing **Chaff Grenades** in the center area. At the opposite end of the corridor, near the stack of crates, there is a floor-level duct where a **Ration** has been stashed. When you're finished in this corridor, ascend the stairs to Deck-D.

Camera Weaknesses

141.12

OTACON

After Snake notices the camera, immediately call Otacon on the Codec for some tips on how to deal with cameras.

Deck-C Crew's Quarters Tactics

A surveillance camera is mounted high on the wall in the corridor. Snake is not capable of destroying the device with only a tranquilizer gun, so some other means of circumnavigating the camera is required. If Snake is spotted, an attack team will flood the narrow corridor.

STRATEGY

Deck-C Camera Tactics

There are two ways to get past the device. The easiest way is to use a Chaff Grenade, which will cause electronic interference and temporarily blind the camera. Run past the camera before the effect subsides. The other way to get around the electric eye is to press Snake up against the wall under the camera and side step along the wall directly under it. All cameras have a blind spot directly under them. Since this camera doesn't pan back and forth, sliding under it unnoticed is relatively easy.

02020015560101

U.S.S. DISCOVERY: DECK-D
Deck-D Crew's Quarters Reconnaissance

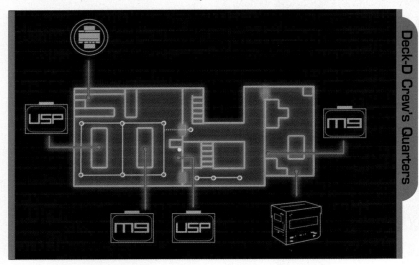

Deck-D Crew's Quarters

(icon)	**Ration**
USP	**USP Ammo**
(box icon)	**Box**
M9	**M9 Ammo**

This area is heavily patrolled and surveyed, so watch your step more carefully than ever! As Snake comes up the stairs, a guard enters the Mess Hall. Don't move until he's inside and the door closes behind him. Then proceed to the doorway, cross the threshold into the cafeteria, and tranquilize the guard from a distance. There is a **Ration** behind the kitchen counter. Crawl underneath the table closest to the door for **M9 Bullets**. There is a box of USP Bullets under the table furthest in, but you'll have to wait until Snake has the USP.

Another box of USP Bullets is under a surveillance camera, so it's better to wait until later before you attempt to get these items. The door just south of the camera leads to the stairs up to the Bridge, but the vigilant camera and the guard posted just beyond the doorway make it difficult to use this route. You are better off exiting the Mess Hall through the same door you entered.

Crossing the corridor to the starboard side, Snake receives an urgent Codec transmission from Otacon. The corridor is rigged with Semtex plastic explosives, set to go off when anything crosses the invisible infrared detection beams. Snake must find some way to get around them.

As you face the IR beam trap, the doorway leading into the food pantry is behind you. At the back of this room, Snake can collect **M9 Bullets** and **Cardboard Box 1**. When the latter item is equipped in the Item Menu, Snake will crouch inside a box that looks like any ordinary orange crate. Use First Person View to see through the box's handle opening. As the name indicates, this is just the first of many area-specific cardboard boxes that Snake will acquire. This box allows you to hide specifically anywhere inside the ship. Used at any position outside the tanker, this box might actually draw suspicion.

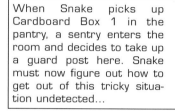

When Snake picks up Cardboard Box 1 in the pantry, a sentry enters the room and decides to take up a guard post here. Snake must now figure out how to get out of this tricky situation undetected...

  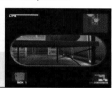

Deck-D Crew's Quarters Tactics

The guards on this level all refuse to turn over their tags unless Snake threatens them with something a little tougher than darts. For now, simply tranquilize the guard on the other side of the sensor array, sneak under the trap, and continue up to the Bridge level. Tactics for obtaining these guards' tags will be described at a later point in the book, when Snake has the advantage.

Box of Tricks

If Snake is heard or if he sneezes, quickly use Cardboard Box 1 to disguise yourself. However, if the guard leaves to go get others, run up to the other boxes marked "The Orange." Try to line up your box with them, so that your box appears to be stacked along-side the others. This is an even more convincing cover.

"Clearings" Are Bad

If Snake is discovered in the pantry and the guard radios for help, the alert will bring in several more guards for a "clearing." This means that an all-out firefight is going to ensue as soon as the soldiers have sighted their target. All that stands between Snake and the enemy is the fruit on the shelf. The guards will gradually blast it away, so use step-out corner shooting to try to knock them unconscious. Don't bother aiming for the heads; you risk standing out in the open too long.

U.S.S. DISCOVERY, DECK-E BRIDGE

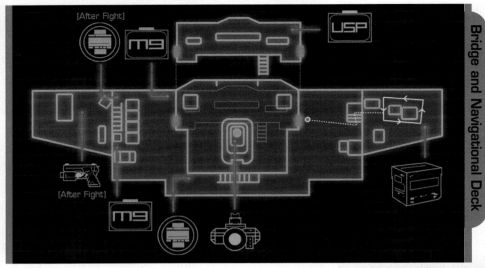

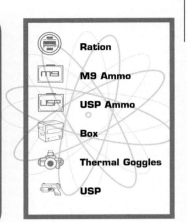

Ration
M9 Ammo
USP Ammo
Box
Thermal Goggles
USP

Snake abruptly cuts off communication when he notices someone standing on the port bow. Move to the watertight door and turn the wheel to open it. Be certain to have Otacon record your game data now, if you haven't up to this point!

 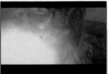 

BOSS FIGHT

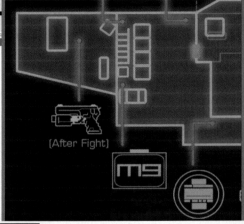

Olga Gurlukovich

Gender:	Female
Affiliation:	General Gurlukovich's Splinter Faction Army
Weapon:	USP 9mm with Barrel-Mounted Flashlight

Olga's a wicked shot! Start off by moving to the crates stacked on the starboard side and press Snake's back against them so that you can see Olga hiding behind the crates nearby. Corner-shots are good enough; don't bother going into First Person View mode. You'll take more damage trying to carefully aim your shots. While Olga is trying to spot Snake, sneak over to the port side of the crates, and you should be able to nail Olga from the side where she isn't looking.

You'll find a **Ration** and **M9 Ammo** nearby in case you need them (see the map). It may seem that the M9 is no good against her, but that isn't true. Although her green life bar never decreases, each dart reduces the small purple bar. This is her "consciousness meter," and you'll win the battle if you can knock her out. After suffering a few tranquilizers, Olga moves to the back of the ship and shoots the cables holding down the tarp. Now she has great cover behind the large canvas fluttering in the wind. Aim for the lower-right anchor of the tarp and sever it with a shot. The wind will blow the tarp away.

If you are successful at releasing the tarp, Olga will shoot the light so that it blares in your face and makes it hard to aim at her. You must move quickly to the other side of the area, where the light is not glaring. From there, you should be able to target and shoot out the light in First Person View, but do it quickly. Olga will move the light again to blind you in your new position, and you'll have to move and start over.

When Olga seems to have Snake pinned down on one side or the other, wait until she ducks behind her cover, then move. From a new position, you should be able get at least one surprise shot to Olga's side.

Be careful when you're standing in the open spaces on the left because Olga will toss grenades to flush you out. Olga warns that she is throwing a grenade by screaming "Take this!" or something to that effect. Immediately get out of your position by rolling left or right.

Olga Compromised

Frame your shot like this for an appropriate reaction from Otacon.

While Olga is unconscious on the deck, stand at her feet and take a photo of her. Snake should make a "kissing" sound after the photo is taken. Retain this shot until Otacon has a chance to look at it...

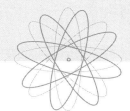

U.S.S. DISCOVERY: NAVIGATIONAL DECK, WING

Olga lies unconscious on the port side deck. Now it's time to see what items the navigation crew left behind that might be useful.

Navigational Deck Reconnaissance

After the battle, Snake collects Olga's empty **USP**. "Shake" Olga's unconscious body to get her **Dog Tags**. Keep shaking her, and you might also get **M9 Bullets**. There is a **Ration** in a small pit behind the stairs.

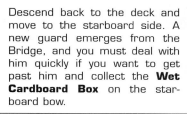

Descend back to the deck and move to the starboard side. A new guard emerges from the Bridge, and you must deal with him quickly if you want to get past him and collect the **Wet Cardboard Box** on the starboard bow.

Move to the stairs at the center of the Navigational Deck, and head up the stairs. At the base of the ladder, press ⓞ to climb. Press upward on the Left Stick, and Snake ascends to the top. The highest platform is where the **Thermal Goggles** are stashed. These are essential for several of the important tasks ahead.

Navigational Deck Tactics

STRATEGY

Navigational Deck Guard

Do not reenter the ship after the confrontation with Olga. Instead, cross the back part of the deck. As you reach the starboard corner of the back wall of the Bridge, a guard emerges from the interior. The guard pauses for a long moment just outside the hatch. Then he begins patrolling the port bow very quickly, without stopping. Shooting this fast-moving guard from a distance is difficult. Therefore, the best opportunity to arrest this man is during the brief moment when he pauses, just outside the hatch. Swift action is required.

U.S.S. DISCOVERY: DECK-E BRIDGE

Return inside, grab the **USP Bullets**, and head downstairs. Before you begin the long descent into the tanker's holds, make sure that Snake doesn't leave wet footprints everywhere, or it will give him away.

U.S.S. DISCOVERY: DECK-D

With Snake entering the area from the Bridge's stairs, the guards' placement and patrol routes have changed somewhat. Remember that there are **USP Bullets** being guarded by the surveillance camera inside the Mess Hall, and more **USP Bullets** lie under the table closest to the electric eye.

Deck-D Crew's Quarters Tactics

It's not going to be easy, but now that Snake has the USP, he can extort Dog Tags from the three soldiers on this deck. Using an unsuppressed firearm may draw unwanted alarms, so you must maintain complete control of the deck at all times.

STRATEGY

Surveillance Camera

To take out the camera properly, you must knock out both guards first. Returning from the Bridge above, the guard who patrols the corridor is now surveying the area near the stairs down to Deck-C. Move to the bottom of the sensor array and tranquilize the corridor guard when he emerges from around the corner. Then move to the rear entrance of the Mess Hall and stand just outside the doorway. The door must be open, but if you step into the room, the camera will spot Snake. Use First Person View to tranquilize the guard inside the Mess Hall, and then toss a Chaff Grenade to confuse the camera equipment. Step into the mess hall, equip the USP, and take out the camera before the electronic jamming wears off.

```
2 0 0 1 5 9 8 0 1 0 1 0 0 2 1 4 0 0
   101      111      20      020
```

Mess Hall Guard

With the camera obliterated, move to the dozing guard inside the eating area and begin to pick him up and drop him. Make sure that he is lying on his back and that you are lifting his upper torso. As he starts to come to, equip the USP and step back a few paces. Even when this guard is arrested, he'll refuse to surrender his tags. Shoot him in the arm or leg, and then execute him once his tags are yours.

Corridor Guard

Hopefully this man is still dozing. If not, tranquilize him again. Drag him into the Mess Hall and begin shaking his upper torso in the same method described for the previous guard. Once you've arrested this man and collected his tags, you must kill him to avoid further interference.

Pantry Guard

The third guard on this floor will not appear until you enter the pantry and move to the location where the Cardboard Box is found. With the other two guards dead and safely stowed in the Mess Hall, draw the third guard into the pantry. Wait until he moves farther into the room, assumes a standing position at the top of the supply shelves, and turns to face the front of the ship. Carefully move up along the shelf and capture the guard from the side. When he refuses to hand over his tags, switch over to the USP and shoot him in the arm or leg. Once you have the last guard's tags, dispose of him as you wish.

U.S.S. DISCOVERY: DECK-C

Deck-C Guard

That's right, a new guard patrols the entire corridor of Deck-C. He isn't hard to take down, as long as you exercise proper timing and caution with the surveillance camera nearby. If the camera sees you capture the guard, or if an unsuppressed shot is heard, the camera will react. As Snake descends the stairs from the mess hall level, the guard moves into the port section of the corridor, directly under the camera. Press Snake up against the corner just below the locker to keep him out of sight of the guard as he patrols towards the starboard corridor section. As he moves past, step out from the wall and capture him. Once you have his tags, do not kill him. Use a suppressed dart instead. After the guard is unconscious, it may be a wise idea to take out the camera with a USP shot.

U.S.S. DISCOVERY: DECK-B

We emphasized obtaining the guards' Dog Tags during your previous visit to this level, but collect them now if you didn't before. Move to the rear corridor, press Snake's back against the port side corner, and use a jump-out shot to tranquilize the guard patrolling in front of the locker. When the drug finally takes effect, drag his body over to the locker and collect the **USP Bullets** inside. Then stuff the guard into the locker, just for fun.

U.S.S. DISCOVERY: DECK-A

As Snake enters the lounge from the top of the central stairs, a lone guard patrols the area below. He makes a thorough search from port to starboard and back, so he's difficult to evade. The sleeping guard in the starboard-side stairwell is hardly protecting the **USP Bullets** behind him. Snake could easily sneak in and steal the bullets without detection, but that isn't any fun!

First, you must neutralize the guard patrolling the lounge area. When the guard passes by on patrol, quickly descend the stairs and hide in the right alcove under the stairs. Equip the M9 and use First Person View to shoot a hole in the glass panel at the opposite end from your position. As the guard patrols back through the area, he notices the new hole and moves in to investigate. Sneaking out of your hiding spot, you can easily take down the guard or arrest him for his tags.

U.S.S. DISCOVERY: ENGINE ROOM

Knowing that visibility is a problem in the Engine Room, the terrorists have positioned guards at every level of the area. Crossing this zone will be a true test of Snake's infiltration abilities.

	Ration
	USP Ammo
	Grenades
	M9 Ammo

Deck-A Crew's Lounge Tactics

Port Side Stairwell Guard

After the lively guard in the lounge is dozing, slowly descend the port-side stairs. Press very lightly on the Left Stick so that Snake slips quietly down the stairs. Arrest the fly-ridden guard from behind, and then move in front of him and threaten him for his tags. The man's poor attitude requires you to put a USP bullet in his arm or leg, just to teach him a lesson. Once you have his tags, move to the starboard-side stairs and descend to the Engine Room.

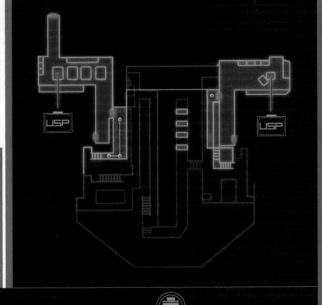

Engine Room Top

Engine Room Middle

Engine Room Bottom

Engine Room Reconnaissance

To reach the Engine Room, move to the starboard stairwell of the Deck-A Crew's Lounge and descend. Enter the door and move up the corridor. Snake spots a very intimidating shadow on the wall. Immediately call Otacon on the Codec, who recognizes it too. Equip the M9 and jump out from the corner—only to find the true source of the shadow—it's the McFarlane Toys Vulcan Raven action figure! Kill the light source by firing a dart at the flashlight. You can activate the figure by shooting it. Vulcan will begin grunting and shooting pellets all over the room. You can knock the figure over by hitting it with darts, but it cannot be turned off. Take a photo of the Vulcan Raven figure with the Camera. If Snake says "Good," then Otacon will make comments later.

In the same room, hop onto the nearby crate to collect more **USP Bullets**. Open the locker on the far left, and a body falls out! Put it back inside to avoid suspicion. Proceed to the starboard entrance to the Engine Room, noting that there is a guard on the other side of the door.

In Normal Mode, there are six guards in the Engine Room. You must reach the small room on the upper-port side, so you need to use a lot of different strategies to get through the area without detection. You need to take out the guards quietly—there's no avoiding it here.

Running out of ammo in this area is hard to do. Use the maps provided to locate various ammo boxes and the **Ration**. There are **Grenades** at the bottom-left corner of the port side's lowest level.

Navigate to the top level of the port side and enter the small room. Proceeding north in the hallway, a guard forces open the previously locked port side door. **USP Bullets** sit on top of a small device.

IR sensor beam traps protect the watertight door in this small room. If you trigger them, explosives will destroy the whole ship. You must deactivate these three IR beam arrays by destroying the control boxes with the USP. If you miss and hit the C4, you're toast.

Engine Room Tactics

Getting through seven soldiers in one area is tough, but if you follow these tactics in this exact order, you should have no problems.

STRATEGY

Top-Level Starboard Guard

This is the easiest man to capture. Stand in the doorway and fire a tranquilizer into the base of his skull. Drag the man into the locker area, all the way into the middle of the room. Start shaking the guard repeatedly until he begins to wake up. Once he's back on his feet, immediately capture him from behind and take his tags. Then tranquilize him one more time and stash his body in one of the lockers. Safely stowed, he won't trouble you any more.

Middle-Level Starboard Guard

Getting the drop on this guard requires Snake to do a little dropping of his own. As the guard is moving from the top part of his route back down toward the corner of the rail, jump over the rail of the top level and hang there. Quickly drop to the floor below, equip your M9, and get the drop on the guard at the corner. There should be just enough room to squeeze between the captured man and the rail. Once you have his tags and he's tranquilized, drag him upstairs and stash his body in a locker next to his buddy.

Lower-Level Starboard Guard

Descend the stairs just behind this guard very carefully, and try not to make any noise. Slip cautiously around the corner and hold up this guard from the side. Tranquilize him when you're finished.

Catch Up on Calisthenics!

Remember, in order to collect all of the Dog Tags in the Tanker scenario, you must get Snake's grip up to level 3. Once you've taken care of the upper two guards on the starboard side, there's no better opportunity. Hang from the rail of the middle level, positioning Snake over the walkway of the lower level just for safety. Pull both trigger buttons to exercise. After 100 chin-ups, your grip should rise to level 2. The increase in strength will make it easier to obtain level 3 in a short time.

 015

Lower-Level Port Side Guard

Having dispatched half of the guards, move to the M9 bullets at the top of the starboard side. Enter First Person View and look to the port side. The guard who patrols the lower area comes into view occasionally. This guard is a very special case, so he must be the first to fall on the port side. If you move to the port side of the engine room, this guard changes patrol routes and moves to the middle level, where he is much harder to capture. From the position near the M9 Bullets, use First Person View to tranquilize the guard from a great distance. Now sneak over to the port side, being careful not to draw attention from the central guard. Flip the sleeping guard over if necessary, and position his body so that when he wakes, he will be facing away from Snake with plenty of room in front of him. Then shake the guard's upper torso until he awakens. Get the drop on the guard, collect his tags, and tranquilize him.

Top-Level Port Side Guard

Since the central guard will provide resistance if captured, go after the guard on the top level of the port side. Move up the stairs to the small, dark alcove just below the top platform. Watch the guard's pattern on the Soliton for a moment. After the guard stares down the steps where Snake is hidden and turns back to the rail, ascend the stairs very quietly by pressing lightly on the Left Stick. As the guard turns to head toward the engine room door, run up behind him and arrest him while he's moving. The important thing about this guard is to capture him when he's not facing the rail, or else there's no room to get between them.

Middle-Level Central Guard

This guard won't surrender until you blow off his hand or foot, so make him your final target in the room. Getting the drop on him is a cinch. Just wait until he's gazing through binoculars at the girly picture posted high on the opposite wall, and then he's a vulnerable target. When you're running past him in this narrow zone, you'll most likely knock him backward from the rail. Fire a warning shot into one of his limbs, and his Dog Tags are yours.

Turbine Area Guard

The guard who saws his way into the small area on the port side of the engine room isn't too hard to overtake, thanks to the lockers here. After he enters the room and radios his superiors, hide inside the open locker and watch the guard through the vents. Just outside the locker, the guard turns to examine the IR beams before heading back toward the entrance. When the guard moves past, step out of the locker, equip a gun, and follow the guard to his stopping point in the corner just below the lockers. Unfortunately, you'll have to kill this guard with the USP so that he doesn't interfere while you disable the IR beams.

Engine Room **IR Beams** c4 Trap

The control boxes for the beams are snuggled away in tight spots. Two of them require that you shoot over C4 bricks, which means that your aiming in First Person View must be sharp. Hop onto the turbine, where you can obtain **USP Bullets**, and take a Pentazemin pill to steady your shots. Equip the Thermal Goggles, and the control boxes will stand out from the rest of the surroundings.

For the uppermost control box, stand on the turbine and look down the right side of the passage. A control box sits high up, behind a C4 patch. To have a better shot at it, stand on Snake's tiptoes by holding both trigger buttons. Aim at the top part of the control box to avoid hitting the explosives. This will disengage the first set of IR beams.

After the first beams are down, keep the Thermal Goggles on and hop off the turbine. Move a little ways down the corridor and look down to the right. The control box for the second IR beam array rests on the floor; you just have to get closer to improve your chances of hitting it. This deactivates the second set of beams.

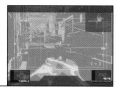

Move as far into the hall as possible. Then crouch and lay Snake flat on the floor, facing the watertight door. With the Thermal Goggles equipped, look to the left side of the passage in First Person View. The last control box is wedged between two C4 packs, and your shot needs to be darned accurate. Take another Pentazemin if it's hard to aim steadily. This should disengage the final IR beam array.

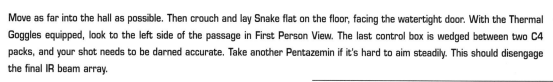

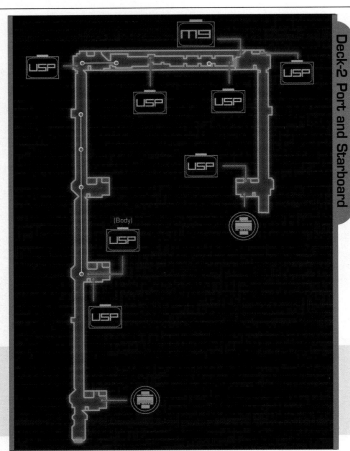

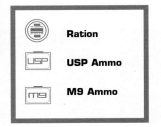

DECK-2, PORT

A general announcement orders the Marines to report to the hold in 10 minutes for the Commandant's speech. Snake must navigate through these narrow passages in order to reach the tanker's central cargo holds.

	Ration
USP	**USP Ammo**
M9	**M9 Ammo**

Deck-2 RECONNaissance

Lights Out

Lighting is the problem here. Guards in these corridors can see a remarkable distance away, especially when you're standing in a well-lit area. Use the M9 to shoot out the light bulbs hanging above the doorways. Check carefully because the electric breakers in this area are jittery and some light bulbs turn on intermittently. Play it safe and shoot every light bulb you can, whether it is illuminated or not.

You'll find that blasting out the light in the first alcove makes this section of the corridor much darker. Grab the **Ration** and continue north—the watertight door here is sealed.

You should halt in the passage before you arrive at the second alcove. From here, shoot out light bulbs that are further down the passage. Use First Person View to aim at the tiny dots of light, then use the Scope to confirm that you blasted them all. Occasionally put on the Thermal Goggles, which will help you spot approaching soldiers.

The watertight door in the second alcove is also sealed. There are **USP Bullets**, and if you shake down the dead crewmember here, he will drop some more. Drag the body into the alcove so you can engage the south corridor guard in some espionage tactics.

Moving north from the second alcove will trigger a guard to follow his patrol route, which extends just past the second alcove. This is a good time for Snake to take down this guard and move on.

Avoiding Unwelcome Attention

Remember that the flashlight on the USP will alert nearby guards, so switch back to the M9 whenever you have tranquilizing to do.

More lit areas should come into view as you approach the northern end of the corridor. Shoot out the lights from as far away as possible, including the one above the watertight door at the end. A guard listening to music will arrive as you reach the corner. Take down this guard quietly, because another soldier is just yards away. There are **USP Bullets** at the corner to help keep you stocked.

Moving east, it's important *not* to shoot out the lights anymore. The sound of smashing bulbs will alert the guard who is dozing between his reports. Carefully sneak up on him between each of his drowsy reports, and attack him from close range. There are more **USP Bullets** near this soldier, and another box sits by the watertight door that leads to the east corridor.

Deck-2 Port Tactics

Patrolling Guard

Be sure to shoot out all the lights with the M9, as previously mentioned. Only in darkness does Snake have any chance of hiding from enemies in these tight areas. When you move past the dead body near the third alcove in the corridor, the guard is triggered to begin his patrol. Use the Thermal Goggles to spot him long before he spots Snake. Make sure you drag the dead crewmember out of the way, since Snake has a tendency to move slowly over dead bodies. Hide behind the small corner in the alcove, and watch the soldier approach the Soliton. When the guard moves past the alcove, he stops before entering the next section of corridor. This is the time to come out of the alcove and surprise him. Unfortunately, you must terminate this guard with the USP so that he'll trouble you no further.

Jammin' Guard

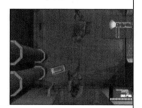

Approaching the northwest corner of the corridor, pay close attention to the Soliton display. A guard boogies into view, engrossed in his tunes. When he stops at the corner and is facing the wall, simply run up from the side and capture him. There should be plenty of room for Snake to get directly in front of the guard and harass him for his tags. Once you have what you want, tranquilize the guard and drag him to the previous alcove. Then, execute him with the USP so he won't trouble you anymore.

Sleep-Talking Solider

Avoid shooting out any more lights in the top corridor, or the guard snoozing on his feet will react quickly to the sound. Move carefully to the corridor section that precedes the guard's position, and press up against the wall to get a corner view of him. Watch him for a moment on the radar, and notice the timing of his eyes opening and closing. Step in when the guard's eyes are closed, and Snake should be able to arrest him from the front.

DECK-2, STARBOARD

Deck-2 Starboard Reconnaissance

It's Quiet——Too Quiet

The second section of corridor that runs around the outside of the Holds area is empty and quiet; this is a bad sign. Equip Snake's Rations, and resume shooting out lights in this corridor—you'll need as much darkness as possible.

There are some **USP and M9 Bullets** in a well-lit area at the first corner. Move down to the first alcove. From here, use First Person View to look as far south down the corridor as possible and shoot out all the lights you can. The firefight you're about to enter demands that you hide well in the dark. After you've taken out as many lights as you can, grab the **USP Bullets** and **Ration** in the alcove and continue south. A short cut scene begins.

Deck-2 Starboard Tactics

Three guards enter and a firefight between Snake and the soldiers breaks out in the hallway. More guards will pour into the alcove after you defeat the first wave, and even more after that will charge at Snake.

STRATEGY

Corridor Standoff Tactics

Equip the Grenades and quickly move forward to the crate that is closest to the intersection. Crouch behind the crate and press Snake's back up against it. When the soldiers disappear out of view for a moment, hold the Left trigger button so that Snake peaks around the crate, then press ⊘ hard for a second and release. Snake will throw a Grenade into the intersection and take out the first wave of guards.

Now equip the USP and press yourself against the crate again. Jump out and enter First Person View. When the single guard behind the crate on the other side of the intersection rises up, fill him full of lead. If you miss him, the guard will throw a Grenade of his own to flush out Snake. This causes heavy damage if the grenade is successful. The second wave of troops should be in the intersection by now, so keep the USP handy and use jump-out shots to nail them when they step into view.

After the soldier behind the crate is dead, leave the crate and run north. You should find two boxes of **USP Bullets** and a **Ration**. As you're standing here, a squad of three troopers will charge at you. Since they have to thin out to get around the crates, start blasting with the USP and you'll kill them one by one.

CARGO HOLDS
1, 2, and 3
Cargo Holds Reconnaissance

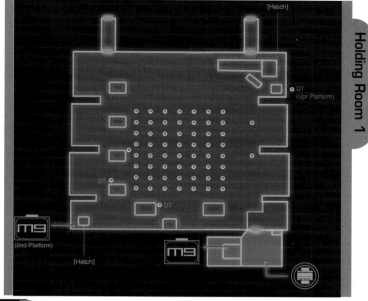

Holding Room 1

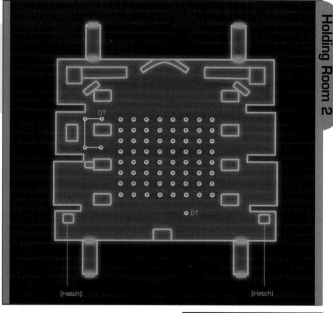

Holding Room 2

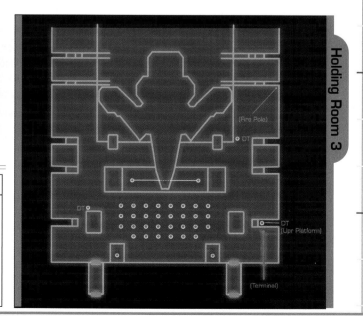

Holding Room 3

Game Over, Man!

If Snake is spotted, he will be arrested and the game will end instantly.

The Commandant's speech lasts exactly seven minutes. Snake must get the photos of RAY before the speech ends, or the soldiers will return to their posts. You can hear the speech in the background as you work. Your mission objective is to capture four photos of Metal Gear RAY: three angles from the front and a fourth shot of the "MARINE" lettering somewhere on the mech.

Above and Below...

On the next page, you'll find our strategies for negotiating through the main floors of the three cargo holds. However, this is not the only path available to you. Investigate these large rooms to find alternate paths, both below the main floor *and* above.

Cargo Holds Tactics

Sneaking through three cargo holds unnoticed is no problem for a stealth expert like Solid Snake. The true challenge is that while Snake must make it from the entrance to Hold No. 3 in 10 minutes or less, he must also arrest five marines scattered throughout the three areas. Each one has a set of valuable Dog Tags. Think it can't be done? Follow these tactics step by step, and the impossible becomes possible!

Hold No. I Port-Side Guard

Open the watertight hatch to find a **Ration** and **M9 Bullets** in a small room. Then descend the two ladders to the ground floor. Navigate along the back wall to the projector. Crouch and crawl under the projector's beam of light, and navigate behind the marine posted nearby. Do *not* attempt to arrest the marine near the projector just yet. Continue to the port side of Hold No. 1, and sneak around the cargo box. Walk carefully across the grating or Snake's footsteps will give him away. Position Snake directly behind the marine posted on the port side of the room, and hold him up for his Dog Tags. The cargo box provides excellent cover while you get in front of the soldier and threaten him. Don't forget to climb the ladder on the port side to reach a box of **M9 Bullets**.

Hidden in Plain Sight

You need not worry about hiding the bodies of sleeping marines in the Hold areas. The other soldiers are too focused on the speech to care, even when looking in the general direction of a sleeping guard.

Hold No. 1 Projector Guard

Once the port side guard is asleep, it's safe to arrest and harass the marine standing near the projector. You should need virtually no help in doing so, since he's wide open and oblivious to all but the Commandant's speech.

Hold No. 1 Third-Level Guard

There's a third officer in the room with Dog Tags, but he's hidden in an impossible spot. ***Your grip level absolutely must be level 3 in order to reach this solider.*** If not, don't waste your time and risk death. The speech is too short to allow you to "level up" here. To pinpoint this hidden marine's location, move forward along the port side of the room and stand parallel to the first row of marines watching the speech. Equip the Camera and look just above the projection screen on the starboard side of the room. After you've got his location, use a well-aimed M9 dart to put him to sleep. As carefully as possible, cross back to the starboard side and climb the first ladder back up to the mid-level platform. Hop over the rail, and Snake grabs an almost-invisible ledge. Shimmy forward across the room until you reach the projector screen, and then hop over the rail. If your grip level is not the highest possible, Snake will fall and die. Drag the snoozing marine toward the door, and then pick him up and drop him continuously to decrease his sleep time. When he wakes up, quickly arrest him, grab his tags, and head through the nearby door.

Hold No. 3 Third-Level Guard

Again, your grip level must be at the maximum level in order to overtake this guard. Use the same method from the previous strategy to shimmy across the top of Hold No. 2, until you reach an

upper door leading to Hold No. 3. Just a few feet inside, a lone guard watches the speech from this upper level. Move slowly across the grated floor to a position directly behind him, capture him, and get his tags. The quickest way to get down to floor level is to continue moving forward in Hold No. 3 until you reach the fire pole on the starboard side of the room. Before sliding down, there's a great opportunity to photograph the Marine logo on RAY's left leg.

Hold No. 3 Dozing Guard

Just below the fire pole's location, a guard is trying hard to stand watch, but he's asleep on his feet. You should be able to arrest him from the side or the rear easily, and then demand his tags.

Hold No. 3 Port Side Guard

The guard on the port side of the room is wide awake and enjoying the Marines' moment of triumph. The only safe way to approach him is by moving along the bottom of the room, where the military cameramen are. Might as well take your photos of RAY from three angles, while you're at it. When you're done, move slowly and quietly along the left side of the room up behind the marine. Then capture him and take his tags. None of the other marines care.

Hold No. 2 Port Side Guard

Exit Hold No. 3 through the port side door, and watch the situation in Hold No. 2 carefully on your Soliton's display. There are two projectors and two screens in Hold No. 2, and the projectors take turns showing the telecast of the speech. When the projectors switch off, all of the marines turn to face the other direction! Entering from Hold No. 3, you should easily spot the guard patrolling nearby. Wait until the marines turn to face the starboard side of the room, and then carefully sneak across the grates and run up behind the marine. Capture him quickly, get in front of him even more quickly, and demand his tags. Once he gives them up, tranquilize him and duck behind the cargo box nearby. By this time, the marines will all turn and face the port side again, and Snake is trapped. Unfortunately, you'll just have to wait in your hiding spot until the marines turn to face the starboard side once again.

Skip the Exercise!

Listen carefully to the speech while capturing Dog Tags in Hold No. 2. If General Dolph starts to lead the group in some neck-stretching exercises, hide immediately! The soldiers will begin to look in all directions, and Snake might be spotted. If you're in the middle of holding up a marine, don't worry. The good soldier will keep his hands raised patiently until you return when the stretches are completed.

Hold No. 2 Projector Guard

From the position of the previous guard, crouch and crawl along the port side of the marine troops, careful not to touch any of them. Get undercover before the marines turn to face the port side again. Once you reach the bottom of the room, the marine near the projectors is easy to sneak up on and capture. But exercise great caution when demanding his tags. You cannot let Snake appear in the light of the closest projector, or everyone will be alerted to his presence. After you hold the marine up, move out to his right side but stay close to him. Place your gun against his face, from a 45-degree angle, in order to take his tags. Once you have this last set, tranquilize the marine and run back to Hold No. 3 to upload the pictures for Otacon's viewing!

Previous Photo Critique Time

The console where Snake needs to upload the shots is situated near the entrance on the east side of the room. If you've taken shots of pinup girls, unconscious Olga, or the Vulcan Raven Action Figure with the Camera, go ahead and try an upload. Otacon's responses to these shots are quite amusing!

1 2 3 6

The Front-Right Photo: Otacon reminds Snake of what pictures to capture. After the scene and the Codec conversation, Snake is stands in the perfect spot from which to capture the "front-right" photo. Simply equip the Camera, frame as much of RAY in the shot as possible, and press ● to shoot. We've provided decent example photos that will get you through this part of the game if you can duplicate them.

Duplicate this shot for best results.

The Front-Center Photo: After taking the front-right shot, sneak around the base of the platform where the cameraman stands and move to the south wall, near the black centerline on the floor. Equip the camera and try to frame as much of RAY as possible in the shot. This is your "front-center" shot.

Duplicate this shot for best results.

Expert Photography

Snake may make a comment after you take a shot. If Snake says "Good," then the photo will satisfy the mission requirements. If Snake says "Alright!" then the photo will receive the best possible response from Otacon after you upload the shots.

Continue sneaking to the left, staying close under the platform where the second cameraman is stationed. Position Snake near the front-left corner of the technician's platform, equip the camera and frame your shot. It's okay if the walkway sticks out in front of RAY's "face" a little bit. The shot will get a better rating from Otacon if you crouch so that RAY's "face" can be seen better under the walkway.

Duplicate this shot for best results.

2 0 0 1 2 5 5

From there, sneak north past the lone guard on the side. We recommend crawling behind the guard, just to be safe. Continue along the west wall to the end, and aim the camera at RAY. Here, you should be able to see the "MARINES" lettering on the side of the mechanical beast. Don't zoom in on it too closely; Otacon wants to see that the lettering is actually a part of RAY.

Duplicate this shot for best results.

False Alarm

At roughly two minutes left to go in the speech, the general will suddenly shout, "Intruder on the Left! Intruder on the right!" Although you hear the alerts, don't sweat it. The General is only drilling his men. However, if you are unlucky enough to be in the open when the men respond to the General, your mission could end right there.

If time runs out, don't panic. The General, loving to hear himself talk, will go on! So, the timing of the speech is not your worst problem—just concentrate on sneaking carefully and getting the photos.

Now return to the command console on the east side of the room, near the entrance, and press  to upload the pics. Otacon will critique them. He will accept photos where you framed as much of RAY as possible in the shot. The "MARINE" lettering is a must for Otacon, so he will send you back if you don't have the shot exactly as he wants it. If he doesn't like one of the angle photos, or maybe two of them, the game will still continue. If Otacon deems all four shots worthless, then he'll send you back to redo them.

General Scott Dolph

General Dolph has worked hard and fought bravely all throughout his military career, believing in the causes of the American people and its government. His inspiring leadership skills make him the perfect commandant to martial the U.S. Marines forces. Though divorced for many years, his beliefs have not faltered and he continues to struggle for peace and prosperity in the world. His personal goal in life is that his troubled daughter might finally see that mankind lives in a peace-loving world, where everyone is safe. The general views the rise of Metal Gear programs around the world as the most powerful threat to freedom that has ever existed. In the past two years, he has worked hard with military intelligence to create the first prototype of a Marine anti-terrorist amphibious battle tank. RAY is a Metal Gear for fighting other Metal Gears. This project represents the culmination of Commandant Dolph's life work.

Colonel Sergei Gurlukovich

The Colonel is the leader of a private Russian military army he assembled following the end of the Cold War. Manpower was easy to come by when thousands of former Soviet soldiers and KGB agents suddenly found themselves unemployed in the late 1980s. The goal of his organization is to restore military power and dignity to Mother Russia, Gurlukovich's self-styled ideal of a military-controlled utopia in the former communist nation.

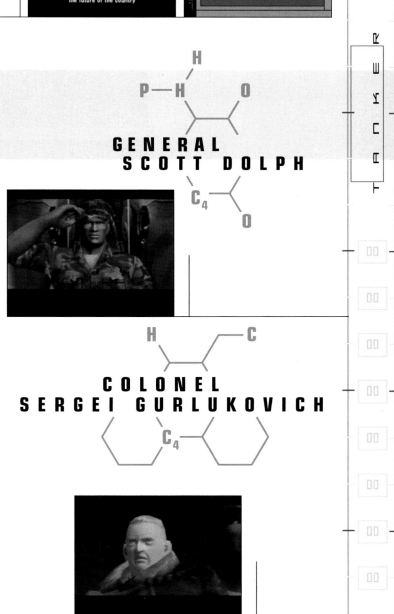

2 part MISSION ANALYSIS

PLANT

Offshore decontamination facility "Big Shell"

Come in from downwind,
then pull up fast!

A VIP from one of the major
conservation groups,

Change of Format

Whereas the Tanker portion of the Mission Analysis was divided into the major areas of the U.S.S. Discovery, coverage of the Big Shell facility is handled in a mission-based fashion. You will often move between multiple areas, some-times revisiting specific sections more than once, as you work toward achieving your objectives.

Strut A:
DEEP SEA DOCK

Chief of Operations

140.85

COLONEL

Colonel Campbell will provide information on Snake's mission objectives, which is helpful if you just booted up the game from a save file. He will explain all of the functions of the con-troller, as well as basic stealth and combat tactics. Campbell is also capable of providing background information on the structure of the Big Shell and profiles on the key players in this operation.

MISSION 01: RECONNAISSANCE

After a quick consultation with Colonel Roy Campbell, commander of this operation, your FOXHOUND operative codename is switched to "Raiden." The Colonel will call several times while you examine the hangar. He'll advise you on basic operations and item usage.

Having infiltrated the Deep Sea Dock at the bottom of the Big Shell's Strut A, the first objective is to get up to the surface of Strut A. There is an elevator to the surface at the north end of the docks area.

Strut A: Deep Sea Dock

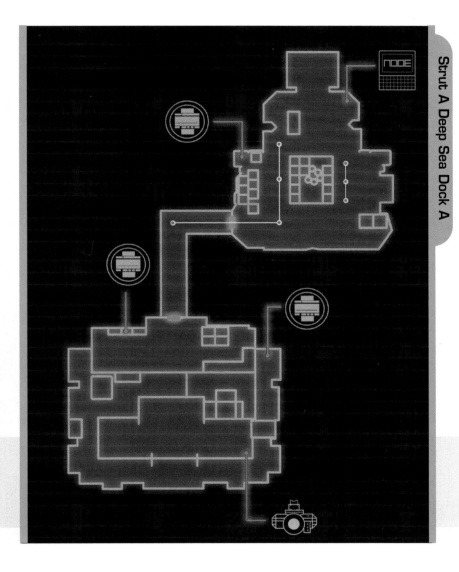

Strut A Deep Sea Dock A

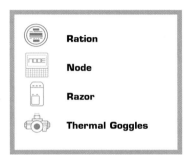	**Ration**
	Node
	Razor
	Thermal Goggles

Shooing Away Sea Lice

If a red bug appears on the Rations icon in your left inventory menu, hold the Left trigger button and press up and down rapidly on the d-pad. This is called "shaking off" the bugs. If sea lice are left to feed on your Rations long enough, they'll leave you without any.

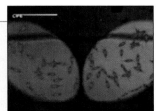

Swimming Controls

Dive into the water and press ⬤ to submerge under the surface. Campbell will call immediately and provide instructions on how to swim. Swim to the lower southeast corner to find the submerged **Thermal Goggles**.

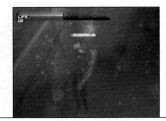

Surface and move to the ladder, then press 🔘 to climb out.

Initial Supplies

Move to the western section of the room and use First Person View to find the vent leading under the platform from this side. Crawl straight through the vent to the other side of the room, where the water pressure tank sections off a small space. Here you will find a **Ration**.

In the lockers on the back wall, Raiden will find another **Ration** in the center locker. One more item to collect remains in the area, and it's partially hidden.

1 0 2 4 0 1 3 2 9 5 0 0 1 0 0 2 1 4 8 6 0 1 8
0 1 4 7 8 7 3 7 0 5 0 1 1

Trail of the Intruder

Open the watertight hatch at the top of the pool area. Raiden spots a sentry that has been attacked. The sentry leaves, so proceed quickly up the corridor and through the sliding door.

The guards in the cargo area have been knocked out cold. Raiden will have to wait until the platform elevator comes back down before he can go up.

Big Shell Nodes

Campbell explains the Soliton Radar system to Raiden. Each time Raiden enters a new floor level, he will have to download the map of the area from the local area Node. When you enter a new area and need to know the exact location of the Node, call Colonel Campbell. Campbell describes the locations pretty well, so don't spend a lot of time searching for Nodes without his help.

First Login

Proceed into the cargo warehouse area. Move up the west side of the room and hop onto the crates to collect another **Ration**.

Since the guards will be unconscious longer than usual, Raiden can shake down their bodies for useful items. Then move to the Node console on the right side of the elevator and login. Raiden is asked to enter a name.

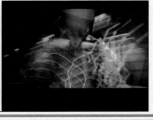

Big Shell Map

After the login, you can view a full map of the Big Shell. The names and functions of Shell 1 and its six Struts are displayed when you highlight them. Move the Right stick to rotate the map.

Identification Confirmed

The name and information you enter at the first Node will be seen again in a special way at the end of the game!

The Unexpected Guest

Raiden's girlfriend Rose will act as mission analyst and record Jack's game data. Whenever you want to find out more about Raiden's past and his relationship with Rose, contact her and save your game.

Deep Sea Dock Tactics

After Raiden logs in, the guards will start to awaken. You should have enough time to run south in the room and hide amid the stacks of boxes on the middle pallet. The guards will radio an alert, and the whole place will go into Caution mode for a time. Don't panic; just stay low on the inside of the pallet and wait for the appropriate moment to move. The guard on the west side of the room will move into the corridor. This is the perfect opportunity to escape from your hiding spot on the pallet and make a break for the elevator. Just make sure that the guard on the east side of the room is not facing the elevator when you go for it, or your movement will draw his attention in this small, well-lit room.

Strut A: Pump Facility
Roof Reconnaissance

Bandage

M9 Ammo

Chaff Grenades

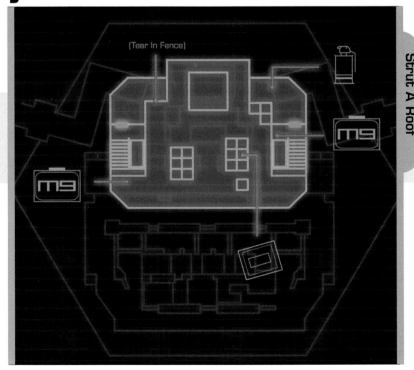

(Tear In Fence)

Strut A Roof

Move down from Raiden's position and hop onto the crates for a **Bandage**. There are **M9 Bullets** in the lower-left corner of the roof, but you'll need the appropriate gun to obtain them.

Move to the upper-left corner, where the Colonel contacts Raiden and points out the hole in the bottom of the fence. Crouch and crawl through the hole. Enter Strut A through the western door.

Poop Alert!

If Raiden runs over an area where there are bird droppings on the deck, he will slip and fall. Also, if Raiden stands in one place too long, one of the temperamental birds might drop a load on his head.

Strut A: Pump Room

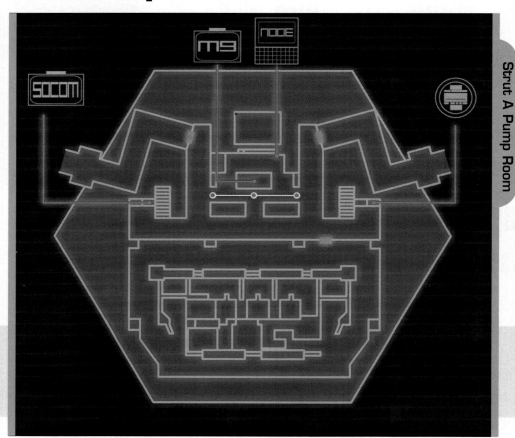

Strut A Pump Room

⊞	**Ration**
SOCOM	**Socom Ammo**
NODE	**Node**
M9	**M9 Ammo**

At the bottom of the stairs, two guards split up. Raiden can spot the location of the Node at the top of the area. Knocking on the partition wall can distract the guard patrolling this area. The best time to knock is when the guard is searching the west side of the room near the entrance to the AB Connector Bridge. As soon as the guard hears the noise, stop hugging the wall so that you can see the guard's movement direction in the top-down camera view. Run around the partition in the opposite direction, and sneak over to the Node to download the map of Strut A.

OSP (On-Site Procurement) in Strut A

As the guard returns to his position, hide behind the central desk. While you're there, crouch and look under the desk to spot a stash of **M9 Bullets**. Remember that they're here in case you need them later in the game.

There are other items hidden in the control room portion of the Pump Facility, some of which you can't collect until later. Under the west stairs, the right locker contains **Socom Bullets**. Leave the locker door open to remind you that they are there. The right locker under the east stairs holds a **Ration**. Another box of **M9 Bullets** is at the top of the stairs. You can obtain some **Chaff Grenades** if you run out to the Roof through this door. A guard patrols the roof, so get back inside quickly.

Brief Diversion

Raiden's current lack of a firearm is probably bothering you. Intelligence reports indicate that an M9 Tranquilizer Gun is located just inside the Strut F Warehouse, where it should be easy to obtain. To provide you with every possible advantage, this Mission Analysis will divert you to the warehouse briefly to obtain this weapon.

FA Connecting Bridge

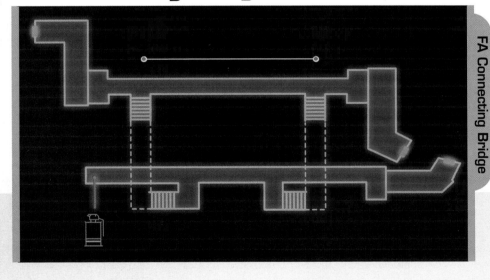

FA Connecting Bridge

 **Chaff Grenade**

Guards and/or automated sentries (Cyphers) monitor most of the connecting bridges between the struts. These bridges are treacherous areas because Raiden is out in the daylight and there are few places to hide. Guards can see further when there is plenty of light, so your objectives in these areas will be harder to accomplish. It's best to get across the bridges as quickly as possible without being spotted.

FA Bridge Tactics

But you can use chaff to set up an interference field. That'll knock its sensors offline for a while.

When Raiden enters the FA Connecting Bridge area, Campbell contacts Raiden about the Cypher. This transmission includes a visual Codec tutorial on how to use Chaff Grenades against Cyphers. Also, notice how Raiden is shown throwing a grenade from behind a wall. This is a good strategy to master if you have the opportunity.

Either employ the Chaff Grenade method demonstrated by the Colonel, or just watch the floating device in First Person View until the Cypher moves below the sight line of the upper level. Either way, run down the first set of stairs on the bridge to the lower platform. Raiden can find **Chaff Grenades** on the closest side of the lower platform.

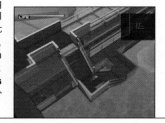

Cross the lower portion of the bridge, throwing a Chaff Grenade as you go. The Chaff disrupts the Cypher and lets Raiden enter Strut F. Make sure you enter the *upper* level—that's where the M9 is located.

Strut F Warehouse

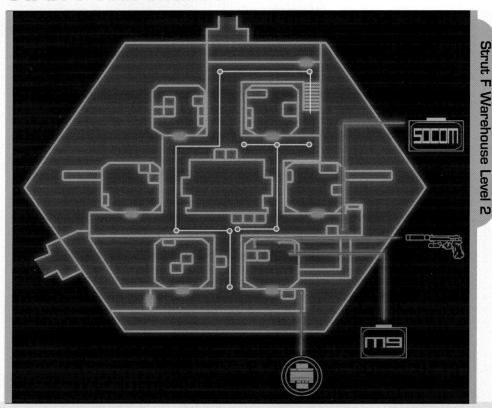

Strut F Warehouse Level 2

Ration	
Socom Ammo	
M9	
M9 Ammo	

Just inside the Warehouse, Raiden spots a guard on duty. The guard radios in every minute or so. If he fails to report, an investigation team will be dispatched. It is important to avoid tranquilizing or killing a guard that must report in. If you must take down a reporting guard for any reason, be prepared to leave the area when the security supervisor demands a status report over the radio. A second investigation team will be dispatched to find out the problem and wake up any sleeping guards.

Warehouse Browsing

Move to the left end of the corridor and collect the **Ration** situated behind the crates. Enter the door that does not have a level marking and find the **M9 Tranquilizer Gun** in the space among the stacked boxes. Then collect the two boxes of **M9 Bullets** in the area.

Now that you have the M9, return to Strut A and proceed to Strut B as ordered. With this firearm, you can get the drop on the central guard in Strut A.

DOG TAGS: Strut-A Control Room Guard

Returning from Strut F with the M9, it's time to collect your first Dog Tags in the Plant chapter. Equip the gun and simply wait until the guard searches the east portion of the room near the FA Connector Bridge entrance. When the guard turns around and walks back to the center, run up and aim your gun at him from behind. Then get in front of him and point the gun at his face to get his Dog Tags.

AB Connecting Bridge

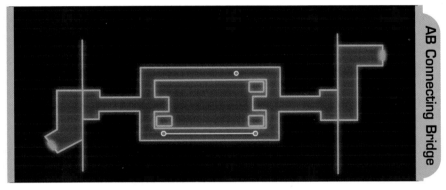

AB Connecting Bridge

Continue on course to Strut B by crossing the AB Connecting Bridge. Raiden notices that two guards are patrolling the platform.

AB Bridge **Tactics**

The top guard is stationary and faces the rail; he will easily spot you if you try to cross by shimmying under him. You must cross through the area where the guard is slowly patrolling back and forth. If the guard is at the opposite end, run to the bottom corner. Then face the rail and press ⑦ to jump over and hang. Shimmy across the bridge to the Strut B side. When you jump back onto the platform, aim for the orange-colored section. If Raiden lands on a section of iron grating, the guard will hear.

Dog Tags Can Wait

Avoid attempting to collect Dog Tags at this time. Both of these guards will resist arrest, meaning you must have heavier firepower to convince them.

Strut B
Transformer Room

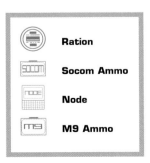

Strut B Transformer Room

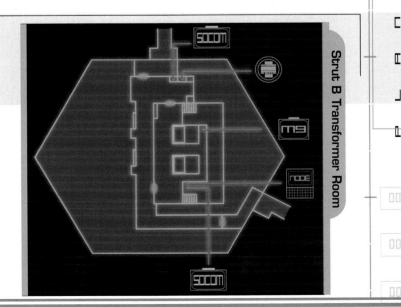

(Ration icon)	**Ration**
SOCOM	**Socom Ammo**
node	**Node**
M9	**M9 Ammo**

Raiden meets Iroquois Pliskin. Pliskin gives Raiden his **Cigarettes** and the unsuppressed **Socom** pistol. Since the gun doesn't have a silencer, stick with the M9 unless you need to destroy an object or a Cypher.

IROQUOIS PLISKIN   (David Hayter)

Raiden's New Partner

Later on, Pliskin will provide expert field advice on weapons and strategy. But for now, the old guy needs a nap. After obtaining Pliskin's frequency during the cinema, tune to the channel and call him repeatedly. Pliskin remains asleep for the time being, but Raiden's reactions are amusing. In the final call, Pliskin screams out in his sleep.

Ongoing Transmission

During the meeting between Raiden and Pliskin, the Colonel radios with a message from SEAL 10 team. They're pinned down on the BC connecting bridge, and they need assistance. Raiden has to go alone since Pliskin needs a rest.

Descend the stairs past the dozing Pliskin and grab the **Socom Bullets** sitting next to the Node. Login and download the Strut B map. A box of **M9 Bullets** is on the north side of the upper level. You might be better off leaving these here until you really need them. If you pick up an ammo box just to receive one bullet, you're shortchanging yourself.

There are three lockers near the exit to the BC Connecting Bridge. The right locker holds **Socom Bullets**, and the center has a **Ration**. If you can't pick up one of these items because Raiden's slot is full, leave the locker open so you remember to pick it up later.

BC Connecting Bridge

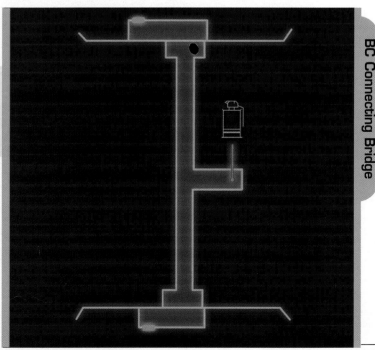

BC Connecting Bridge

 **Chaff Grenade**

Move across the empty bridge, collecting the **Chaff Grenades** dropped by the SEALs. Enter Strut C.

MISSION 02: BOMB DISPOSAL

Colonel Campbell has shifted mission priority to disarming the bombs that have been set all over the plant by the maniacal explosives genius known as Fatman. First, you must find and recruit Navy bomb expert Peter Stillman, who was brought in with the SEAL team. Under his tutelage, it shouldn't be hard to learn what to do and carry out the Colonel's orders.

Strut C Dining Hall

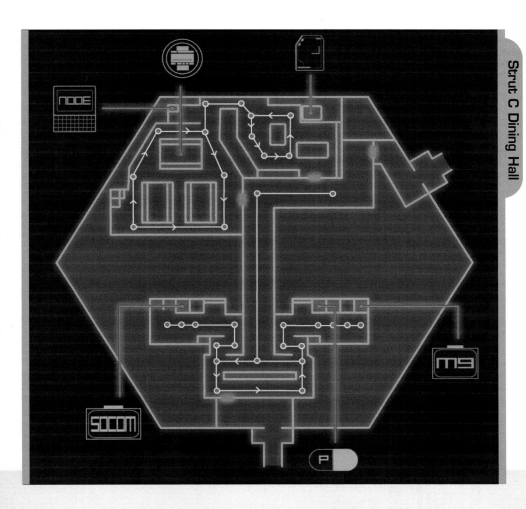

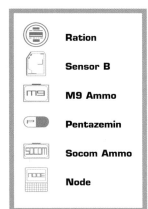	Ration
	Sensor B
	M9 Ammo
	Pentazemin
	Socom Ammo
	Node

A smart infiltrator will search the bathrooms for useful items—even the Women's! Check the left stall in the Men's Room to find some **Socom Bullets**.

In the Women's Bathroom, check the left toilet stall for **Pentazemin**. The far right stall holds **M9 Bullets**.

A poor old man who got dragged along for this picnic.

The Bomb Squad Guy

Continue up the center hallway past a Lv1 door. Raiden meets Peter Stillman, who is going through the kitchen looking for bombs. Stillman explains to Raiden and Pliskin how to clear the C4 bombs from all of the Big Shell's struts. There is a bomb in every strut, and Raiden must clear the ones labeled A through F. Stillman equips Raiden with the **Coolant** and the **Sensor A**. He also gives the rookie the **Lv1 PAN Card**. Start searching for bombs in Strut C.

Bomb Markers

Any time during what we're calling Mission 2, the map will have small markers indicating which buildings have not yet been cleared of bombs.

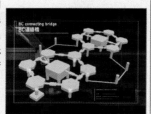

Explosives Expertise

Dial Stillman's frequency on the Codec. He'll give you some pretty obvious clues about where the first bomb is hidden, and he'll even make fun of you for going into the Women's Bathroom.

Beginning the Search

Move into the eating area and download the local map from the Node. Equip Sensor A, and you'll spot a greenish cloud on the map. Fatman's bomb is located somewhere in the cloud, which hovers over the Women's Bathroom.

If you're hungry, there's a **Ration** under the top table in the cafeteria section. Also, you can mess with Stillman's temper by pressing up against the pantry door where he's hidden and knocking. If you try to open the door, he gets even angrier.

The Strut C Bomb

Enter the Women's Bathroom and stand near the right-hand sink. Look up in First Person View, and you'll immediately spot the bomb. It's tucked into a crevice above the toilet, and it's reflected in the mirror. Just aim the Coolant at the bomb and keep spraying it until the device clicks off.

Strut C Tactics

After you meet Stillman and Pliskin in Strut C, leave the level through either exit and then reenter. Guards have taken up posts around the dining area, and it's time to collect some Dog Tags. But don't try these yet unless you have the M9.

What makes this guard difficult is his timing and patrol route. The cramped and curvy entrances to the restroom are a place where you're likely to foul up a capture. As the guard comes down the central corridor toward the BC Connecting Bridge entrance, stand just inside the Men's Room. As soon as he faces the Women's, run out behind him and get the surprise. Even if he starts moving toward the Women's, you still have time, but once he gets inside the bathroom, abort. There's hardly any room in there to perform the capture correctly, so don't risk getting spotted.

Getting the drop on this guard is somewhat easier than trying to snipe him from a distance. Simply wait outside the south Lv1 door. Once the guard passes the door heading to the bottom corner of the room, run through the door and a few steps toward him. Then capture him by aiming the handgun. Use the dots on the radar to better judge your distance, and wait until he faces west so that you don't have to squeeze between the guard and the wall.

BC Connecting Bridge

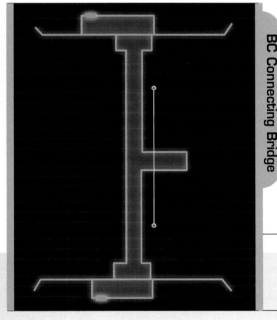

BC Connecting Bridge

A Cypher now patrols the damaged bridge, so be cautious. Use either a Chaff Grenade to get through this area, or use the Socom to knock out the Cypher altogether. To take a Cypher out in one shot, you must hit it directly on the camera.

You must dispose of five more bombs. Due to the enemy placement on the bridges and in the struts, plus the number of quick cutscenes that point out enemy placement, it seems that the easier way to go is counterclockwise through Struts B and A, then F through D.

Strut B

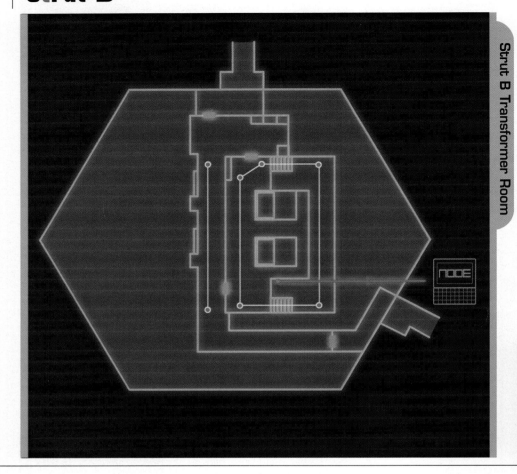

Node

Two new guards patrol inside and outside the Transformer Room. Because of their long patrol routes, these guards are pretty easy to take down.

As you move south in the corridor, you might hear a sudden beeping. This is the signal from Fatman's bomb. Inside the north door of the Transformer room, the top transformer's door is open. When you close it, you'll find the second bomb. Use Coolant to freeze it.

Strut B Tactics

DOG TAG: Strut B Transformer Room Guard

Getting the better of the sentry in the Transformer room isn't too hard. On his route, he pauses by the north door near the lockers and stares for a moment. Simply run through the door and get the drop on him.

DOG TAG: Strut B Corridor Guard

Due to the high number of floor gratings in the corridor, it is necessary to set up a complex trap for the guard. Cross south through the Transformer Room and enter the corridor through the lower-west door when the guard is moving upward in his route. Open one of the transformer doors in the corridor, press Raiden's back against it, and crouch ( ) so that Raiden cannot be seen through the door's opening. As the guard passes moving south, stand and press to get the drop on him.

Strut B

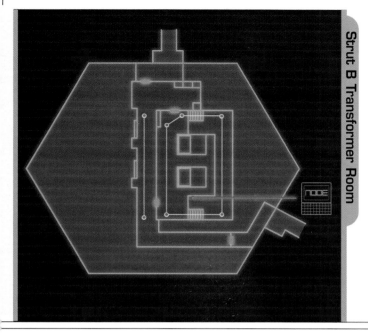

Strut B Transformer Room

Node

Two new guards patrol inside and outside the Transformer Room. Because of their long patrol routes, these guards are pretty easy to take down.

As you move south in the corridor, you might hear a sudden beeping. This is the signal from Fatman's bomb. Inside the north door of the Transformer room, the top transformer's door is open. When you close it, you'll find the second bomb. Use Coolant tofreeze it. Then call Stillman for relevant conversation, and check in with Pliskin.

Strut B Tactics

DOG TAG: Strut B Transformer Room Guard

Getting the better of the sentry in the Transformer room isn't too hard. On his route, he pauses by the north door near the lockers and stares for a moment. Simply run through the door and get the drop on him.

DOG TAG: Strut B Corridor Guard

Due to the high number of floor gratings in the corridor, it is necessary to set up a complex trap for the guard. Cross south through the Transformer Room and enter the corridor through the lower-west door when the guard is moving upward in his route. Open one of the transformer doors in the corridor, press Raiden's back against it, and crouch (⬤) so that Raiden cannot be seen through the door's opening. As the guard passes moving south, stand and press 🔘 to get the drop on him.

AB Connecting Bridge

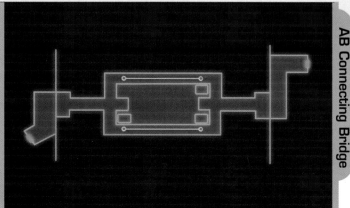

AB Connecting Bridge

```
1 0 2 4 0 1 3 2 9 5 0 0 1 0 0 2 1 4 8 6 0 1 8 7
 0 1 4 7 8 7 3 7 0 5 0 1 1
```

Now that Raiden has the Socom, there is a way to get the Dog Tags from at least one of the AB Connecting Bridge Guards. One of the two guards must be tranquilized so that when you fire warning shots at one guard, the other will be asleep and unable to hear.

AB Bridge Tactics, Part 2

Approaching from either end, run out onto the bridge just a few feet, so that Raiden stands just outside the guard's cone of vision when he pauses on your side of his route. Enter First Person View and tranquilize the closest guard. Then run to the area behind the guard that is still active, jump over the rail, and hang. Shimmy across the platform a little, so that the guard crosses above as you are shimmying to a position a few feet behind him. When the guard stops at the end of an iron grating, quietly jump onto the platform behind him. Nudge the Left Stick just a little to shake off the jump, and then draw the Socom on the guard. When he taunts, fire a shot into his hand. Then you'll get his tags. Now eliminate the guard and drag him out of view. Move over to the sleeping guard. Equip the Coolant and spray it in the guard's face for a few seconds. When he wakes, run back inside the closest entrance and wait for the guard's cone of vision to change from yellow to white. Now you can employ the same strategy with this guard that you used on the last one. This complex strategy may take a practice run to master, so save your game beforehand.

Strut A Pump Room

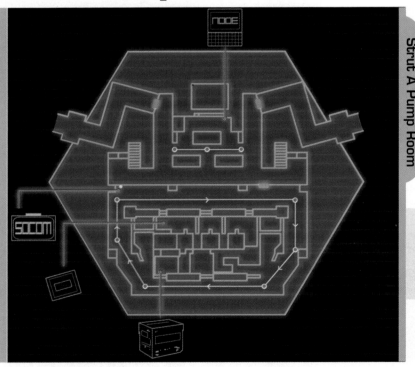

Strut A Pump Room

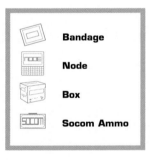

	Bandage
	Node
	Box
	Socom Ammo

With Sensor A equipped, you can tell that Fatman's bomb is hidden somewhere in the mechanical room to the south. Without being seen, move past the guard in the cubicle area or hold him up for his Dog Tags if you haven't already. The Lv1 PAN card will allow Raiden into the machinery room—just be certain that the guard inside is nowhere near the door. Move to the south corner of the room and run over the stairs into the central area of pipes. Crouch and crawl under the pipes, moving upward and then over to the left. A **Bandage** is on the far side of this pipe maze.

From the Ration, crawl back to the red pipe and crawl south until you reach a small square area where the bomb is located. Stay flat on the floor to avoid detection and use the Coolant to deactivate the detonator.

At this point, you may have to take care of the guard; see the following Tactics section. Then move to the bottom-left stairs and crouch on the other side. Crawl to the right under some pipes, then stand and hop over the obstacle to reach **Cardboard Box 1**.

Emerging from the lower part of the pipe maze, and with the guard tranquilized or neutralized, stand on top of the lower-left stairs and aim for the surveillance camera in the top-left corner of the room. Shoot it out, and then claim the **Socom Bullets** that sit under it.

Pump Room Tactics

DOG TAG: Strut A Pump Room Guard

Hide amongst the pipes on the right side of the room until the guard passes the bottom-right corner. Then follow him to the bottom-left corner where he stops, and aim your weapon to get the drop on him. Be sure to capture him before he walks into the camera's range.

FA Connecting Bridge

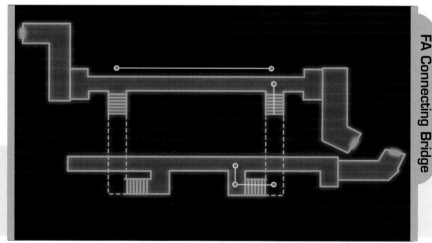

A lone soldier has joined the Cypher in patrolling the bridge. To enter Strut F closest to the Node location, use the lower entrance on the Strut F side of the bridge.

FA Connecting Bridge

FA Bridge Tactics

STRATEGY

FA Bridge Cypher and Guard

Wait until the guard is patrolling the lower part of the bridge, and then use the Socom to blow the Cypher out of the sky. With the M9 handy, move out to the halfway point of the bridge. When the guard comes back up to the top, tranquilize him and enter Strut F through the bottom level.

DOG TAG: FA Bridge Guard

After destroying the Cypher with the Socom, run to the top of the stairs, crouch and hide behind the small corner as shown in the screenshot. When the guard comes up the stairs, stand up and nudge the Left Stick a little, then aim your weapon to capture the guard. There's plenty of room to get in front of him and demand those Dog Tags. This guard will resist capture, so fire a warning shot or blow his hand off.

Strut F **Warehouse**

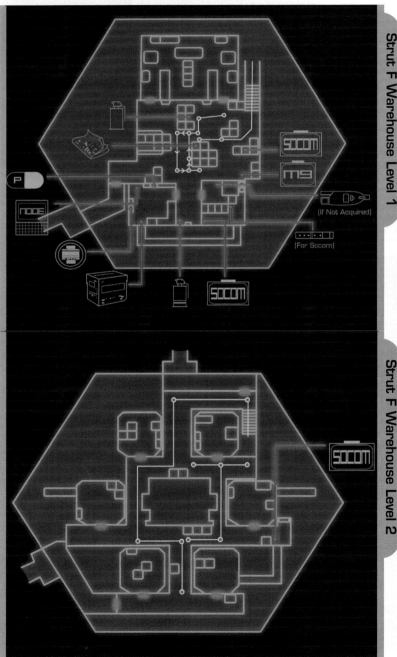

SOCOM	Socom Ammo
M9	M9 Ammo
	Mine Detector
	Supressor
	Stun Grenades
	Box
	Ration
P	Pentazemin
	Book
	Chaff Grenades
NODE	Node

3 0 0 1 6 5 0 2 4 0 7 4 5
8 7 0 2 0 0 1 5 8 8 0 1 0 1 0 0 2 1 4 0 0 3 8 7

0 0 3 2 0 0 2 0 0 6 9

Enter the Warehouse again, this time through the lower B1 level. Immediately press Raiden's back up against the nearby boxes so that the guard does not catch sight of him. When the guard moves north in the room, slip around the crates and into the south passage. A box of **Chaff Grenades** is at the bottom of the passage. Enter the left Lv1 door.

Download the map of the Warehouse from the Node. **Cardboard Box 2** sits in the bottom corner of the room. Of the lockers on the left, the one that is unlocked contains a **Ration**. As for the locked locker, if you stand in the space above it and hit the door repeatedly from the side with single punches, the door will fall outward and you can get the **Book** inside. This naughty magazine will keep any guard distracted for quite some time. In the top row of lockers, the one on the right holds **Pentazemin**.

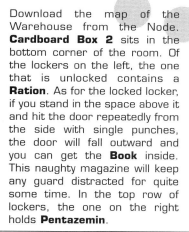

Use First Person View to locate the vent shaft at floor level. Crawl into the shaft and navigate to the east room. When you emerge, collect the **Socom Suppressor** and **Socom Bullets**. Equip the Socom in the right menu and the Suppressor in the left, and the silencer will be permanently attached to your gun. Climb over the crates and grab the **Mine Detector** on the other side. Some **M9 Bullets** have been stashed under the shelves behind the Mine Detector location.

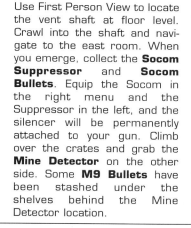

Strut F's Bomb

Equip Sensor A, and Fatman's signature appears on the left side of the first floor. The bomb is planted in the middle of a fortress of stacked crates. The only way to reach it is by dropping from the rail above. For success, you'll have to take out all the guards, including the one that reports. Then defuse the bomb quickly and get out of the Warehouse before an investigation commences.

Warehouse Wares

Other items scattered around the warehouse include the **Socom Bullets** on top of a crate. Just get on the crate to get them. **Stun Grenades** are partially hidden among the crates between the two Lv2 doors. You can drop from above to collect **M9 Bullets** in the bottom-right corner of the lower level. You can obtain another **Book**, which is on top of the crates in the center of the room, by dropping from the top-level rail, as well. On the second floor, return to the room where you got the M9 and crawl through the vent. With the Soliton radar, it's much easier to avoid enemy guards as you emerge from the vent. A box of **Socom Bullets** is at the end of the shaft.

To Each According to Need

Take only what you need from the Warehouse when you really need it, because you will have to return to Strut F several more times before the day is done.

Warehouse Tactics

Warehouse B1 Guard

Make this guard your first target. Enter the Warehouse through the B1 level entrance from the FA Connecting Bridge. Sneak around this guard and download the map from the Node. After you collect the Mine Detector from the lower-right Lv1 room on B1, wait until the guard pauses for a long moment directly outside the door. Run out of the southeast room and capture the guard from behind. Try to catch him as close to the south end as possible so that the guards above cannot see what you are doing. After you have threatened him, tranquilize him and drag him into a locker inside the southwest Lv1 room. *Do not execute him*, or the blood will attract the wrong kind of attention.

Warehouse 1F Guard

After tranquilizing the guard who only patrols B1, exit the Warehouse through the B1 door, out to the FA Connecting Bridge. Move to the top entrance and come back into the Warehouse. The guard who only patrols the upper level moves in a U-shaped pattern around the east side of the rail. Return to the room where Raiden obtained the M9 and crawl into the duct. This duct emerges in a small alcove to the left of the main area. This guard occasionally checks the alcove, so make sure that you aren't seen emerging from the vent. Hide behind the low crates. Once the other guard moves down to the B1 level, prepare to move on the 1F guard. As the guard moves north along his route, catch him by surprise from behind. When the guard moves north in his patrol route, run out from your hiding space and surprise him from behind. Move in front of him and quickly demand those Dog Tags. This guard should cave easily.

Warehouse Reporting Guard

This guard must report in every few minutes or an attack team will be dispatched to investigate. If they find the guard dead, a full clearing of Strut F commences. However, if they only find the guard asleep, they wake him up and leave! To obtain this guard's tags, crouch and hide on the south side of the stack of boxes in the south corridor. When the reporting guard walks south and stops at the bottom of the corridor, quickly stand and step up behind him to make the arrest. Once you have his tags, quickly get to work on diffusing the bomb in the area.

EF Connecting Bridge

 AKS-74u Ammo

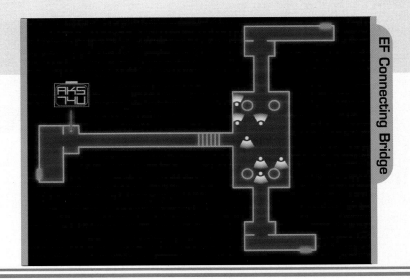

EF Connecting Bridge

Raiden watches as a guard ascends to a high lookout point on the Heliport. From there, the sentry uses binoculars to search the bridge for intruders. Where is a long-range sniper rifle when you need one? Carefully aim the M9 at the guard and put him out of commission in order to cross.

There are two ways to detect Claymores, either with the Thermal Goggles or a Mine Detector. Crawling across a Claymore allows Raiden to pick it up. There are **7 Claymores** to collect on the bridge.

Strut E **Parcel Room, 1F**

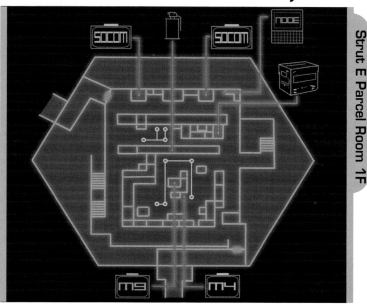

Strut E Parcel Room 1F

Node	**Node**
Box	**Box**
Stun Grenades	**Stun Grenades**
SOCOM	**Socom Ammo**
M9	**M9 Ammo**
M4	**M4 Ammo**

Wait in the south alcove and peek around the corner. Look for the guard with the U-shaped patrol route in the south area to come into view. When that guard turns and heads north, it's time to move. Navigate carefully through the west side of the area, using the large conveyors as cover. Move to the top-right corner of the room, where the Node is located. Download the map of Strut E. There are several items to pick up here, but the guards also have extremely good visibility despite all the fast-moving boxes. Use the following strategies to take them down so you can collect the items.

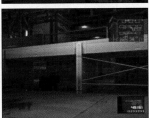

Cardboard Box 5, which is the *Zone of the Enders* box, is on top of the conveyor to the northeast. To get **Stun Grenades**, crawl under the conveyor behind the guard that makes periodic reports. Naturally, both guards should be heavily slumbering before you try for either of these items.

At the south end of a bunch of Tokugawa boxes in the lower center of the room, there are **M4 Bullets** that you can collect later on. Crawl under two of the shelves at the top end of the room for two boxes of **Socom Bullets**. If Raiden is desperate for **Rations**, there are some in a small vent at the bottom of the western stairs.

Rations are in a vent at Raiden's feet.

Parcel Room Tactics

DOG TAG: Parcel Room Patrolling Guard

To obtain this guard's tags, you essentially have to rush him. Move to the second large machine from the top on the east side of the room, near the stairs entrance. When the guard reaches the eastern end of his route, run down and catch him. Adding to the difficulty is the fact that as you run south, machinery and other tall pieces obstruct your view. Use the radar to determine if you are close enough to the guard to draw. This strategy can be intimidating, but it seems to work every time.

DOG TAG: Parcel Room Reporting Guard

To get the drop on this guard, you must first take out or tranquilize the other guard. Rushing up to this guard is no problem because he stares north for the longest time. From the east side of the room, watch this sentry carefully. Wait for him to examine the south side of the room, and then turn back. This is when to run up behind him. But wait; it is even better to stand right there and allow the guard to radio in his next report. Then aim your weapon to capture him. When you get in front of the guard, he will refuse to cooperate. You must shoot the guard in the hand or the shoulder to get your point across.

Strut E Heliport

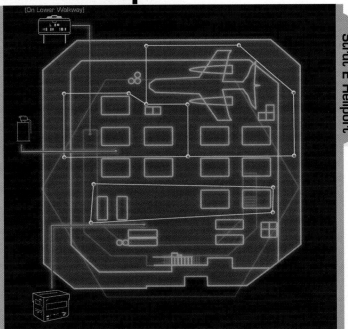

[On Lower Walkway]

Strut E Heliport

📦	**Box**
	Stun Grenades
	Claymore Mines

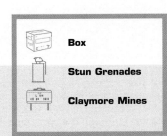

After the cut-scene, go back down the stairs and cross to the left side. Someone has knocked out the guard that is posted here! Shake down the guard's body to get an item, and grab the **Claymores** on the other side of him.

Return to the stairs and ascend to the heliport. From the top of the stairs, move to the left and collect **Cardboard Box 3**. **Stun Grenades** are between two freight cars on the west side of the building.

The terrorist's Harrier fighter jet is parked here, and two guards make wide sweeps of the area. Using Sensor A, you can see that Fatman's scent is all over the Harrier. Move to just under the wing of the fighter, crouch, and use First Person View. The bomb is stuffed way up under the jet, directly under its landing gear. Position Raiden under the Harrier's wing and use the Coolant on the bomb.

Heliport Tactics

DOG TAG: South Heliport Guard

The guard who patrols the portion of the Heliport closest to the stairway entrance makes a long cross from east to west. At some point on this route, you can position Raiden behind one of the freight transports where the guard will pass. As the guard keeps moving, run out from your hiding place and chase down the fast-moving guard.

DOG TAG: North Heliport Guard

This guard patrols around the Harrier jet, which makes his route a little difficult to follow. But there is a point directly between the Harrier and the freight containers where the guard stops and stands facing north for a long moment. This is the best time to run out from behind a container and surprise the guard from behind.

DOG TAGS: Lower Walkway Guard

After you've diffused the bomb under the Harrier, the guard who looks out over the DE Connecting Bridge is alert and actively patrols a long route. He will move down the walkway almost to the stairs, so stay put just out of sight range. When the guard turns and heads back to his lookout point, run steadily behind him until Raiden finally catches up. Then hold up the guard and get those tags. Tranquilizing this guard before moving on also makes it easier to cross the DE Connecting Bridge!

DE Connecting Bridge

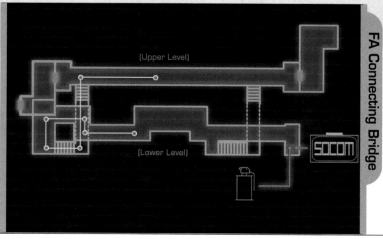

(Upper Level)

(Lower Level)

FA Connecting Bridge

Stun Grenades	
Socom Ammo	

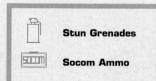

If the lookout on the Heliport above has been recently put to sleep, then crossing this narrow path is much less treacherous. Descend the first set of stairs on the left and move back to the ending to collect **Socom Bullets** and **Stun Grenades**.

DE Bridge Tactics

Strut D Sediment Pool

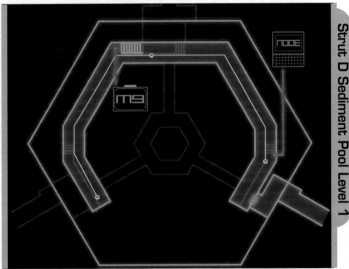

Strut D Sediment Pool Level 1

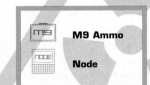

M9	**M9 Ammo**
NODE	**Node**

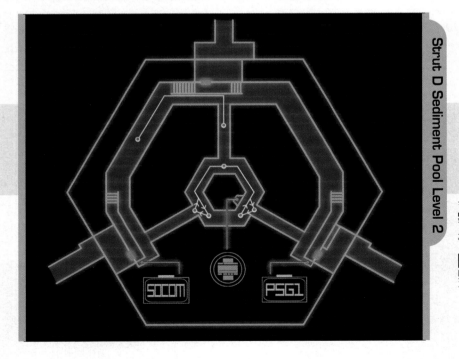

Strut D Sediment Pool Level 2

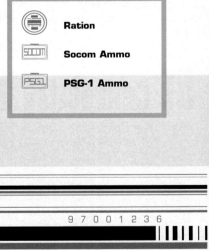

(ration)	**Ration**
SOCOM	**Socom Ammo**
PSG1	**PSG-1 Ammo**

97 00 1236

Enter Strut D through the lower entrance from the DE Connecting Bridge. The local network Node sits just inside the doorway. Download the essential Soliton Radar map of the area and exit the way you came in. Now reenter the Sediment Pool through the Lv1 entrance.

A box of **PSG-1 Bullets** is just below the upper level entrance. From this location, you can safely study the patrol routes and movement patterns of the three guards. A **Ration** is in the center of the area, and **Socom Bullets** are near the CD Connecting Bridge exit. A box of **M9 Bullets** is behind the stairs under the Shell 1-2 Bridge exit.

Taking Out the Trash

There is a gate that can swing out for waste disposal below the Lv3 door that leads out to the Shell 1-2 Connecting Bridge. This is a good location to drag the bodies of unconscious guards. Just don't dispose of any when the reporting guard is directly below. The bomb is located on the lower level under the CD Bridge exit. There are hatches in the floor you can open. Although Fatman's signature odor covers the entire southwestern section, the bomb is located under the last hatch. It's not hard to completely avoid the bottom guard and get over to the bomb before he completes his route. If it comes to it, a little beauty sleep never hurt anyone, either.

Sediment Pool Tactics

DOG TAG: Sediment Pool Central Guard

Go after the center guard first and spread out from there. From just inside the DE Bridge exit, use First Person View to study the center guard's movement pattern and especially his timing. When he is on the opposite side of the center cage from Raiden's position, move to the level just below the entrance, where the PSG-1 Bullets sit. When the guard faces southwest, it's time to move. Run up to the center cage and press Raiden's back into the small niche where the Ration sits. As the center guard moves north, run out and catch him. You can't let him get too far, or the other guard might spot the two of you. Once you have the guard's tags, tranquilize him and drag the body behind the center cage, out of view of the next guard.

DOG TAG: Sediment Pool North Guard

First, take down the central guard and position Raiden behind the cage opposite the north guard's southernmost stopping point. At this position, the guard will face south for a long time. Then he will search left and right a few times. Move out from behind the cage and stand a few feet closer in. Finally, he turns and faces the Shell 1-2 Connecting Bridge exit for a long moment. This is when you should run up behind him and try to surprise the guard. Best of luck.

DOG TAG: Sediment Pool Lower Level Reporting Guard

Because the lower guard makes such long trips back and forth on the bottom level, he has a great ability to spot Raiden from yards away. The trick to getting the drop on this soldier involves literally getting the drop. Move Raiden to one side of the upper level or the other, wherever the reporting guard is currently patrolling. Wait for the guard to reach the end of his route. Watch on the radar as the sentry turns and moves back in the other direction. At this instant, jump over the rail and

hang. Press ⬤ to drop, and then quickly press ⑦ to catch the lower level's rail. Hop onto the platform and run up behind the reporting guard. Once you have this guard's tags, high tail it out of Strut D before someone starts demanding a status report.

CD Connecting Bridge

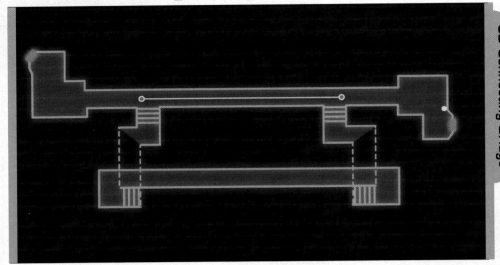

1024013295001002

Stepping out of the smelly disposal area, Raiden spots a surveillance camera mounted directly overhead! Swiftly equip the suppressed Socom and use First Person View to shoot the camera.

A lone guard patrols the entire length of the bridge. Wait until he checks the Strut D side, and then turns to go back. Run out and try to get the drop on him!

Booby Trapped Bridge

Use extreme caution crossing the lower bridge; its floor panels are rigged to drop out from under you as you step on them. There are a few methods to cross safely. You can hang and shimmy by hand from outside the rail. If you move quickly, you can run across, but you can do this only once—the panels that drop will be gone the next time you want to cross. Probably the easiest way is to press your body against the rail and sidestep along the length of the bridge.

Strut C Dining Hall

Return to the Kitchen area and find **Sensor B** in the pantry. When Pliskin defuses the last C4 bomb in the Shell 2 strut, the *real* bombs begin counting down. Now you must return to the bottom of Strut A and find the hidden bomb using the new Sensor B. You'll see a countdown of 400 seconds begin ticking away on the right side of the screen. If you don't make it in time, everyone dies!

Strut A Roof

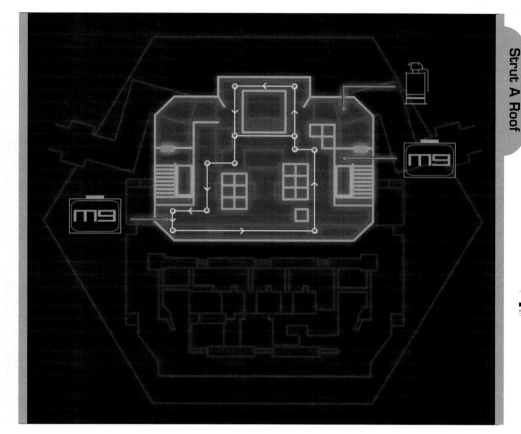

	Chaff Grenades
M9	**M9 Ammo**

14860187

The elevator to the docks has returned to the roof. The guard at the south end won't be much of a nuisance if you get on the elevator quickly. However, the guard does have a set of Dog Tags, and he disappears for a while after the coming events. Better to get the drop on him now if you've got a few seconds to spare. Move to the back of the elevator and it will begin to descend.

Strut A Roof Tactics

 DOG TAG: Strut A Roof Guard

To capture the guard on the roof, enter from either side and carefully follow him around the roof, hiding behind crates when necessary. When the guard stops at the center point in front of the elevator, it's a great time to run out and capture him.

Strut A Deep Sea Dock

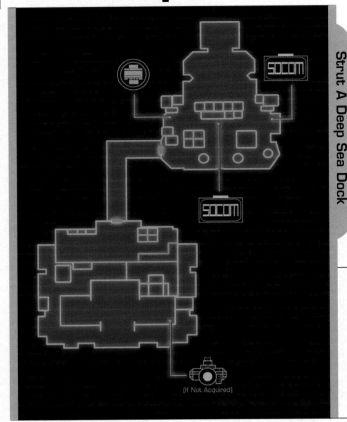

Ration

Thermal Goggles

Socom Ammo

Notice that the crates at the dock have all been rearranged. New items are available, too, including a **Ration** and two boxes of **Socom Bullets**. Move through the dock and the short corridor back to Raiden's entry point.

The bomb is located on the underside of the suspended deep sea sub. To defuse it, stand just south of the sub on the side of the pool behind the rail, and use the Coolant from a distance. Move back toward the elevator.

BOSS FIGHT

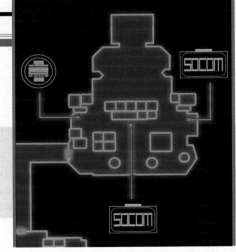

Fortune

Gender:	Female
Affiliation:	Dead Cell Leader
Weapon:	Lockheed RG-590 Experimental Aircraft Rail Cannon

When Raiden nears the elevator, Fortune emerges. She begins to blast every object in the area with her large rail cannon. What's worse is that Fortune can't be hit by Raiden's attacks. Avoid taking a direct hit, because the damage is massive.

Hurry, kill me please!

Don't waste any ammo in this exhibition match, just dodge her attacks and stay away from fires that break out. Keep moving, rolling from one side of the room to the other. If you allow Fortune to pound away at one hiding spot, then soon you won't have anyplace left to hide.

Suddenly the battle ends and the Colonel calls. Fatman has planted a new bomb on the Strut E Heliport and has asked for Raiden to join him there now.

Strut A Roof

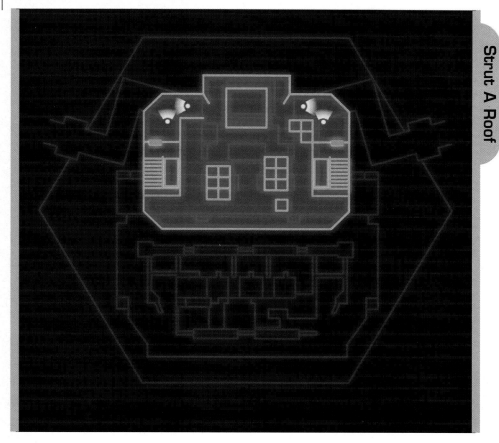

Raiden has 400 seconds to get back to Strut E. The trip is not far if you go through Strut F. On the roof, equip the Mine Detector in order to see the new Claymores that have been set in front of each doorway.

Strut E Heliport

Restock your **Socom Bullets** at the top of the stairs because you will desperately need them in a few moments. The bomb you seek is placed conspicuously in the middle of the floor. Defuse it with the Coolant, and Fatman appears.

900175034   08415
013980101002170 0397
11370   02006

BOSS FIGHT

Fatman

Gender:	Male
Affiliation:	Dead Cell Explosives Expert
Weapon:	Semtex C4 Packs with Timed Detonators, UZI 9mm

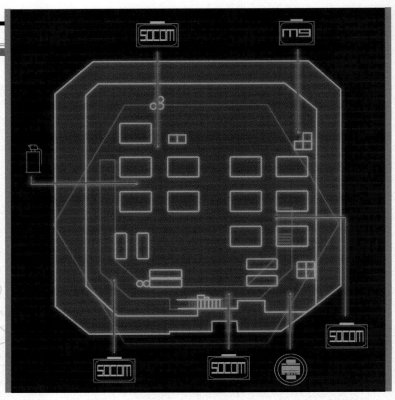

- **Ration**
- **Chaff Grenade**
- **Socom Ammo**
- **M9 Ammo**

During this tricky battle, Raiden must defuse bombs as he avoids Fatman's gunfire, and he has to figure out a way to kill the giant man, as well. Keep Sensor A equipped at all times, and use a Ration manually when necessary. Fatman will set two or three bombs around the Heliport.

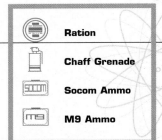

As Fatman tries to set more bombs, chase him down and fire at him with the Socom. Or, if Fatman stops in close range of Raiden, try to knock Fatman down with punches and kicks. Either way, once Fatman is down, equip the Socom and enter First Person View. When Fatman struggles to his hands and knees, shoot him in the head to inflict damage. If he charges at Raiden, flip-jump out of the way. The same goes for when he fires a volley of shots at Raiden.

If Raiden is at the right place at the right time, shooting Fatman with the Socom can prevent him from setting a bomb.

In the last half of the battle, Fatman will hang around one of the locations where he set a bomb and will try to defend it. First, knock Fatman down with Socom fire or punches and kicks, and then put a bullet in his head as he tries to recover. He should skate away, allowing you to freely defuse the bomb.

When the battle ends, Fatman sets one last bomb. The secret is that it's under Fatman, so drag away his bloated carcass to reveal it. Fatman should drop **Peter Stillman's Dog Tags**. Defuse the final bomb.

MISSION 03: HOSTAGE SITUATION
Strut E Heliport

Raiden encounters a Cyborg Ninja wearing an exoskeleton.

I'm like you...I have no name.

The Ninja spells out how to find the President—by going to Shell 1 and finding a hostage named Ames. You'll have to disguise yourself in the **B.D.U.** (body disguise uniform) that the Ninja hands you. Also, you'll have to acquire an AKS-47u. The Ninja gives Raiden a **Cell Phone** so that he can contact Raiden again. When the Ninja calls, the phone buzzes and the controller vibrates. The phone will display an email message. Now you just have to go find the appropriate gun, and the new **Lv2 PAN card** that the Ninja gives you will help. Return to the Strut F warehouse after detouring briefly to engage some new guards.

This security card will unlock all level 2 security doors,

Spankin' New Guards

Following Fatman's grand finale, there are new guards posted on three bridges. So, instead of heading back to the Shell 1 entrance by the quick route, we'll show you how to bag the Dog Tags from the three new guards.

DOG TAG: New DE Connecting Bridge Guard

The guard you've already taken the tags from is patrolling the top level of the bridge, so aim from a distance to put him to sleep. The new guard patrols the lower area, and he can see well in all directions. Entering from the Strut E side, sneak down the stairs to the first corner and wait for the guard to walk toward Strut E. The sentry then turns and walks past the stairs. Sneak down the stairs and catch the guard as he is moving toward Strut D, then squeeze in front of him to demand the tags. Your gun may be sticking through his face, but he will still cower and beg for mercy.

DOG TAG: New CD Connecting Bridge Guard

Entering from Strut D, the guard you've already taken down is patrolling closer to Strut C. Take the old guard out of the equation with a tranquilizer. Move onto the bridge and hide behind one of the low walls on either side of the entrance. When the new guard climbs the stairs, he patrols toward Strut C first. Allow him to patrol toward Strut D. Then, as he's going back to the stairs, run out and get the drop on him.

DOG TAG: New BC Connecting Bridge Guard

First, hide inside the shelter of the Strut C entrance and use the suppressed Socom to blow the Cypher out of the sky. Then watch the guard carefully. After he patrols the short section of destroyed bridge, he comes toward Strut C. Hide until he turns and heads back for Strut B, then run onto the bridge and catch up with him.

EF Connecting Bridge

Don't Rely on the Disguise Yet

Although Raiden can now disguise himself as a Russian mercenary, his uniform indicates that he is supposed to be stationed inside Shell 1. So, the disguise is not useful in other areas of the Big Shell. Use the same sneaking methods as before to return to the EF Connecting Bridge.

This bridge connects not only the two Struts, but is also the east entrance to Shell 1. However, Raiden still needs to find an AKS-74u like the guards use, or his disguise will be incomplete. The Lv2 PAN card allows Raiden to enter doors inside the Warehouse that he couldn't previously.

Another Mechanical Foe

Note that a Gun-mounted Cypher enters the area as Raiden reaches Strut F. This formidable surveillance attack equipment will be waiting when you come back...

Strut F Warehouse

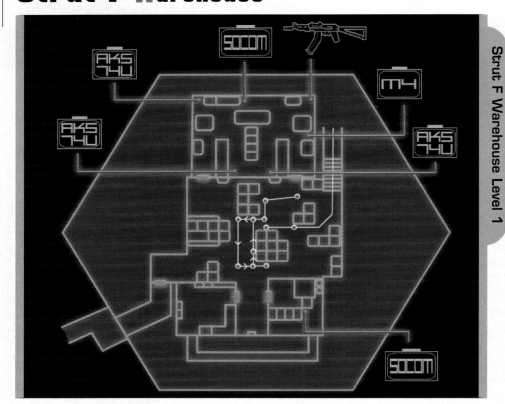

AKS-74u	
AKS-74u Ammo	
Socom Ammo	
M4 Ammo	

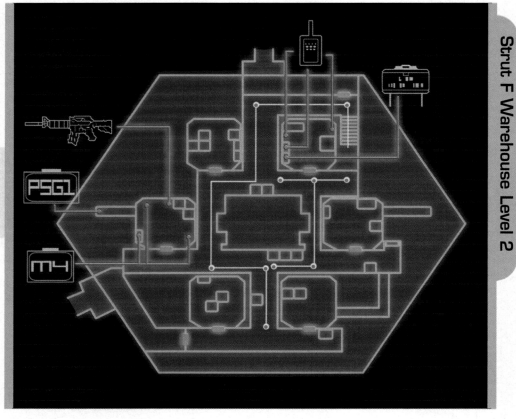

AKS-74u	
Claymore Mine	
C-4	
PSG-1 Ammo	
M4 Ammo	

The northern Lv2 room on the upper level has two lockers where you can conveniently stuff sleeping guards. There are **Claymores** in the lower locker, and there is **C4** in the upper locker. Two more boxes of **C4** lie on the floor in the room.

Carefully navigate to the west side of the upper level, and enter the Lv2 room here. *Do not move too far into the room*—there is an IR beam array wired to Semtex explosives scattered around the room. The control box sits on top of the lockers, so use the suppressed Socom to take it out. The **M4 Assault Rifle** is on the other side of the beams. A box of **M4 ammo** lies nearby, and another one is in the locker. Some **PSG-1 Bullets** are in the small crawlway on the west side of the room.

To reach the lower level, we recommend exiting out to the FA Connecting Bridge and then reentering through the bottom door. Sneak into the north room with the two Lv2 doors. The **AKS-74u** is in the northeast corner of the room. Three boxes of **AKS-74u Bullets** are scattered around the room, there are **Socom Bullets** to the north, and **M4 Bullets** on the east wall. There is a new box of **Socom Bullets** in the southeast Lv1 room.

Strut F Tactics

The Dog Tag strategies for these three guards have already been described, and you already have a good idea of how to take down these guards.

EF Connecting Bridge

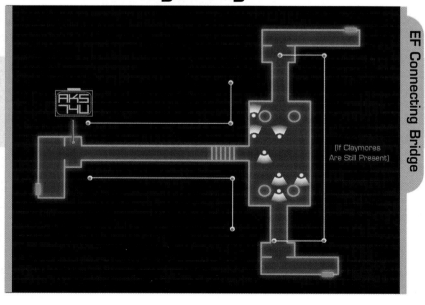

EF Connecting Bridge

(If Claymores Are Still Present)

 AKS-74u Ammo

A guard will climb the stairs and act as a lookout over the bridge. Raiden must carefully tranquilize him before moving on. While you are taking care of that, a Gun Cypher will move into view. Use the Socom and aim for its camera. If you're out of Socom Bullets, the M4 Assault Rifle works even better. Run onto the bridge and use First Person View to find the Gun Cypher that now appears over near Shell 1. Shoot out this robot sentry, and then move to the top of the stairs on the left side. Use First Person View to locate another new Gun Cypher that will make life difficult if you try to cross the bridge.

Remember the Rigged Bridge

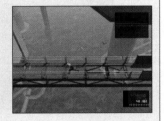

In a moment, you'll see why it's important to take out all the Gun Cyphers. As Raiden crosses the bridge, the floor panels will fall out. If Raiden just keeps running, he should get across safely. But if a Gun Cypher hits him and he is stopped for even a second, he'll fall to his death.

AKS-74u Bullets are on the bridge outside Shell 1. Outside the Shell 1 door, equip the AKS-74u and the B.D.U. Raiden is now disguised and ready to infiltrate.

Shell 1 Core, 1F

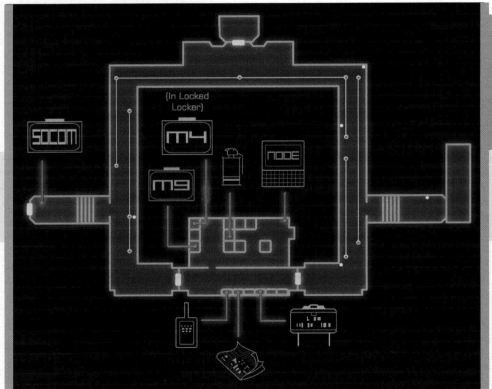

Shell 1 Core 1F

Chaff Grenades	
C-4	
Book	
Claymore Mines	
Node	
Socom Ammo	
M9 Ammo	
M4 Ammo	

Maintaining Your Cover

With both the B.D.U. and the AKS-74u equipped, don't bump into any of the guards, or your cover will be blown! If you do bump into a guard, knock him out with kicks and punches and put your disguise back on before any other guards spot you. If you can move some distance away and disguise yourself again before the guard gets back up, not even the guard that previously spotted you will be able to identify you again.

Also, do not crouch and crawl in front of other soldiers, do not perform Raiden's signature rolling kick, and keep the AKS-74u equipped at all times. If you do anything that's out of the ordinary for a guard and a fellow soldier notices, quickly change your behavior back to normal. Stand perfectly still and let the curious soldier examine you. After a moment, he will blow it off and return to his duties. If you run from a soldier that is asking you questions, he will sound the alarm. Just stay calm and play your cards right.

Navigation in Disguise

Dog Tags Can Wait

Now is not the time to obtain Dog Tags or take down guards. There will be a better time for this later, and full strategies will be described.

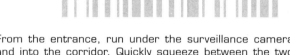

From the entrance, run under the surveillance camera and into the corridor. Quickly squeeze between the two guards patrolling here without letting either of them bump you. Move south (toward the screen), and follow the corridor to the center room.

A box of **Chaff Grenades** is floating on some crates, and the local network Node is in the upper-right corner of the room. Download the map to the Soliton Radar, then search the lockers for items. In the south row of six lockers, you'll find **C4**, a **Book**, and **Claymores**. In the top-left row of three lockers, there are **M9 Bullets**. The top locker is locked. Punch the door until it falls off to reveal **M4 Bullets**.

Proper Identification

Leave the locker area through the west door, and head up the corridor past the single guard and the surveillance camera. On the left side of this corridor is a small diversion. There are some **Socom Bullets** by the door.

Move to the elevator and press ⓦ. The camera scans Raiden's terrorist uniform and permits him access. If he doesn't have the uniform or the AKS-74u equipped, the alarm will sound.

Board the elevator and press the B2 button. Going on the hint that Rose has given us, we're going to search the lowest level first for a Directional Microphone.

Shell 1 Core, B2 Computer Room

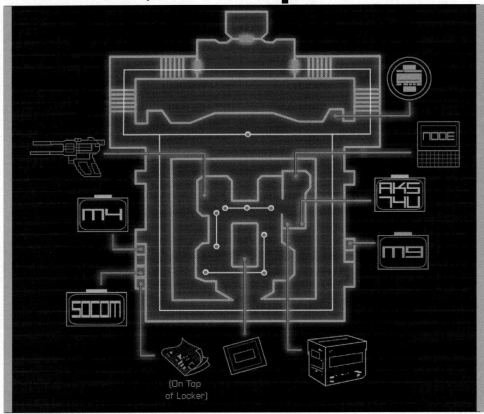

Directional Mic.

Ration

Node

Book

Box

M4 Ammo

M9 Ammo

AKS-74u Ammo

Socom Ammo

Bandage

(On Top of Locker)

Ride the elevator down to B2 first. Even though you've been instructed to search the B1 level for Ames, you'll first need some essential equipment.

Move down the east stairs toward the Computer Room, which is a heavily guarded area. One guard patrols the outside of the technician's area, and sometimes he will move around the square as if he is running laps. Be wary of his varying patterns and stay out of his way to avoid discovery. There's a **Ration** in the small alcove near the patrolling guard in the east area.

Move down the east corridor outside the computer area, and search the first locker on the right for **M9 Bullets**. Continue down and left into the technician's area. The **Directional Microphone** is located in the northwest corner of the computer area, near the squawking parrot. Move to the right, squeezing past the patrolling guard. The local network Node is in the northeast alcove. Download the map of the area and collect the **AKS-74u Bullets** and the **Cardboard Box 4**, which looks like a crate of McFarlane Toys. A **Bandage** is hidden under the central control panel. To take it, position Raiden on the east side of the center control panel. Wait until no guards are around, then crouch and crawl under the table to get it. Carefully watch the radar, and don't emerge until the coast is completely clear.

The four lockers in the west hallway also have items. **Socom Bullets** are in the second from the bottom, and **M4 Bullets** are in the last locker on the right.

Shell 1 Core, B1

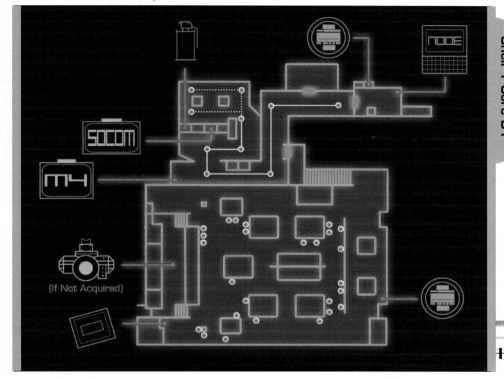

Shell 1 Core B1

Ration

Stun Grenades

Node

Thermal goggles

Bandage

Socom Ammo

M4 Ammo

(If Not Acquired)

2 0 0 2 0 0 1 5 1 9 3 7 1 0 0 2 1 4 0 5

Exiting the elevator, Raiden spots a soldier using the retinal scanner to enter the hostage area. From there, enter the room to the right of the elevator. Inside, download the map of the area from the local network Node, and find the **Ration** stowed in the right side locker.

In the corridor, avoid any guards and navigate to the southwest corner, to find a box of **M4 Bullets**. The other guards don't mind if you do a little looting, as long as you stay in uniform. Search the lockers inside the break room for **Stun Grenades** and **Socom Bullets**.

Move outside the break room into the southwest corner of the corridor, and watch what the guards in this area are doing. One will leave the break room and patrol the corridor. When he returns and declares "All Clear," he will move to a position inside the break room and remain still, while another guard moves out to inspect the hall. The three men take turns patrolling in this manner.

The Retina Scanner

To fool the retina scanner system on the door to the hostage area, Raiden must grab a real guard in a chokehold and shove his face up to the device. Luckily, all of the guards make a stop directly in front of the scanner! Position Raiden directly opposite the scanner, equipped with BDU and AKS-74u, facing the scanner. When the guard stops in front of the scanner, tap the Right trigger to unequip the weapon, and then grab the guard in a chokehold. Raiden automatically places the guard's face against the device, and you now have access to the hostages.

The Hostages

As you descend into the room where the hostages are held, make sure the B.D.U. and the AKS-74u are equipped. There is one patrolling guard in the hold, who reports in on his radio. Do not attempt to overthrow this guard—an alarm sounds automatically. There's a **Ration** against the wall on the far-left side of the room, and there's a **Bandage** below the podium on the right side of the room. If you didn't find the **Thermal Goggles** previously, they will be behind the podium on the stage.

This is how to look for Ames: When the guard is patrolling the other side of the room, equip the Directional Microphone and point it at the various hostages. If the guard spots Raiden with the Directional Microphone, he will immediately sound the alert.

Since Ames wears an electronic pacemaker, you need to listen for an electronic beep that accompanies the person's heartbeat. Once you have found Mr. Ames, press the Action button (🔘) to address him. If you address the wrong person, they will become scared and cry out. This will draw the attention of the other guard, so equip your AKS-74u and don't look suspicious. Either run away before the guard gets to where you are, or stand there and don't move while the guard asks you a bunch of questions before giving up. If you can't determine which hostage is Ames, the answer is at the end of this section.

Private Conversations

Raiden then overhears a conversation between Ocelot and the terrorist leader, Solid Snake. During the scene where you listen in with the microphone, move it back and forth to hear each person better, or position it directly between them to hear both equally. The subtitle font size is at its largest when the signal is at its strongest.

Johnny Sasaki Returns!

During the scene in which Raiden listens to Ocelot and the terrorist leader, move the microphone toward the Lavatory to the left of the control room. Someone is having a pretty rough time in the restroom. Listen to his story carefully, and you'll realize that he's the poor guard everyone kept knocking out in Metal Gear Solid.

Wrath of the Ninja

Ocelot is coming! Ames gives Raiden the **Lv3 PAN Card**. He wants you to use it to reach Shell 2, where the President is held on the first floor. You have 10 seconds to equip your AKS-74U. Don't move! Just stand there innocently, or Ocelot will know!

Shell 1 Core, B1

Raiden no longer has the Balaclava facemask, so the costume is now useless. Caution mode is in effect, so the patrol patterns of the guards have changed. It's time to start taking on guards and collecting Dog Tags, so read the three sections of tactics that follow for expert advice.

Ames is the hostage at the bottom of the room, facing the south wall, leaning against the table with the boxes marked TDV-900HG. He's the only hostage with a unique hairstyle!

Do not return to 1F until the caution alert has been canceled. If you go up to 1F while security is this tight, an attack team member will be patrolling outside the corridor. Raiden will very likely have to take on the whole floor if he is discovered. Although blasting your way out of Shell 1 can be enthralling, don't take risky chances.

Shell 1 Core, B1 Tactics

DOG TAG: Shell 1, B1 Elevator Guard

This guard patrols the space in front of the elevator only while the Caution Alert remains in effect, so you have to move on him swiftly. Position Raiden just around the corner from the guard; press Raiden's back flat against the wall. When the guard turns and heads east, run down the corridor and catch him just outside the door of the eastern Node room.

DOG TAG: Shell 1, B1 Lower Corridor Guard

This guard will patrol the lower corridor only when the Caution Alert is still in effect, so you must move on him quickly. Position Raiden around the corner from the east end of the guard's route, with your back pressed flat against the wall. When the guard turns and starts to move west, quickly run around the corner and catch him.

DOG TAG: Shell 1, B1 Break Room Guard

Press Raiden's back up against the front of the lockers and knock. As the sentry comes to investigate the noise, run into the corridor and hide on the east side of the doorway, well out of the soldier's view. As he stares at the lockers, charge in and arrest him.

Shell 1 Core, B2 Computer Room

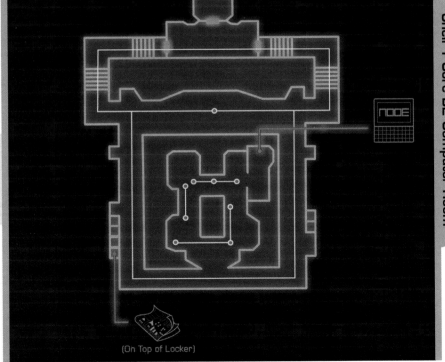
(On Top of Locker)

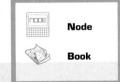

Shell 1 Core B2 Computer Room

NODE	**Node**
	Book

Now you can start collecting Dog Tags from the soldiers here. The challenge to get each of these guards alone in this wide-open space is very amusing. Save your game beforehand, because you will probably need a few tries.

DOG TAG: Shell 1, B2 Outer Perimeter Guard

The guard who patrols outside the control area is the easiest to catch. Just wait at the top of the stairs for him to turn and head west, then catch him. If the guard is patrolling quickly around the area as if he's running laps, then hide in one of the tiny spaces by the lockers in either of the side corridors. When the guard runs past, jump out and aim at the exact moment that he is directly in front of Raiden's position. This is a little trickier, but still not as tough as the three guards inside the control area.

DOG TAG: Shell 1, B2 Net Surfing Guard

The guard who patrols from monitor to monitor, looking at hot girls on the Internet, is the easiest target of the three. First, move to the southwest corner outside the computer room. Equip a naughty Book, and lay it in the southwest corridor. Try to place it a short distance from the wall, but far enough out that Raiden can run around the corner and get behind the guard. Once the Book is placed, move to the lower wall and press Raiden's back against it. When the guard is surfing the net on the south computer, knock on the wall at the corner to draw his attention. As he comes outside to the point where Raiden knocked, run around the corner and stand out of view. The guard will spot the Book on the floor and move over to it. When you see the guard's cone of vision disappear from the radar, move out from the corner and capture him. Squeeze between the guard and the wall. After he gives up the tags, crouch and shoot a dart into his chin to knock him out.

DOG TAG: Shell 1, B1 West Computer Area Guard

Once you have used the net-surfing guard's vices against him, wait for the guard who patrols north to south on the west side of the computer area to move south. Run in front of the doorway from west to east, so that the guard sees your movement. Hide around the corner as the guard comes out to investigate. As soon as the guard's cone of vision returns to white and he heads back, run around the corner and try to capture him outside the computer area. Once you have the tags and have tranquilized him, drag the body back outside the computer area, behind the partition.

DOG TAG: Shell 1, B1 North Computer Area Guard

After taking down every other guard in this area, move into the computer area and flatten Raiden's back against the *Policenauts* poster. When the guard is facing east or south at the east end of his route closest to the Node, knock on the poster. As the guard moves to investigate the noise, run around the central consoles and get behind the guard. Before he dismisses the sound and turns back, capture him!

Shell 1 Core, 1F

 Node

 Socom Ammo

 M9 Ammo

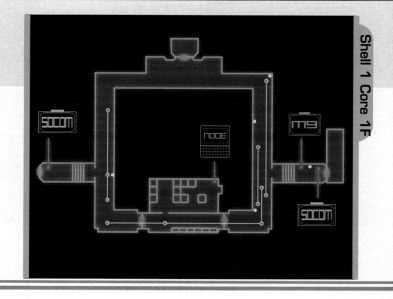

Shell 1 Core 1F

Do not return to this corridor until the Caution Alert previously invoked by Ocelot has ended. If you return to this level too soon, there are too many soldiers to deal with. But after the alert ends, the attack team will leave.

Getting down the corridor is tricky. Take out cameras with the suppressed Socom, and knock out the soldiers with the M9. If you want to collect Dog Tags, the Alert must be absolutely over. Now is the time to do it.

In the east exit corridor, use the Socom to knock out the camera while Raiden is still standing inside the hallway. **Socom Bullets** and **M9 Bullets** are below the camera.

DOG TAG: Shell 1, 1F Northeast Corridor Guard

The first soldier to take out is the one who patrols the north part of the east corridor, and occasionally turns left and patrols near the elevator. Use the Socom with the silencer to knock out the camera in the northeast corner. Then move to the corner's edge and flatten your back against it. When the solider stops at the northeast corner of his route, step away from the wall, nudge the Left stick toward the guard a bit and surprise him. There should be plenty of room to squeeze between the guard and the wall to demand his Dog Tags. After putting the guard to sleep, drag his body just around the corner to hide it.

DOG TAG: Shell 1, 1F West Corridor Guard

After taking down the northeast corner guard, move to the west corridor and position Raiden at the top corner. When the guard is patrolling the south end of his route, step out and use the Socom to destroy the surveillance camera. Then hide behind the corner until the guard stops at the north end of his route. When the guard turns back and starts south, run down the corridor and catch him as quickly as possible.

DOG TAG: Shell 1, 1F South Guard

This soldier appears only when Raiden is leaving Shell 1. He patrols through the locker room on the south side of the area, and emerges into the hallways on either side. Having taken out the guard in the west corridor, wait until this guard emerges from the locker room on the west side. Then follow him into the locker room, where he stops just a few feet into the door. Capture him there before he moves too far east.

DOG TAG: Shell 1, 1F Southwest Corner Guard

Having overtaken both the guard who patrols the locker room and the guard who monitors the northeast corner, this guard should become a little easier. Step just outside the east door of the locker room, and aim the Socom at the camera high on the corner. It's a bit easier to hit when it's searching the south. Just make sure that the guard isn't nearby when the camera fizzles out, or he will spot Raiden very quickly. Once the camera is out, press Raiden's back to the corner and wait for the guard to come south. When he turns and heads back north, run around the corner and up behind him to catch him unawares.

MISSION 04: THE CROSSING

Going on the information divulged by Colonel Ames, Raiden must now blaze a path to Shell 2. As the terrorist leader Solid Snake indicated, the Shell 1-2 Bridge is wired with IR sensor beams and Semtex explosives set to go off when anything crosses the beams. To eliminate all of the explosives efficiently and cross the bridge, Raiden must find a sniper rifle. Perhaps the Lv3 PAN Card Ames gave to Raiden will be helpful.

Strut F Warehouse

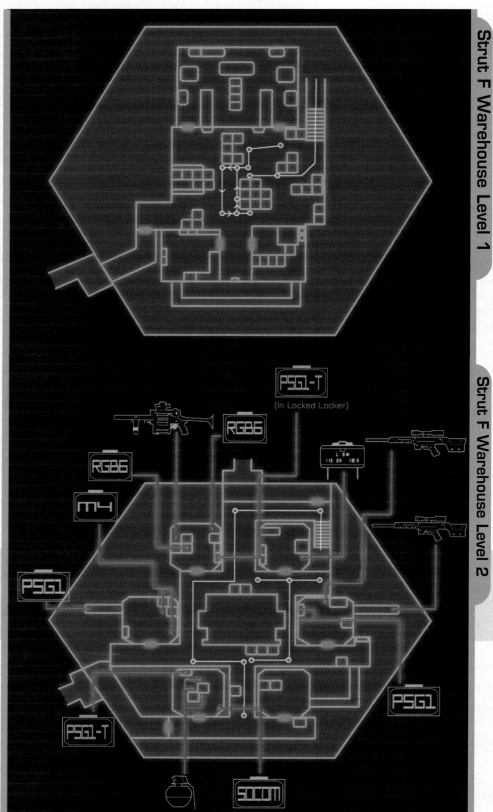

RGB6

PSG-1

PSG-1T

Grenades

Claymore Mines

RGB6 Ammo

PSG-1 Ammo

PSG-1T Ammo

M4 Ammo

Socom Ammo

PSG1-T
(In Locked Locker)

RGB6

RGB6

M4

PSG1

PSG1-T

PSG1

SOCOM

00320020069 |III|III|I| |III||I|I|IIIIIIIIII| 42301 03005

With Colonel Ames' Lv3 PAN Card, Raiden can now ransack the remaining rooms in the Strut F Warehouse. Use the same tactics described previously to take the guards out of the equation. New **Claymores** have appeared in the northeast Lv2 room.

In the northwest Lv3 room, Raiden will find the **RGB6 Grenade Launcher** and two boxes of **RBG6 Grenades**. Although optional, this weapon makes a certain upcoming boss fight much easier. There is a locked locker that contains **PSG-1T Bullets**, if you can punch off the door. These are extremely rare to find, so don't forget that they are here.

Two boxes of **M4 Bullets** have appeared in the middle Lv2 room on the west side. Remember that there are **PSG-1 Bullets** in the crawlspace as before. Raiden finally finds the **PSG-1 Sniper Rifle** and a box of **Bullets** for it in the middle Lv3 room to the east. More **PSG-1 Bullets** are in the locker. The **PSG-1T**, a sniper rifle that fires tranquilizer darts, is in a crawlspace on the east side of the room. Since bullets for this gun are so rare, save all that you can get for later events.

The Lv3 room by the FA Connecting Bridge contains a much-needed box of **Socom Bullets**, three boxes of **Grenades**, and **PSG-1T Bullets** are in the locker.

Strut D

Remember that there are **PSG-1 Bullets** by the EF Connecting Bridge entrance. Equip the M9 and tranquilize the guards on the central bridge, then grab the bullets and enter the door on the north side, which leads to the Shell 1-2 Connecting Bridge.

Shell 1-2
Connecting Bridge

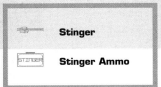
Stinger

Stinger Ammo

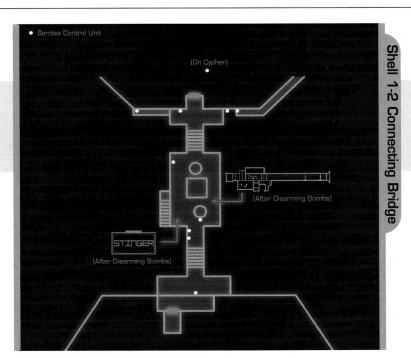

Shell 1-2 Connecting Bridge

Pliskin finally contacts Raiden after a long silence, explaining how Raiden must shoot all the control units to disengage the infrared sensors on the bridge. Call Pliskin again and he explains that you need a sniper rifle. He also tells you where to get one if you don't have it.

Sniping Basics

Becoming an expert sniper overnight doesn't just happen, but Raiden must adapt quickly if he is to move on. When you equip the PSG-1, Raiden instantly shifts to scope view. As you look through the scope, press ⬤ to zoom in, ⬤ to zoom out, and ⬤ to fire. The closer you zoom to an object, the harder it is to miss. Aiming is quicker when you look in the general direction of the target in First Person View beforehand. To aim more accurately, use a Pentazemin to steady your hands. The Pentazemin lasts only about one minute, so keep them handy.

Since there are no live targets in this situation, you shouldn't need to use more than one Pentazemin. You can shoot most of the C4 control boxes with just the Socom anyhow.

To the right is a list of the control boxes you can hit with the Socom. Take these out first:

This section shows the C4 control boxes that are easier to hit with the PSG-1 sniper rifle:

A control box is directly above Raiden's location over the doorway. This is the easiest Socom shot.

One is attached to the small, white-striped pump a few feet beyond the beams. Raiden views it with his scope during the previous scene. This is the second easiest Socom shot.

There are two control boxes nestled on the left side of the bridge among C4 packs and the IR beams. Shoot the white tops of them to avoid hitting the C4.

Move directly to the left of the Strut D doorway. Equip the PSG-1 and zoom in on the Sons of Liberty flag on the far left. Eventually, the breeze will flap it out far enough to reveal the control box behind it. After you get a glimpse, estimate its location in relation to the flag, and fire.

From the same position left of the Strut D doorway, look directly ahead. Some birds are clustered around a control box below the Strut G entrance. Fire a warning shot to make the birds scatter. If that doesn't work, you may have to shoot one. Then shoot the box.

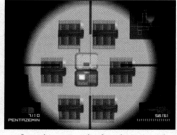

Another one is further up the same wall, snuggled in the middle of six C4 bundles. Zoom in extremely close to it and fire.

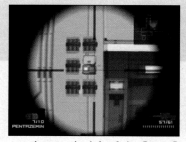

Just to the left of the Strut G entrance, a control box is nestled among five C4 bundles. Zoom in extremely close and shoot.

Move to the right of the Strut D doorway, and look down at the bridge. A control box is on the floor of the bridge at the other end. You can only see its profile. Zoom in extremely close on the box to avoid hitting the Semtex behind it. Target the top portion just to be safe.

The last one is attached to the top of a Cypher that's moving in a triangular pattern over Strut G. Zoom in extremely close and follow the Cypher to one of the corners of its path. Make sure you hit the control box and not the camera to which it is mounted, or the Cypher will emit a signal and destroy the bridge!

BOSS FIGHT

AV-88 Harrier II

Pilot   Solidus Snake

Weapons: AIM-9 Sidewinders; AGM-65 Maverick
               Missiles; GAU-12 25MM Six-Barrel Gun Pod,
               300 Round Capacity with Lead Computing
               Optical Sight System (LCOSS)

Grab the **Stinger Launcher** and the box of **Stinger Missiles** Pliskin throws down. Be sure to equip the Rations so that Raiden can hopefully survive severe damage. Throughout the battle, if Raiden runs low on Rations, Pliskin will throw down more from the chopper. Don't hit the Kastaka with a Stinger by mistake, or the free items will stop coming. If the Kasataka is destroyed, the game ends. Be ready to click off the Stinger at any moment by tapping the Left trigger button Raiden has to be able to run and dodge attacks, and at some points in the battle, this is more important than targeting the Harrier II.

Now examine the Soliton Radar and note the positions of both the Harrier II and the Kasatka on the radar. The fighter jet is the big red arrow and the Kasatka is the small red dot. Turn Raiden to face the general direction of the Harrier II, then equip the Stinger. In normal view, the Stinger will analyze your target's weak points and mark them in its radar eyepiece as small squares, even at extremely long range. Align the center crosshairs on that square, and the Stinger will lock onto the target. Fire, and the missile will fly after that target until the rocket runs out of fuel. To quickly remove the Stinger's scope from your eye, press and hold the White button. This helps if you are worried about attacks from the side. The Stinger can still track targets via sonar in this mode.

When the Stinger draws a bead on the Harrier and the fighter jet is in the open, fire. If the Harrier is circling around, the missile will follow it for a while and then fall away. During the first course of the battle, Solidus flies the Harrier some distance away, then soars in and buzzes the bridge. Raiden will be knocked off his feet and take damage if this happens, so find the target quickly and launch a Stinger. When the Harrier is charging and a missile hits it, the jet is knocked off course and must abort the attack run. Solidus will also try to hurt Raiden with heat from the Harrier's jets. Simply aim the Stinger anywhere at the fighter's underbelly and fire. You'll inflict more damage if you can target one of the highlighted areas in the Stinger's scope, but the most important thing is to drive off the Harrier before its exhaust jets cause Raiden too much pain.

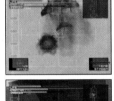

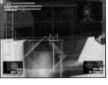

After it loses a quarter of its stamina, the Harrier will release a volley of missiles. The best thing you can do is run toward Strut D, because the entire middle section of the bridge will be blasted out. Generally, Raiden cannot seem to outrun this particular attack. However, anytime the Harrier releases missiles after this, just drop off any edge to the level below and hide behind the pumps and pipes. The downside is that there is hardly any way to attack from this level, so when the Harrier moves off, run back up to the top level. If the Harrier closes in while Raiden is emerging from below, it will pin him down with machinegun fire. After a few minutes of this, Pliskin radios that he will take care of it and fires a grenade at the plane just to drive it off. If you stay under cover when the Harrier tries to pin you down, Pliskin will help you out every time.

When the Harrier dips below the bridge, it will rise, and Solidus will attempt to hit Raiden with gunfire. The Stinger will display four targets under the plane, so just move the crosshairs left or right until the Stinger locks onto one. After you fire that missile, try to lock onto another target and fire.

The most important key to winning this battle is to rely on the Soliton Radar. Constantly monitor the Harrier's position on the radar, and keep changing Raiden's position to better see it through the Stinger's scope. If the Harrier flies from one side of the bridge to the other, unequip the Stinger, turn, and equip it again. This is faster than turning in First Person View. Continue chipping away at the Harrier until you prevail.

MISSION 4: THE CROSSING 87

Treacherous Passage

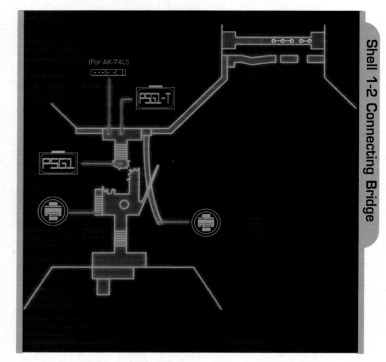

Shell 1-2 Connecting Bridge

	Ration
	AKS-74u Supressor
PSG1	PSG-1 Ammo
PSG1-T	PSG-1T Ammo

300010

The Shell 1-2 bridge is on fire and in pieces. Move left to the burning area, and the Cell Phone will start to ring and buzz. Equip the Cell Phone to receive an email from the Ninja. Use the Coolant to put out the fire, then quickly run down the stairs to get a **Ration**. Quickly run back up, before Raiden falls into the ocean with the collapsing stairs.

Move to the right railing, leap over it, and hang. Shimmy out until it seems Raiden is directly over the orange pipe below. Use First Person View to confirm your position directly over the pipe, then drop down. Carefully work your way back along the pipe toward Strut D, where you will find another **Ration** at the end. Now carefully move back to where you were.

When you reach the first gob of bird droppings on the pipe, move slowly or crawl around this area so that Raiden doesn't slip off and fall. Just past that area, stand and face left. Use First Person View to line up perfectly with the platform opposite your position. Raiden can do his amazing torso-axial jump over to the left platform. There are **PSG-1 Bullets** on the left edge of this dangling gantry. Move up to the doorway and use the Coolant again to put out the fire blocking access to the **AKS-74u Suppressor**—now you have a silenced machinegun! **PSG-1T Bullets** are nearby.

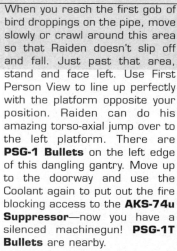

Head left and drop onto the platform where the pipe connects. Press ⊙ to pull yourself up onto the walkway. As Raiden moves around the outside of Strut G, the catwalk begins to fall apart. Keep running until you reach the end.

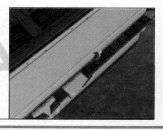

 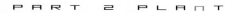

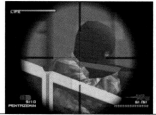

At the top of the narrow catwalk, flip over the rail and hang. Drop to the catwalk below. Two soldiers will emerge on the bridge above. Use the sniper rifle to take them out. Make sure neither one gets the chance to radio in, or you'll become a sitting duck. Do a torso-axial jump over the first gap. At the second gap, jump over the rail and hang, then shimmy across to the end.

Strut L Perimeter

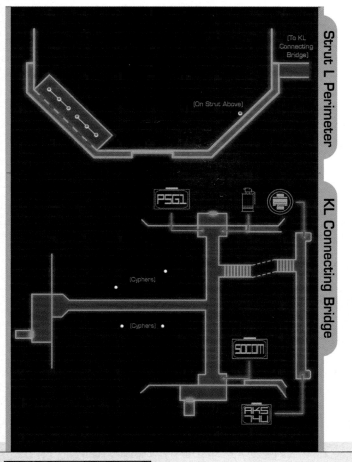

Strut L Perimeter

KL Connecting Bridge

	Ration
	Chaff Grenades
PSG1	**PSG-1 Ammo**
SOCOM	**Socom Ammo**
M4	**M4 Ammo**
AKS 74U	**AKS-74u Ammo**

Two guards will move from window to window, looking out over the catwalk. If they spot Raiden, they will radio for a few Gun Cyphers to come take him out. Crouch, press Raiden's back against the wall, and sidestep under the windows. When part of the catwalk threatens to give, go back instead of forward. Crouch under the window if a guard is about to pass. When the nearest guard is walking, jump over the rail and hang. Shimmy to the right until you can't go any further. Watch the guards in the windows; when they are far enough away and walking, jump back onto the platform. Crouch immediately and hide from the soldiers by pressing Raiden's back against the wall. Continue crouch-stepping under the windows.

After the windows comes a gap that is too long to jump over. Press Raiden's back against the wall and sidestep across the gap using the thin ledge. Careful, though—if Raiden steps out from the wall, he'll fall off. When you get to the obstruction, just crouch and continue under it.

Nature Calls

Past the long gap, a guard above your position decides he has to go to the restroom and just can't wait. The only question is, will you waste your time waiting for him to finish, or will you just hold your breath and run under it? Actually, you have another option or two. You can flip over the rail, hang, and then shimmy along the edge. Or, you can fire a shot at the platform on which the guard stands; this might startle him enough to make him pause.

Once you've crossed under this guard, you should use First Person View or a Corner View and look around. You can't miss spotting the small fleet of Gun Cyphers hovering above the KL Connecting Bridge. Use the silenced AKS-74u to take them out. Press ⬤ lightly to aim the weapon with laser sighting, and then press harder to fire. Drop over the rail and grab the **AKS-74u Bullets**. There's a **Ration** at the other side of this path. Climb up the stairs. There are **PSG-1 Bullets** and **Chaff Grenades** near Strut K's malfunctioning entrance. You'll find **Socom Bullets** near Strut K.

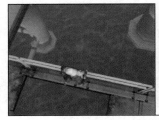

To cross the damaged bridge to Shell 2, do a torso-axial jump over the first gap. At the second gap, press Raiden against the upper railing and sidestep across.

MISSION 05: PRESIDENTIAL RESCUE

As he enters the Shell 2 Core, Raiden watches as Olga Gurlukovich electrifies the floor in front of the room where the President is being held. This brief mission involves knocking out the electric current in order to reach the President of the United States.

Shell 2 Core, 1F Air Purification Room

1 0 2 4 0 1 3 2 9 5 0 0

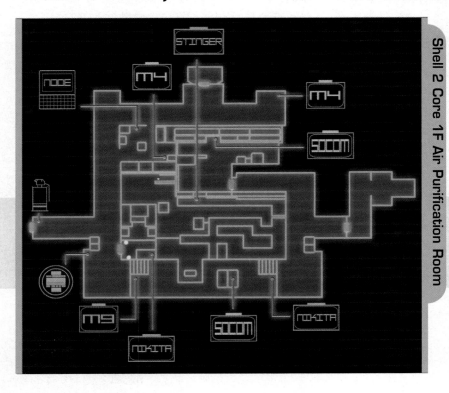

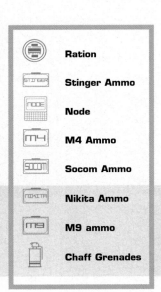

Shell 2 Core 1F Air Purification Room

	Ration
STINGER	Stinger Ammo
NODE	Node
M4	M4 Ammo
SOCOM	Socom Ammo
NIKITA	Nikita Ammo
M9	M9 ammo
	Chaff Grenades

97001236

02001255

Finding the Nikita

Move down the stairs to the west and notice the two holes in the north wall. These vents will be utilized later. Hop onto the box for **Socom Bullets** if you need them. The Nikita Rockets will have to wait for a while. Continue left to find **M9 Bullets**, and go upstairs.

There's a **Ration** at the top of the stairs. Step close enough to the door across the hall to open it but don't go inside; two Gun Cameras are mounted above, on the other side of the threshold. Use the Socom to shoot them out. There are more Nikita Rockets in here, but again, you need the firing mechanism first.

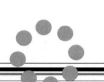

02001598010567300110400

■■■■■■■■■■■■■■■■■■ 0

Continuing north, diverge into the left corridor to find **Chaff Grenades** near the malfunctioning west exit. Continue north in the corridor until you find a small employee break area. Pick up **M4 Bullets** and login to the local Node.

Hail to the Chief

Now press up against the east wall of the break area; the camera will shift to partially reveal the President's room. Knock on the wall, and he will respond. Continue knocking on the wall, and he will remain there several minutes listening. Knock too rapidly, and he will get annoyed and walk off. Also, if you gaze upon the wall where you were knocking, you'll see a two-level map of the entire ventilation system on this floor.

Shell 2 Core, B1 Filtration Chamber No. 1

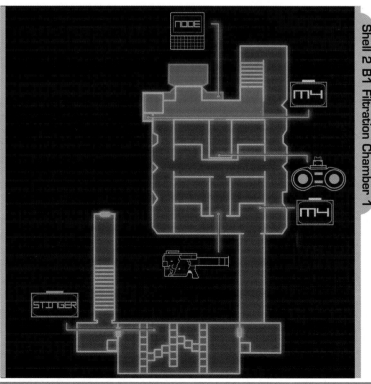

Shell 2 B1 Filtration Chamber 1

STINGER	Stinger Ammo
	Night Vision Goggles
M4	M4 Ammo
	Radio Guided Missile
NODE	Node

2001598010100021400
010 | 101 | 111 | 20 | 020

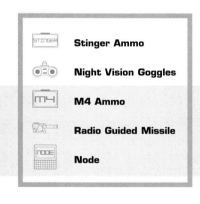

As you exit the elevator on B1, login to the Node and be thankful—this section requires you to swim underwater. The Colonel calls to remind Raiden of the swim controls.

When you're underwater, look for light spots on the floor or on the Soliton Radar map. These indicate air pockets directly above. Press ⚫ to swim, press the Left Stick up to go up, down to go down, and right or left to turn either way. You can make hard turns with the Right Stick—press right or left to turn 90˚ instantly, or press down to turn 180˚ degrees completely around.

Dive into the water and swim through the first doorway on the right. Continue up the passage just a short way, and then turn into the dark left passage and collect the **Night Vision Goggles**. Continue west and surface at the skylight to catch a breath. Then swim south and take the next left. A sea mine floats in the center of the corridor. Equip the Mine Detector. All the mines in the area show up as little red dots on the radar. Touch one of them and BOOM! Swim south from the first mine, and under the next doorway is the **Nikita** remote missile launcher. There's more to explore here, obviously, but your objective is to rescue the President. Return to 1F with the Nikita.

Shell 2 Core, 1F Air Purification Room

Move south past the President's room to the small, dark room with the Gun Cameras that you disabled. Step onto the block and grab the **Nikita Rockets**. Also, remember that there are more **Nikita Rockets** by the stairs where you saw the vent holes in the wall.

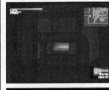

In the dark room with the Gun Cameras, step onto the block and face the vent on the opposite side of the room. Fire a Nikita into the vent, and guide it through the twists and turns into the President's room. Destroy the large circuit breaker in the northeast corner. If you want to slow down the missile, press left or right to change its direction a little. You can also use the vents by the stairs, but the vent in the Gun Camera room offers a duct path that's easier to navigate.

The President explains the involvement of the Patriots, Solidus, and the new model Arsenal Gear. Then Johnson hands over the **Lv4 PAN Card**. He tells Raiden to find Emma Emmerich and gives him an **MO Disk** containing a virus for the AI of Arsenal Gear.

This is Card 4. It'll give you access all the way to Emma's location.

After the scenes, search the President's room for **Socom Bullets**. There's a vent at floor level in the south wall. Climb in and grab the **Stinger Missiles**. Go back to the elevator and return to B1.

MISSION 06: THE CHILD GENIUS

Holding the virus contained on the MO Disk, Raiden needs to find the last living systems programmer on the Arsenal Gear project. The President said that Emma was rumored to be in captivity on the flooded B1 level. Only she can upload the virus to Arsenal Gear's system.

Swim back to the place where you obtained the Nikita launcher, and a new **Ration** should be in the same spot. At the T-intersection, swim to the left and continue into the corner to locate **M4 Bullets**. Continue swimming south, where two mines float in the corridor. Carefully swim under the first mine and over the second. Don't press the Swim button frantically. Just tap ⚫ occasionally to propel Raiden slowly through the treacherous waters. Reaching the end, catch your breath at the skylight. Then look beneath you in First Person View to find two watertight hatches. Open the west door. Peter Stillman's body floats out, marking the location of his tragic demise.

In the room strewn with girders, there is a confusing maze to swim through. Reach the first skylight for some air, and then look around in First Person View to find the gap low in the girders. Swim to the south wall, and then left. Follow this opening until you see the light of the next skylight on the floor. You'll find more **Stinger Missiles** there. Continue swimming west to the watertight door and open it. The next room has a skylight, but a mine floats on the surface. Instead of getting air there, just swim to the right and go up the stairs to the exit.

BOSS FIGHT

Vamp

Gender:	Male
Affiliation:	Dead Cell Knife Specialist
Weapon:	Throwing Knives, Serrated Hunting Knives

You've seen this guy in action, so you know that bullets are mostly ineffective. Equip the RGB6 and the Rations. Aim with First Person View and blast Vamp where he hovers over the water. He will swim around for some time. Do yourself a favor and equip the Socom whenever Vamp is underwater; blast out the lights all around the upper level of the room. Vamp will use an attack later on that is detrimental to your survival—he is capable of pinning Raiden's shadow to the floor with a knife. If his shadow is pinned, Raiden can't move. Then Vamp can hit Raiden with all the throwing knives he wants.

Socom Bullets, two boxes of **M4 Bullets**, a **Ration,** and a box of **RBG6 Shells** are positioned around the room. Except for the Rations, don't pick up these items until you absolutely need them. There's no use picking up a box of ammo if all you receive is one bullet.

```
0 1 3 2 9 5 0 0 1 0 0 2 1 4 8 6 0 1 8 7
7 8 7 3 7 0 5 0 1 1
```

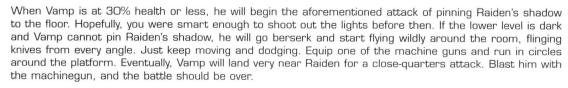

After you first knock Vamp into the water, spend some time blowing out any remaining lights around the room with the Socom. Stand at the entrance to the room on the south side as you do this. When Vamp leaps out onto the lower level, equip the RGB6 and fire a grenade at him. Use First Person View, and be sure to raise your aim to compensate for the arcing trajectory of the shell. The force of the blast will blow Vamp back into the water, and the attack does tremendous damage. Stay at the entrance to the room to see what Vamp does next. If he leaps all the way up to the upper railing, start moving around the room. He will begin throwing clusters of knives at Raiden, and it's just better to concentrate on dodging for a round. Eventually Vamp will get tired of this, and he'll leap back into the water. During his next attack, he will most likely jump onto the lower platform. Position yourself by the entrance again, and aim at the same spot on the other side of the platform where he landed last time.

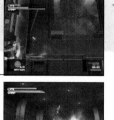

When Vamp is at 30% health or less, he will begin the aforementioned attack of pinning Raiden's shadow to the floor. Hopefully, you were smart enough to shoot out the lights before then. If the lower level is dark and Vamp cannot pin Raiden's shadow, he will go berserk and start flying wildly around the room, flinging knives from every angle. Just keep moving and dodging. Equip one of the machine guns and run in circles around the platform. Eventually, Vamp will land very near Raiden for a close-quarters attack. Blast him with the machinegun, and the battle should be over.

Shell 2 Core, B1 Filtration Chamber No. 2

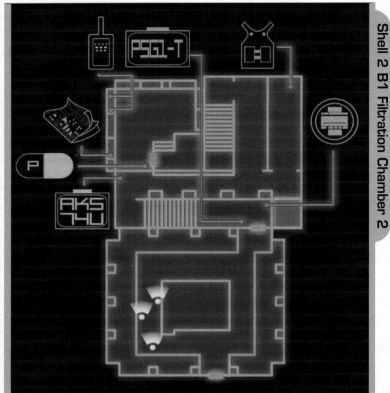

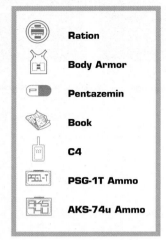

	Ration
	Body Armor
	Pentazemin
	Book
	C4
PSG1-T	**PSG-1T Ammo**
AKS 74u	**AKS-74u Ammo**

5 9 8 0 1 0 1 0 0

0 0 3 2 0 0 2 0 0 6 9

After the battle, grab whatever items are left in the room and proceed north. Grab the **Ration** in the hallway and descend the stairs into the water. Unfortunately, you don't have the Soliton Radar map of this section! However, if you equip the Mine Detector, you will be able to see the Node in this area as a little blue dot not too far away.

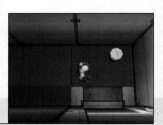

4 2 3 0 1 0 3 0 0 5 5

Swimming straight ahead from the bottom of the steps, you'll enter a small room where there's a mine and a box of **AKS-74u Bullets**. Return to the corridor and catch a breath at the skylight. Enter First Person View, and Raiden will spot Emma Emmerich waiting in a small control room. Swim all the way to the end, where there are three doorways. At the end, swim to the left and under the mine to find the **Body Armor**. Across the hall, there are some **PSG-1T Bullets** in a room with two mines. Now get some air at the skylight. Look down in First Person at the two doorways, and swim through the one on the left. Climb the stairs and go into the control room.

Hide and Seek

Emma must be hiding in one of the lockers, because she's nowhere to be seen. Download the map from the Node and grab the **Pentazemin** sitting at the bottom of the steps. You can check to see if Emma is in a locker by knocking on it. She will let out a small yelp. Start with the locker on the far left, where you'll find another **Book**. There are two boxes of **C4** in the top-left locker. Emma is hiding in the center locker of the top row.

Emma's Return to **Swimming**

After the cut scenes, swim with Emma back to the room where Raiden fought Vamp, stopping at every skylight along the way for air. Emma's breath and life are too short to risk long swims. Once you're out of the water, press ⓜ to make Emma grab Raiden's hand, then lead her into the next area.

With the Mine Detector equipped, you can see that the west side of the chamber is full of **Claymores**. Don't lead Emma in that direction for any reason.

Notes on Emma

When Emma is partnered with Raiden, there are several things to keep in mind. Raiden cannot hold a weapon or fight while he's holding Emma's hand. If you need to scout ahead, leave Emma in a safe place where enemies won't find her. If Emma's life meter is low, let her rest for a while. While Emma is sitting down, her life meter will recharge.

Emma's **Second** Swim

After Emma explains everything Raiden ever wanted to know about computer viruses, swim through the first water area, stopping at every skylight. When you reach the elevator area, the floor is covered with sea lice. Emma won't cross the path. You'll have to consult your peers to figure out what to do here.

Emma's Fear of **Bugs**

If you try to drag Emma through the sea lice a few times, the Ninja's Cell Phone buzzes. The Ninja says you can drive away the sea lice with the Coolant. So now you know two ways to get Emma back up to 1F. Use punches and kicks to knock her unconscious, then drag her through the lice onto the elevator. Or, use the Coolant spray to drive off every last bug. The first method doesn't take as long. Whichever way suits you best, don't miss the new **M4 Bullets** in the south corner of the area.

Shell 2 Core, **1F** Air Purification Room

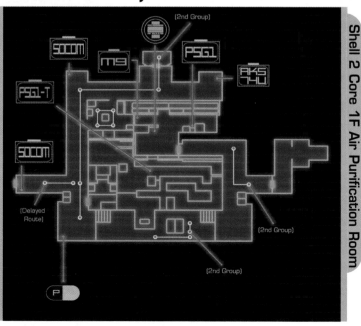

Shell 2 Core 1F Air Purification Room

☰	**Ration**
◖	**Pentazemin**
PSG1	**PSG-1 Ammo**
AKS 74U	**AKS-74u Ammo**
M9	**M9 Ammo**
SOCOM	**Socom Ammo**
PSG-T	**PSG-1T Ammo**

Leave Emma on board the elevator and go take care of the two guards that have taken up patrols on this level. Collect the new items that have appeared here while you're at it. Then lead Emma to the employee break area. New guards will appear as you lead Emma toward the exit, so find good places for her to hide and go take care of business.

Shell 2, 1F Tactics

Crossing the lobby of Shell 2 with Emma is a risky adventure. Raiden must leave Emma in safe locations, then scout ahead to take out enemy guards with extreme prejudice. After you take out guards in this area, shake down their bodies for really good ammo.

DOG TAG: Shell 2 Break Area Guard

Arriving on 1F, leave Emma on the elevator and scout ahead. There are new **AKS-74u Bullets** to the far east from the elevator. You can easily take the guard patrolling the employee break area when he is facing west. At this location on his route, the guard usually stops and does some stretches. Wait until his cone of vision disappears from the map, then charge at him. After you've arrested the man and confiscated his Dog Tags, execute him with the Socom. It will simplify matters if you don't have to worry about guards in this area waking up while you are slowly walking Emma around. You should drag the dead body beneath the table in the middle of the break area. New **Socom Bullets** have appeared northwest of the break area.

DOG TAG: Shell 2 South Area Guard

While Emma is resting on the elevator, go all the way to the south area and stop at the top of the stairs. A guard patrols east to west near the south wall. Wait until he turns and heads off, then move down the stairs and press Raiden's back against the nearest corner. When the guard returns, wait for him to turn and head east again before you run out and capture him. After you've bagged the tags and killed the guard, drag his body to the west side of the south area. Now you're ready to go back and get Emma off the elevator.

DOG TAG: Shell 2 Malfunctioning Door Guard

Get Emma off the elevator and lead her into the employee break area. You should notice a guard's cone of vision in the corridor to the south. Leave Emma and quickly run down to the small corridor with the malfunctioning west door. The guard stands and stares transfixed at the door for long periods, allowing ample time to catch him from behind. After you have captured his tags and shot him in the face, collect the **Socom Bullets** that have appeared by the door. Now return to the break area, collect Emma, and lead her south down the corridor to the top of the stairs.

DOG TAG: Shell 2 North Corridor Guard

Reaching the top of the west stairs in the south area, a new guard will arrive on the elevator! Leave Emma in the small, dark room at the top of the stairs, and run north with your Socom ready. Just below the break area, stop and watch for the guard in First Person View. He stops and turns at the northwest corner. As he is headed back toward the elevator, cut through the break area and catch him from behind. Execute this guard, and then return to the south area. Notice the new box of **Pentazemin** that has appeared in the southwest corner of the area.

DOG TAG: Shell 2 Vent Shafts Guard

Before taking Emma out of the dark room, head down the stairs into the south area and look for the new guard that follows a very short patrol route near the ventilation shafts. Wait on the other side of the blocks until he is facing north, then run around the block and catch him by surprise. Execute this guard, then run back and take Emma out of the small, dark room.

DOG TAG: Shell 2 Exit Guard

As Raiden and Emma cross the south area and climb the stairs on the east side, let go of her hand and move behind the boxes stacked below the exit corridor. A new guard will emerge from the exit area. After he stares around for what seems like an eternity, he turns north and heads toward the formerly electrified floor. This is when you can easily get the drop on him. You can tranquilize this guard if you wish, because you're about to leave.

KL Connecting Bridge

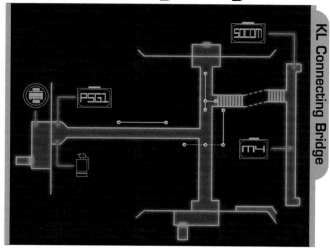

KL Connecting Bridge

![Ration]	**Ration**
![Chaff Grenade]	**Chaff Grenade**
SOCOM	**Socom Ammo**
PSG1	**PSG-1 Ammo**
M4	**M4 Ammo**

2 0 0 1 5 9 8 0 1 0 1 0 0 2 1 4 0 0

10	010	101	111	20	020

Leave Emma just outside the door while you scout ahead. Stand just outside the doorway and shoot the two Gun Cyphers from a distance before they spot you. Then grab the items around the doorway, including a new **Ration**, **PSG-1 Bullets**, and **Chaff Grenades**.

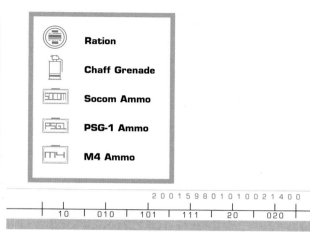

Cross the connecting bridge to the main bridge, where a soldier will suddenly appear. After you take him out, search the lower bridge for **Socom Bullets** and **M4 Bullets**.

0 2 1 4 8 6 0 1 8 7

Put out the fire in front of Strut L with the Coolant, and lead Emma across. At the Strut L entrance, Emma gives Raiden the **Lv5 PAN Card**.

KL Connecting Bridge **Tactics**

DOG TAG: KL Connecting Bridge Guard

Cross the connecting bridge to the main bridge, and crouch behind the low wall on the north side. Crouch-step to the corner and study the guard's movements behind you. When he faces the stairs on the right, stand and run out from behind the corner. Capture him, and then move to the top of the stairs in front of him. The guard resists arrest, so shoot him in the hand to get the tags. Then execute the guard, because you'll still be in the area for a while collecting items and dousing fires.

Strut L Sewage Treatment Facility

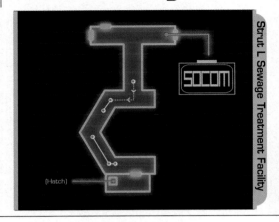

Socom Ammo

Leave Emma near the entrance and scout ahead. **Socom Bullets** are at the end of the hall. Two guards are inside the main room; both have Dog Tags. These are some of the most difficult guards in the game to hold up, also best of luck getting those tags! See the following Tactics section.

Once you've got the guards bedded down, take Emma south to the watertight door and move over to the floor hatch.

Strut L Tactics

DOG TAG: Strut L Guards (Both)

First, equip the M9 and tranquilize the guard on the opposite side. Now quickly run forward and wait near the inside wall, just around the corner from the nearest guard. When he turns to patrol the south, run around the corner and catch him. Once you've got his tags, tranquilize him but don't kill him. Drag his body out into the hallway near the exit where you left Emma. Now return to the dozing guard near the watertight door. Spray the Coolant in his face until he starts to wake up. Quickly run back into the hallway, and wait for him to resume his route. This guard is a bit trickier. Watch his route carefully from the safety of the corridor and learn the timing of his movements. When you know that he is at the northern point of his route and about to turn, run in and capture him near the watertight door. Whew—that strategy takes some guts!

Strut L Oil Fence

Emma and Raiden climb down the long ladder outside the base of Strut L. To get back to Shell 1 from here, the two must cross the Oil Fence using the pontoon bridges that connect Strut L to Strut E. In a few minutes, Snake will arrive to give you some backup, but you must handle it on your own for now. Using the sniper rifle, Raiden must clear the way for Emma.

 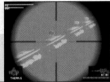 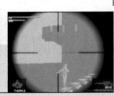

Sniping Tips Revisited

Equip the Thermal Goggles to better see Claymores and sentries. First, shoot the four Claymores nearest Strut L. Then look for sentries on the platform ahead. If they stop, don't zoom in; you want to be able to see if others show up. It's also important to shoot at nerve endings, such as in the shoulder. If you can disable a guard's arm, he can't fire or use his radio. Be sure to double-tap the Left trigger button once in a while to reload the rifle, and check the platform occasionally to see if additional bullets or Pentazemin has appeared adjacent to Raiden's position. Use First Person View to narrow down your initial aim before you raise the sniper rifle's scope to your eye. Finally, laying down on the ground can help steady your aim.

When Emma reaches the first column and starts to cross behind it, you'll need to worry about additional soldiers on the column and Gun Cyphers that might float into view.

Around this time, Snake will call. You can spot him lying on the upper part of Strut E, willing to help you with the sniping. Just call him on the Codec when you want him to join in, and he will snipe whatever is in your scope. This is especially helpful if you run out of bullets or Pentazemin.

BOSS FIGHT

Final Vamp

Gender:	Male
Affiliation:	Dead Cell Knife Specialist
Weapon:	Serrated Hunting Knife

You can't keep a thirsty vampire down. When Emma almost reaches safety, the Romanian knife wizard takes her hostage in a desperate last stand. For Emma's safety, switch over to the PSG-1T. That way, if you hit her by accident, she won't take as much damage. Besides, it's really cool to see 10 or 12 darts sticking out of Vamp's face. You don't need the Thermal Goggles for this, so keep the Pentazemin ready if you have any left—it really comes in handy. Aim for Vamp's head and shoot as rapidly as possible. If you lose your aim on the head, target Vamp's shoulder when he twists Emma to the side. After you have knocked his purple "consciousness bar" down to half, take another Pentazemin even if Raiden still seems steady. When the purple "consciousness bar" under Vamp's life bar runs out, the battle ends.

MISSION 07: DELIVER THE DISK

With Emma seriously wounded, Snake takes the girl and runs ahead to the Shell 1 Computer Room on the B2 level. Raiden crosses the oil bridge on his own and enters the lower level of Strut E. From here, Raiden has 300 seconds to reach the B2 Level of Shell 1.

Strut E Parcel Room B1

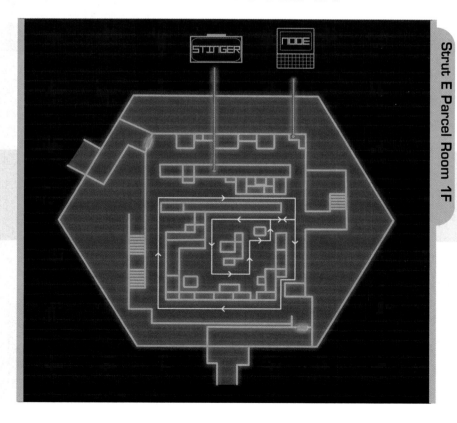

Strut E Parcel Room 1F

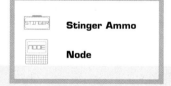

Stinger Ammo

Node

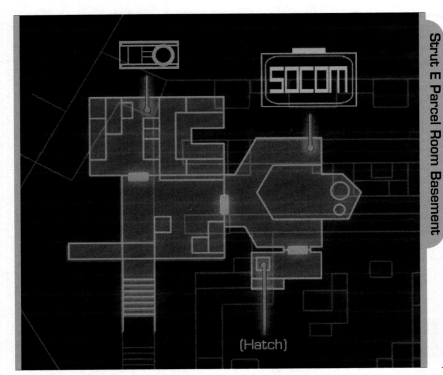

Strut E Parcel Room Basement

(Hatch)

	Digital Camera
	Socom Ammo

The clock is ticking, so get a move on! You have 300 seconds to reach the B2 level of Shell 1. **Socom Bullets** are at the top of the B1 platform. Exit through the Lv5 door, and enter the other one in the corridor.

Say Cheese!

The **Digital Camera** is in the small parcel storage room. While it's a little late to start taking pictures, this item will be mighty helpful in your next game. Check the Secrets and Bonuses section of this guide for more details.

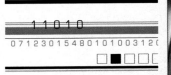

Run up to the first floor, but be wary of the new guard left behind to patrol this area. He is listening to music and distracted, but still reacts to the sight of Raiden. Once you've sneaked up and claimed his tags, move to the conveyor close to the DE Connecting Bridge entrance. Crawl under the machine to find a new box of **Stinger Missiles**, and claim any other ammo you didn't get on previous trips through here.

Parcel Room Tactics

DOG TAG: Parcel Room Boogie Guard

The last guard in the game with Dog Tags is deceptively tricky, mostly due to the wide patrol route he follows. The strategy that seems to work the best is to move from the stairs up to the north conveyor, where the missiles are found. Hide behind this conveyor until the music-loving guard crosses the area below. Running around the conveyor, Raiden must capture the guard before he turns and heads south.

Shell 1 Core, 1F

Watch out for mines on the south side of the corridor. Move up to the elevator before time runs out. Check your Rations for parasites after you run through the sea lice. Entering the elevator takes Raiden immediately through a series of scenes in the B2 Computer Room. From there, this band of extraordinary men prepares to enter the freight elevator, which descends deep into Arsenal Gear.

MISSION 08: ARSENAL GEAR

Arsenal Gear: Stomach

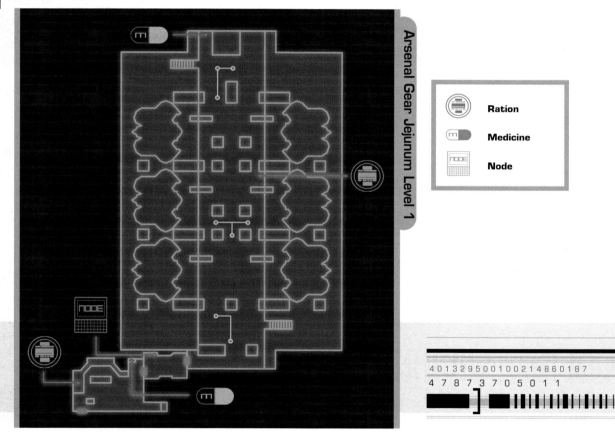

Arsenal Gear Jejunum Level 1

	Ration
	Medicine
	Node

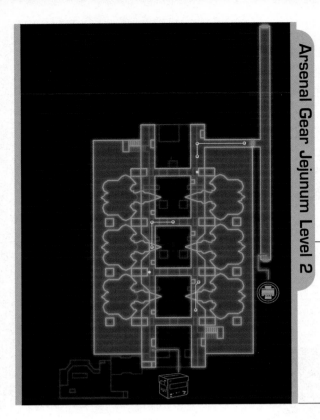

 Ration

 Box

Raiden finds himself strapped to a torture table facing Ocelot and Solidus. During the torture event, tap ⊙ as quickly as you can to avoid losing any health.

Afterward, Olga socks Raiden in the stomach for a few points of damage. When Raiden is alone, moving left or right causes him to yank against his restraints. Call Rose and Raiden is released. Snake is waiting for Raiden at the end of a long corridor full of guards. Getting through this long and open area alone is the challenge of a lifetime.

The 'Bare' Essentials

With one hand occupied covering his privates, Raiden's abilities are seriously compromised. He cannot hang from rails or even fight hand-to-hand very well. He is also unable to perform the chokehold, so don't get caught attempting to do something you're unable to.

Once you're released from the manacles, move to the locker near the exit and find the **Medicine** inside. If Raiden runs around naked for an extended period, he will start sneezing. Use the Medicine to cure his cold, so that he does not accidentally give away his position. Outside the torture room door, download the Soliton Radar map from the local network Node.

Arsenal Gear: Jejunum

Get around the guard patrolling the area outside the Stomach. When the guard turns and moves north, run from Raiden's starting position all the way to the giant cargo container on the right. Flatten Raiden's back against the south edge of the crate and knock on the metal surface to attract the guard's attention. As the guard approaches the crate from the left side, move around the opposite side and continue north. At this point, you have to decide whether you are going to go up the stairs to the right or continue through the lower portion of the Jejunum. We've provided strategy for either choice in the following two sections, starting with the lower level.

Lower Level Subterfuge

If you decide you'd rather ascend the stairs to the right of your current position, skip this section and read the following "Upper Level Hiding" section. If you are moving on through the bottom level, then best of luck to you. Move all the way up to the large container on the right and hide behind it. Sometimes the second guard on the lower level looks north and pauses. At this opportunity, move to the first low container on the right. Crouch and crawl behind it, continuing north. Find a **Ration** just past the next large container on the right.

Move up to the next large container on the right. Start keeping tabs on the position of the guard on the upper level. If the red dot indicating his position is close to the connecting bridge above, do not move for a while. Also, watch the last guard on the lower level. When he is on the west side of the large central container, move to the front of the container and press your back against it. Knock on the container, and the guard will come to investigate. Whichever side he moves to, run around the opposite side of the container and run up the stairs. By the way, there is more **Medicine** in the upper-left corner of the lower level, but you can carry only one.

On the top level, stay behind the large container on the western rail, and peek around the corner at the guard on the opposite side. Study his movement pattern carefully. It will be difficult to get past him, because he patrols directly in front of the exit! Once you have memorized his pattern, move to the bridge and stop. Watch the surveillance camera's cone of vision, and as it moves away from the bridge, run at the camera. Using the blind spot directly beneath the device, move to the south side of the column on which the camera is mounted. Press Raiden's back against it and resume watching the guard near the exit. After he searches near Raiden's location and moves north, run for the exit. Most likely, the guard will notice the movement and come to investigate. However, if you keep running through the exit, there will be no Alert.

Upper Level Hiding

If you've already followed the strategy for investigating the lower level of the Jejunum and you've made it through the exit, skip ahead to the "Arsenal Gear: Ascending Colon" section. However, If you choose to ascend the first set of stairs, there is also a good way to break through on the upper level.

Out in the Open

At all points in the upper level, you must monitor the movements and sight lines of the guards above as well as below. Guards on both levels can see you.

Move from the top of the stairs, across the narrow catwalk, to the west side of the room, where you can reclaim the **Z.O.E. Cardboard Box**. In areas where there is only a camera, simply run under it and navigate close to the column underneath to stay in the device's blind spot. Move up the west side of the room to the middle catwalk bridge and wait for the guard on the other side to move north. Head across the catwalk then, provided that no other sentries are directly below the catwalk bridge, and run as far up behind the guard as you can. Equip the Z.O.E. Box very quickly and remain still as he turns and passes moving south. This doesn't always work; if the Box is too much of an obstruction in the guard's path, he'll likely examine it and discover you. If the Box provides successful cover, then unequip it as soon as the guard passes south of you, and move north from there along the east side of the room. There is a gap in the floor, which you can cross with a torso-axial jump. However, the hole drops down to the location of a **Ration** below.

Across the gap, set down on the other side of the last column, where a camera views the situation overhead. Press Raiden's back against the lower part of the column. Watch the guard near the exit carefully. When he patrols the south area near Raiden's hiding spot and then moves north, run under the camera's blind spot and make a break for the door. The guard will most likely notice something and come to investigate, but you can rush out the exit before he actually confirms sighting Raiden.

Arsenal Gear: Ascending Colon

Run south in the corridor, toward the game camera's position, to find a **Ration**. Then run north. You may notice that a video clip of a girl overtakes the Soliton Radar. If you answer a Codec call, this will disappear. Keep running up and down in the hall and answering the Colonel's weird messages until Rose calls. After the conversation, Solid Snake emerges. Fully decked out in his trademark sneaking suit and bandana, he looks ready to take care of business. He returns all of Raiden's former equipment, plus a little gift from the Ninja, the **High Frequency Blade**.

Get used to the control of the ninja blade now while you have a few minutes. Control the blade using the Right Stick. Press to execute an uppercut, down to cleave, and left and right to slash from side to side. If you press the stick up or down, Raid will hold the blade in position until you move the Right Stick again or release it. Press the Right Stick as a button, and Raid will thrust with the sword. Rotate the Right Stick all the way around, and Raiden will execute a spinning slash. To blo press ⬤. Raiden can even block bullets with the sword. When the sword icon in the right menu is red, the sword will cau damage to an enemy's life bar. Press ⬤ and the sword icon will switch to blue. In this mode, Raiden attacks with the blu edge of the sword and knocks enemies unconscious. Blunt mode has only one particular use...

DOG TAG: Solid Snake

The final Dog Tags of the game are the hardest to come by, because you have to obtain them from the one and only legendary counter-terrorist, Solid Snake! To get Snake's Dog Tags, switch the HF Sword over to the blunt edge. Attack Snake with the sword, then run away. Snake gets angry and will attack with punches and kicks. He will even draw his Socom and fire! Dodge his attacks using Raiden's torso-axial jump. If possible, use the jump to hurt Snake, as well. After Snake has taken a series of blunt strikes, he will be knocked unconscious. Shake down his body to make his tags drop out.

Arsenal Gear: Ileum

Together, Snake and Raiden will have to blast their way through tons of soldiers in the minutes to come. Luckily, Snake has his Infinite Ammo Bandana. So, if you run out of bullets, he'll throw you some. Just stick with the same weapon the whole time and stay close to Snake.

Infinite ammo.

Keep the Rations equipped to avoid dying during the melee. Use a machinegun, such as the M4 or the AKS-74u. Duck behind cubes and rectangles on either side and in the center. Basically, you should charge down the aisle firing, running from cover point to cover point to avoid enemy fire. Use the step-out technique to nail enemies as they cross.

The Arsenal Tengus with the swords will be able to block bullets. Engage them at close range with punches and kicks, and they shouldn't get back up. Also, if Tengus get shot from two different angles, they can't defend themselves.

Use First Person View to take out snipers perched on the rails above. Watch out for falling bodies; they cause damage. When you reach the end of the row, just keep blasting until the all clear chime sounds. Stay close to Snake so that he will throw you more bullets. If Snake dies, the game ends. Don't let him do all the fighting, or he will take all the damage, as well.

Technical Advice

141.12

OTACON

Hal will be your strategic advisor as Raiden and Snake face off against the Tengu hordes. Through various conversations, he will suggest tips for fighting the Tengus and provide extremely accurate technical data on their weapons and armor. He even has tips for how to use the HF Blade against Tengus, but you will take less damage and kill more enemies using a machinegun.

Arsenal Gear: Sigmoid Colon

Grab the **Ration** and move into the next chamber. Tengu Commandos surround Snake and Raiden, so there's no way out but to fight. Again, equip a machinegun. Stay close to Snake so that he can throw you Rations and hopefully ammo. Try not to hit Snake, and flip out of his line of fire. Luckily, he enters this room with another full bar of health.

Stay at the bottom of the screen as much as possible if Snake will allow, since that provides better visibility.

Use kicks and punches to take out Sword Tengus. If the ammo seems to stop coming and Raiden runs out, switch over to a fun weapon like the RGB6. Start blowing up clusters of enemies, but don't let Snake get caught in the blast.

Another good way to break through this chamber of death in style is to use the HF Blade. Press to block bullets from the front, and get used to fighting with the sword. You practically have to be an expert with the sword by the time you reach the final battle.

Fission Mailed?

A few times during the fight, a facsimile of the Game Over screen will appear. This is just Arsenal's AI messing with Raiden's head some more. We suggest sitting really close to the screen and keeping close tabs on the fight because the battle will continue, even while this frustrating interference is in effect.

Final Battles Ahead!

Try not to consume too many Rations during all the wetworks. After the firefights, you'll face a major skirmish with a deployment of Metal Gear RAYs, followed by an even more intense final showdown!

Arsenal Gear: Rectum

Raiden climbs the ladder out of the Sigmoid Colon, arriving at a level that seems ripped straight from one of his VR training missions. As you listen to Solidus's voice, consider using your time to equip the HR Blade and practice your moves. While this is not yet the final boss fight, the HR Blade will be the *only* weapon you can use when that time comes, so you must become proficient with it quickly.

BOSS FIGHT

Metal Gear RAY Army

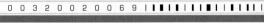

Contact Otacon frequently at the start of the battle. He provides some of the clues and strategies listed here. Equip the Rations and the Chaff Grenades. Raiden can run while throwing a Chaff. The electronic jamming will make it harder for the RAYs to hit Raiden with missiles, and they will be unable to lock on with their machineguns.

You can avoid machinegun and missile attacks by performing the torso-axial jump at just the right instant. RAYs have different warnings for each type of attack. The machinegun attack comes after a RAY hides its head behind its arm for a moment. When a RAY launches homing missiles, Raiden can hear the sonar targeting lock of their guidance system. Before a RAY fires its rail gun, it must open its faceplate and draw in outside energy. The only attack that really comes with little warning is when a RAY fires missiles from its knees. But you can avoid this attack by using the Chaff Grenades and staying close to RAYs that have jumped into the ring with Raiden.

After you have set off a Chaff Grenade, equip the Stinger Missile Launcher. You'll notice targets outlined at the RAY's knees and head. The way to attack a RAY and cause maximum damage is to fire one missile at the knee, then one at the head. When a RAY is hit in the knee, it buckles over from the impact. The head will lean over the impacted knee and the faceplate will open. So, after you have fired a missile at the knee, raise the Stinger's scope just slightly, and the head should fall into the lock-on area. Missiles that strike a RAY's head while its faceplate is open inflict a tremendous amount of damage.

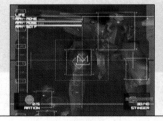 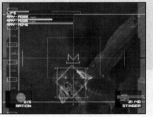

After you've reduced one of the RAYs to half its health, it will jump into the central ring with Raiden. By jumping away at just the right moment, Raiden can avoid damage from the force of this entrance. The RAYs' strategy shifts at this point. While the RAY inside the ring attacks with machinegun, rail gun, and knee-fired missiles, the RAYs outside the ring will target homing missiles at Raiden. By staying in fairly close range of the RAY inside the arena, the RAYs outside the ring won't risk firing missiles. If you continually throw Chaff Grenades to maintain the electronic interference, then the only attack you have to worry about from the RAY in the ring is the rail gun, and possibly an occasional stomp of its feet.

Raiden climbs the ladder out of the Sigmoid Colon, arriving at a level that seems ripped straight from one of his VR training missions. As you listen to Solidus's voice, consider using your time to equip the HR Blade and practice your moves. While this is not yet the final boss fight, the HR Blade will be the *only* weapon you can use when that time comes, so you must become proficient with it quickly.

BOSS FIGHT

Metal Gear RAY Army

Contact Otacon frequently at the start of the battle. He provides some of the clues and strategies listed here. Equip the Rations and the Chaff Grenades. Raiden can run while throwing a Chaff. The electronic jamming will make it harder for the RAYs to hit Raiden with missiles, and they will be unable to lock on with their machineguns.

You can avoid machinegun and missile attacks by performing the torso-axial jump at just the right instant. RAYs have different warnings for each type of attack. The machinegun attack comes after a RAY hides its head behind its arm for a moment. When a RAY launches homing missiles, Raiden can hear the sonar targeting lock of their guidance system. Before a RAY fires its rail gun, it must open its faceplate and draw in outside energy. The only attack that really comes with little warning is when a RAY fires missiles from its knees. But you can avoid this attack by using the Chaff Grenades and staying close to RAYs that have jumped into the ring with Raiden.

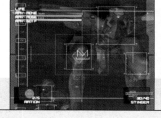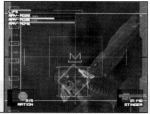

After you have set off a Chaff Grenade, equip the Stinger Missile Launcher. You'll notice targets outlined at the RAY's knees and head. The way to attack a RAY and cause maximum damage is to fire one missile at the knee, then one at the head. When a RAY is hit in the knee, it buckles over from the impact. The head will lean over the impacted knee and the faceplate will open. So, after you have fired a missile at the knee, raise the Stinger's scope just slightly, and the head should fall into the lock-on area. Missiles that strike a RAY's head while the faceplate is open inflict a tremendous amount of damage.

After you've reduced one of the RAYs to half its health, it will jump into the central ring with Raiden. By jumping away at just the right moment, Raiden can avoid damage from the force of this entrance. The RAYs' strategy shifts at this point. While the RAY inside the ring attacks with machinegun, rail gun, and knee-fired missiles, the RAYs outside the ring will target homing missiles at Raiden. By staying in fairly close range of the RAY inside the arena, the RAYs outside the ring won't risk firing missiles. If you continually throw Chaff Grenades to maintain the electronic interference, then the only attack you have to worry about from the RAY in the ring is the rail gun, and possibly an occasional stomp of its feet.

11010

071230154801010003120038 9

607201208868

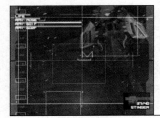

Target the RAY inside the ring with the Stinger, continuing the same strategy of shooting the knee and then the open face. After each successful attack, unequip the Stinger and move. If you are short on Rations, sometimes one will spawn in the center of the arena. Stinger Missiles will appear on the outskirts of the ring when Raiden gets low.

MISSION 09: SONS OF LIBERTY

BOSS FIGHT

Solidus

Otacon is still available by Codec to provide Raiden tips on how to beat Solidus. The strategy covered here will supplement Otacon's advice.

The way to survive this battle is to use 🔘 effectively and plan a series of counterstrikes and escapes at key moments. A **Ration** sits in the upper-front corner of Federal Hall's roof, and that's all you get. Equip your remaining Rations in the left menu, and keep the HF Blade in sharp edge mode (red). Charge at Solidus, holding 🔘 to block his sword swipes. After Solidus's swords have bounced off Raiden's defense, he will have overextended himself. The most damaging attack Raiden can inflict is to combine a series of up and down, left and right slashes. Don't try anything too fancy, like the spin move. As Raiden continues to slash, he will gradually turn left or right. Press 🔘 and Raiden will auto-face Solidus while defending himself. Because Solidus is missing his left eye, he is less likely to see and defend against attacks from his left.

There are a few attacks that Raiden cannot defend against. When Solidus streaks across the roof, leaving a trail of fire in his wake, only luck will prevent Raiden from being set ablaze. Being on fire will continually reduce Raiden's health, so keep doing torso-axial rolls to shake out the flames. Use this move to jump over streaks of fire, as well. During the first round of the battle, Solidus often follows up a fire streak with a volley of tentacle missiles. Hold 🔘 and charge at Solidus, and the blade should deflect the missiles. This positions Raiden for an excellent counterstrike opportunity. When Solidus leaps onto the wall of the connecting building, run away! The megalomaniac will land with tremendous force, knocking Raiden to the ground. If one of Solidus's tentacles manages to grab Raiden, press 🔘 rapidly and wiggle the Left Stick to get free.

After Raiden has reduced the wretch's life bar by half, Solidus casts off the tentacles. Doing so increases the speed of his fire streak attack. Solidus will streak around the roof, setting the entire area ablaze. Then he will taunt Raiden and streak directly at him, delivering an unbelievable power punch. The key to avoiding this attack is to stay in one place while Solidus is fire-streaking around and prepare for the final charge. Raiden must flip out of the way at just the right moment. If you do this correctly, Raiden should be positioned near Solidus' side or back for an excellent counterstrike opportunity. How do you prevent Solidus from repeatedly streaking all over the place? During the second round, you must focus on engaging Solidus at close range. If Raiden can keep him busy, then he will not have the chance to start a triple fire streak. Defend against Solidus's sword slashes and counterstrike when he has overextended himself.

Mission Complete

This Mission Analysis contains the keys to the future. What you do with those keys is up to you. No one can make your decisions for you. Life is too short and too precious to let anyone control you. Take control by using the strategies you've been given and unlock the secrets of the Patriots by turning to page 176.

MISSIONs
BASICS

Introduction

Welcome to the world of VR (virtual reality) training missions. All of Foxhound's most elite soldiers are trained using the latest in VR technology. Essentially, a simulated environment is created to train a soldier on a specific aspect of warfare. Whether he needs to practice his sneaking tactics or learn to use a specific weapon, it's all available. Now you can hone your skills for use in Metal Gear Solid 2: Substance. We recommend that you play through the VR Missions first to brush up on the basic tactics you'll use in the main game itself. After facing over 500 scenarios with seven characters, you'll be a hardened soldier ready to face the toughest challenges the game can offer.

Fundamentals

During each mission, you receive a score according to your performance. This score is based on how quickly you complete a level, the amount of ammo remaining for all weapons, and whether or not you're lethal (known as the No-Kill bonus). There are also three top scores assigned to each mission. If you place within the top three, you'll displace all scores beneath your own. For example, let's say the top scores for a level are 10000, 9000, and 8000, and you score 11000. The new scores for the level will change to 11000, 10000, and 9000.

To be nonlethal, you must do your best to either tranquilize your enemies or pound them to a pulp. This becomes more difficult in later missions, and sometimes it's not feasible unless you want a big challenge. In earlier stages, being nonlethal is quite possible. Give it a try for a higher score.

When it comes to sneaking, you can be extremely creative with your techniques. For the most part, you can be right next to a guard as long as you don't enter his cone of vision. This enables you to pull off some audacious maneuvering tactics that you wouldn't otherwise think possible. Explore the limits of the guards' awareness to find out what you can do.

Characters

Although there are seven characters to play as in the VR Missions, only two of them are available when you start the game. You must complete a certain percentage of the missions to unlock each remaining character. See each character description for details on how to obtain him.

Raiden

Raiden is available at the start of the game as a selectable character. He has the full range of mission types, and the difficulty for each one falls in the easy range. He can easily get the No-Kill bonus. Raiden's missions form the basis for all the other characters, so pay attention as you go through them.

Raiden (Ninja)

Raiden dons the ninja suit, which essentially limits him to the use of the HF Blade for the entire set of missions. Of course, this cuts down on the time you need to spend searching for weapons because you always start with the blade. It also means that all combat must occur at close range, making it impossible to eliminate guards from a distance. Modify your tactics accordingly. Ninja Raiden becomes available after completing 50% of Raiden's missions.

X Raiden

For a change of pace, Raiden drops his outfit altogether and bares it all to the world. He is now X Raiden! X Raiden only has one set of missions, known as Streaking Mode. You cannot use any weapons as X Raiden, and you must completely avoid the enemy to avoid embarrassment. X Raiden becomes available after completing 100% of the Raiden (Ninja) missions.

0320020069

Snake

Solid Snake is the other character who's available from the beginning. Snake typically faces more enemies on each level than Raiden, but the difficulty is not much greater. He also has the entire range of missions at his disposal.

Pliskin

Snake's alter ego, Pliskin, is armed to the teeth when he faces his VR Missions. He leans more toward lethal force, but stealth is still possible with a little effort. In most cases, Pliskin's missions are modeled after Raiden's with some minor differences, such as less ammo or more guards. Pliskin becomes available after completing 50% of Snake's missions.

Snake (Tuxedo)

In true James Bond fashion, Snake dresses in a tuxedo for a set of missions. He always begins each level with an M9, so he can easily dispose of guards without killing them. These missions are based on Snake's missions, with less ammo and more guards in some cases. You must complete 100% of Pliskin's missions to unlock Snake (Tuxedo).

Snake (MGS1)

The final hidden character is none other than Solid Snake in his Metal Gear Solid 1 outfit! MGS1 Snake is by far the most difficult character to use. He never has radar or enough ammunition. But that's not all! The guards you'll face can see across entire levels and have hearing well beyond any normal human, and their weapons deal massive damage with a single shot. They can also survive direct hits with a Stinger rocket! Essentially, the only effective way to deal with these guards is to shoot them in the head, heart, or groin, or to snap their necks.

Most of the MGS1 Snake levels are so difficult that the same strategy may not work twice. Perfect timing, creativity, and complete stealth are the only way to succeed. Are you up to the challenge?

Mission Types

There are two main mission types: VR Missions and Alternative Missions.

VR Missions

VR Missions consist of various training scenarios that hone your ability in a certain skill. There are five main subcategories of the VR missions.

Sneaking Mode

The Sneaking Mode missions require you to make it to a goal point without being detected. If a guard sees you, you fail the mission. There are two types of sneaking missions. The first type requires that you simply make it to the exit undetected, and the second forces you to eliminate all guards on the level without being spotted.

Weapon Mode

Weapon Mode missions focus on destroying targets with various weapons used in the game. The missions vary slightly depending on the character you choose. Each weapon has five missions that you must complete before you can proceed.

First-Person Mode

First-Person Mode is like playing a different game entirely. You complete each mission through the eyes of the character you've chosen, rather than the standard third-person perspective. There's a whole new set of skills that you must master to complete these missions. Only Raiden and Snake have First-Person Mode missions.

Variety Mode

The Variety Mode missions range from the unusual to the outlandish. Here you'll face such challenges as sniper missions, giant monster soldiers, and dropping down the side of a building. Be prepared for anything.

Streaking Mode

Exclusive to X Raiden, Streaking Mode isn't a set of missions, but rather a single string of five sneaking missions in a row… with a catch. You have one time limit for the entire set.

Alternative Missions

Alternative missions take place in VR reconstructions of the Tanker and the Big Shell from the actual game. They test your skills in several different ways, particularly in dealing with guards in the irregular terrain of both areas.

Bomb Disposal Mode

Bomb Disposal Mode challenges you to locate several C4 charges placed around the level and disarm them with the Coolant spray. Two types of sensors are used on the missions. One type enables you to locate bombs on your radar, and the other requires you to locate them by a beeping tone.

Eliminate Mode

Eliminate Mode is similar to the Eliminate All VR missions, but with a few key differences. Most importantly, the guards cannot call for reinforcements, and you can be spotted with no penalty (well, other than the angry guards chasing you). More importantly, you're dealing with areas from the game, each of which presents its own challenges.

Hold-Up Mode

Twin brother to Eliminate Mode, Hold-Up Mode requires you to, well, hold up guards. Successfully holding up a guard makes him vanish, which means you can cruise through these levels quickly after finishing Eliminate Mode.

Photograph Mode

Exclusive to Raiden and Snake, Photograph Mode tests your photography skills by requiring you to take a specific picture. These missions aren't high on the difficulty scale, but most of them are fun.

How to Use This Guide

A basic strategy for Raiden is described for every level in the game. Since the other characters have levels based on Raiden's missions, only those characters with significant differences have their own strategies listed separately. Otherwise, refer to the primary Raiden walkthrough to get an idea of what to expect.

Good luck!

Missions

SNEAKING MISSIONS

Level 01

1024013295001002148860187
0147873705011

Mission Parameters	
First Place Score	15500
Time Limit	2:00
Enemy Count	1
Difficulty	1

Raiden

This level is by far the easiest of the training missions. Run up to the end of the hallway, stopping at the corner. Wait for the lone guard to advance to the right until he stops, then run behind him and proceed to the goal. No problem.

Snake

Stay to the right of the hallway, rolling to get past the guard before he turns to face you.

Pliskin

For the most part, Pliskin's levels are identical to Raiden's, except he always starts with a silenced USP. To attain the score requirement, you can't kill anyone.

Snake (Tuxedo)

Even though he's now in a tuxedo, Snake's missions are the same as regular Snake. Tuxedo Snake starts every level with an M9 and James Bond-like music.

Snake (MGS1)

With no radar and incredibly fast, alert guards, MGS1 Snake's levels are a true test of your skills.

Level 02

1711002106 8

Mission Parameters	
First Place Score	15500
Time Limit	2:00
Enemy Count	3
Difficulty	1

To get the highest score on this and future levels, you must time the guards' movements.

Raiden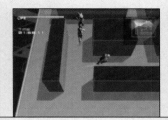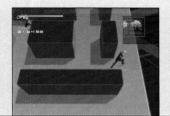

To achieve the highest score for this level, you'll need to use a bit of trickery. Walk up from the starting point until you're just about even with the guard on the other side of the wall. Back up against the wall and knock. The guards in the area come to investigate, leaving an opening available to rush to your goal. Run back down, wind through the second path from the bottom until you reach the far right, and make a quick sprint to the goal. Timing is everything, so if you don't get it the first time, keep trying.

Snake

Run up and to the right until you reach the second hallway from the bottom. Roll past the rightmost guard and race to the goal.

Level 03

0101002140038700021

Mission Parameters

First Place Score	17500
Time Limit	2:20
Enemy Count	3
Difficulty	2

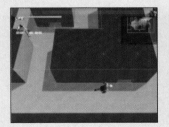   

Raiden

Run to the far right and head up to catch the first guard. Throw him to the ground, and then continue up to the second guard. Perform a somersault to knock him down, then make your way up to the goal.

Snake

Go up the first hallway to the right leading up, and stop behind the first guard until the path leading up is clear. Back up against the wall next to the hallway leading up until you can squeeze behind the guard on duty here. Continue to the goal.

Level 04

Mission Parameters

First Place Score	17500
Time Limit	2:20
Enemy Count	3
Difficulty	2

Raiden

Begin the level by tossing a magazine and waiting for the guard to walk toward the sound. Make a break to the right, and then proceed up the middle pathway. Cut behind the guard standing to the right and run to the goal.

Snake

Back up against the box-shaped structure near the starting point, and knock to draw the lower guard's attention. Run up and cut to the right, tossing a magazine behind the two guards in the next hallway. One guard should move in to investigate; roll through the other one to quickly reach the goal.

Level 05

Mission Parameters

First Place Score	18000
Time Limit	2:40
Enemy Count	5
Difficulty	3

Raiden

From the starting point, run up and across the line of sight of the guard at the top of the screen. Wait until he crosses the noisy grating, and then somersault into him to knock him down. Run across the grating, and then wait in the top corner until the guard to your right turns away from you. Sneak up behind him and throw him to the ground, and then hop over the ledge to your right. Drop down to reach the goal.

Snake

Move to the right, just a bit from the starting point, until the guard above spots you. Run up to the right of the hallway he walks down, rolling across the grating once he's past. Drop over the topmost railing and climb hand over hand to the right until the guard turns to the left, and then hop up. Drop over the ledge again, this time the one to the right. Release your grip to fall onto the goal.

Level 06

02020015560101002140 0165

Mission Parameters

First Place Score	19000
Time Limit	2:40
Enemy Count	4
Difficulty	2

Raiden

With the right strategy, this level is a breeze. Climb onto the first ledge to your right, and then climb onto the ledge above. Somersault to the platform directly above, and then somersault to the platform on the right. Somersault to the platform above again, and then continue right and somersault over once more. Walk up to the top right of this platform, drop down, and then climb up the final ledge to the goal.

  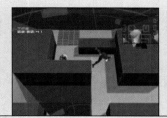 

Snake

Go up the left side, rolling over the pools that leave footprints. Wait until the first guard spots you, and then run across the trap door and head to the top of the level. Roll across the grating when the guard is turned away, and then roll across the second grating. Pull yourself up to reach the exit.

Level 07

1024013295001002148601 87
0147873705011

Mission Parameters

First Place Score	15500
Time Limit	2:40
Enemy Count	3
Difficulty	5

This strategy is particularly audacious and takes patience and skill. No one said getting the highest score would be easy!

Raiden

Although it's tempting to stow the body near the starting point in a locker, don't do it. Run down and to your right, somersaulting over the unconscious guard's body. Somersault upward once to get a little speed, and then somersault over the dark squares in your path until you reach the top of the hallway. Back up against the center of the top wall and knock on the wall to get the guard's attention. Back down the hall a bit and wait at the corner. The guard will come to the end of the hallway and look to the left. The instant he looks up, run behind him and sprint like mad down the hall.

Proceed all the way down, and then go right as fast as you can. Up and to the right, you can see a guard on your radar. Make sure he's facing upward, and run behind him as well. He should turn to the left, and then your path to the goal is clear. If you can finish this level with a first-place score, pat yourself on the back. You've earned it.

 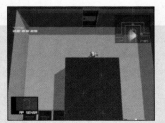  

Snake

Roll across the unconscious body, and then roll across the puddles to reach the wall in the center. Knock until you have both guards' attention, and then run behind them when they reach the top of the wall. Run all the way down the hall and cut to the right, running behind the guards you encounter until you reach the goal.

Level 08

Mission Parameters	
First Place Score	18000
Time Limit	2:40
Enemy Count	4
Difficulty	3

Speed is the key to this level. Don't hesitate or you won't make it in time.

Raiden

Begin this level by putting your gun away. You won't need it. Speed up the stairs to your right, following the walkway around to the next set of stairs. Somersault down the stairs and run up, hugging the wall a bit to avoid the camera. Toss the guard in front of you, and then run up the stairs above. Stay to the right side of the structure at the top of the stairs until you reach the goal.

Raiden (Ninja)

Since it takes time to put the sword away, leave it out. Follow the same path described in Raiden's mission, but this time pause until the first guard on your right turns away from you. Then run behind the guard patrolling here while being mindful of the camera on the left. Give the guard on the final platform a moment to move past the stairs, and then run up and to the left to reach the goal.

Snake

Run up the middle path and take the left fork, running behind the first guard you encounter. Wait a moment at the top of the wall for the guards to face away from you, and run up the stairs to the goal.

Level 09

11010

071230154801010031200389

Mission Parameters	
First Place Score	35500
Time Limit	5:00
Enemy Count	3
Difficulty	1 or 5

There are two strategies for this level. The first gets you a *really* high score, and the second will merely get you a *very* high score. Choose according to your skill level.

Raiden

Option A

The easier of the two paths, this method still gets you a first-place score. Put your weapon away and wait for the guard just above you to face upward. Once he does, make a break up and to the right, somersaulting as you pass the opening between the walls. Once you've gone all the way to the right, rush up and to the left, and then go straight up. Flip into the guard above you, and then get to the goal.

Option B

Only those with patience and sharp skills should try this strategy, but the payoff is an incredibly high score. Again, put your weapon away and wait for the guard just above you to face upward. This time, charge the guard and flip into him to knock him down. You must time this flip perfectly, or else you'll be spotted. Somersaulting too early or late guarantees your failure. Assuming your timing is correct, simply continue upward until you reach the goal. Prepare for many, many restarts to get this one right.

Snake

Grab the box and run up the hallway. Knock on the wall to your right and equip the box. Stand still until the left guard walks past, and then run up (while still in the box) and go for the goal.

Level 10

Mission Parameters	
First Place Score	27000
Time Limit	4:00
Enemy Count	5
Difficulty	4

Raiden

Put away the magazine and head up the stairs to the left. Hug the walls as you move up and to the right, being careful to step around the grating on the floor. Run behind the guard to your right, and then flip across the bridge to avoid making any noise. Make sure you're as far up as possible when you cross the bridge, so you can get the attention of the guard below. Move up to the ledge just past the bridge, and drop down once the guard below moves onto the staircase. Once you land, simply run up and to the left to reach the goal. Don't worry about dodging the pools of liquid, because no one is around to detect you.

Snake

Run up the middle of the level, climbing over the boxes on the right wall. Watch out for the cameras! Wait for the guard to pass, and then hop down and run to the right. Go up all the way to the left, timing your movements to avoid the guards. Move back up and climb up the ledge to reach the goal.

ELIMINATE ALL MISSIONS

Level 01

Mission Parameters	
First Place Score	16500
Time Limit	2:00
Enemy Count	1
Difficulty	1

87020015980101002140000387

In the Eliminate All Mode, the exit for each level will not appear until all the guards are eliminated. Also, to get the No-Kill bonus for each level, use the M9 tranquilizer weapon to render the guards unconscious.

Raiden

This mission is very simple. Start out by grabbing the M9 and equipping it. Rush up the hall and go into First-Person View once you reach the end of the hall. When the guard comes into view, tranquilize him and then rush to the top of the zone. If you take out the guard quickly enough, you'll get a first place score.

Pliskin

For Pliskin's missions, the M9 is even more difficult to reach. This makes getting the No-Kill bonus tougher. The guard placement is the same as in the Raiden missions. All of these mission descriptions will tell you where to find the M9. In the first mission, the M9 is located in the opening to your left.

Snake

Duck into the first opening on the right and grab the M9. Equip the weapon, wait for the guard to turn away, and pop a tranquilizer into his neck. Run for the goal.

Snake (Tuxedo)

After making you deal with the Pliskin missions, the developers decided to go easy on you. Tuxedo Snake starts with the M9 each time, so you can start eliminating the enemy right away. Since Raiden has the M9 closest to him when he starts a mission, follow his strategy for these missions.

Snake (MGS1)

MGS1 Snake must contend with the usual lack of radar and incredibly alert guards. You need a lot of patience to complete these missions. For every mission, the M9 is at the farthest point of the level. Being lethal just started looking a lot more feasible.

Level 02

400110731

Mission Parameters

First Place Score	15000
Time Limit	2:00
Enemy Count	3
Difficulty	2

Raiden

Pick up and equip the M9, and then shoot the guard to your right. Run up and take out the other guard to your right. Move to the right until you can go up again, and then go into First-Person View and take a long shot at the guard in front of you. Don't miss or you won't get first place. The exit is located to the far right of the level.

Snake

The M9 is located in the top-left corner. Grab it and tranquilize the guards in a clockwise pattern. Run quickly for the goal.

Pliskin

The M9 is located in the center aisle to the right.

Level 03

607201208868

Mission Parameters

First Place Score	17000
Time Limit	2:20
Enemy Count	3
Difficulty	2

Raiden

Move to your right, grab the M9, and equip it. Shoot the guard directly above you, and then move up the hallway. Shoot the guard up and to the left. Run up until you reach the top of the area, and then hang a left. Turn left once you reach the end of the hall, and take a very long shot at the guard down from you. Head back to your right to leave the area.

Snake

Walk over to the right of the opening above and knock on the wall. Scoot back to the starting point and wait for the guard to investigate the noise. Run behind him and up, grabbing the M9 just to the left. Equip it and take out the guards starting with the one that investigated the knock earlier. Continue shooting and moving upward until you reach the goal.

Pliskin

Head to the top-left corner of the level to get the M9.

Level 04

Mission Parameters

First Place Score	17000
Time Limit	2:20
Enemy Count	3
Difficulty	3

97001236

Raiden

Start by walking to the far right of the box-shaped structure to your right, then knock on the edge. Make sure you're as far to the right as possible without exposing yourself. Circle around the box and grab the M9 in the hallway. Face down and shoot the guard who comes to check out the noise, and then move up and to the left to take out the guard waiting there. Continue up and then take aim to your right to knock out the guard. Run toward the last guard to find the exit.

Snake

Knock on the wall near the starting point, and then run over to the right to find the M9. Take out the guards nearby and go for the exit.

Pliskin

Again, the M9 is located in the top-left corner.

Level 05

Mission Parameters

First Place Score	18000
Time Limit	2:40
Enemy Count	5
Difficulty	4

Raiden

Proceed up and to the right, grabbing the M9 in the area. Face down and go into First-Person View. Tranquilize the guard to the right, and then shoot the other one immediately to the left. Get out of First-Person View and move back to the left, taking out the guard above. Somersault across the grating above you and turn to the right. Go into First-Person View again and take out the guard below. Run up and face right again, firing on the guard just in front of you. Once he's down, continue right and drop off the ledge at the end of the walkway. The exit is just below.

  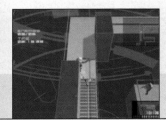 

Raiden (Ninja)

Draw the attention of the first guard by walking in front of the grating. When he's in range, slice him. Somersault across the grating above and sneak up behind the guard to the far right. This should draw the attention of some guards below. Run back to the starting point and slice the enemies as they come up the stairs. If there are any stragglers, get their attention. While staying on the top level, run up to the far right until you see the goal and then drop down.

Snake

Drop over the ledge to the right of the starting point, timing your fall so that you land on the guard below. Pick up the M9 and take down the other guard on the bottom. Run back up to the top and take down the remaining guards. Drop off the ledge above the goal to reach the exit quickly.

Pliskin

The M9 is in the top-left corner of this level. See a pattern?

Level 06

```
100016502117    020200155601010021400165800:
```

Mission Parameters	
First Place Score	19000
Time Limit	2:40
Enemy Count	4
Difficulty	3

Raiden

If you've finished Level 06 of the Sneaking missions already, the strategy for success is the same. Climb to the top of the platform to your right and grab the M9. Shoot the guard standing to the right, and then shoot the guard above your position. Leap to the box located up and to the right, and then hop over to the platform above. Shoot the sleeping guard below and to the right, and then leap to the next platform on your right. Shoot the guard down and to the right, and then climb down and head for the exit. To leave this area, you have one more ledge to scale.

Raiden (Ninja)

Since you have no gun, you must stalk each guard individually. Your best bet is to sneak up to a corner near the guard, knock, and slice. The guard placement here is identical to the Raiden mission, so follow the same general path of hugging the left side and following the top. Pull up to reach the ledge at the goal.

Snake

Run up the left side and cut to the right when the guard spots you, moving across the trap door to reach the M9. Shoot the guard just below you, and then make your way back up and to the right. Take down the remaining guards and head for the exit.

Pliskin

Go right down the corridor next to the starting point to get the M9.

Level 07

Mission Parameters

First Place Score	17000
Time Limit	2:40
Enemy Count	4
Difficulty	3

0200159801056730011 0400

Raiden

Speed is of the essence here, so don't waste any time. Run to the lower-left locker next to the starting point and get the M9 inside. Immediately spin around to the right and shoot the guard waiting behind you. Follow the hallway up, being careful to jump over the squares that leave tracks. Hold up the guard who comes around the top corner, and then put him to sleep. Head down and quickly shoot the guard down the right corridor. Run down that same corridor, following it down and to the right. One more guard awaits above you. Just take him down and follow the hallway to the exit.

Raiden (Ninja)

Again, use the order described in the Raiden mission for tracking down the guards. Remember that you must get much closer to each guard to take him down.

Snake

Run up to the wall at the top center of the level and knock. Wait for the guards to walk up and leave, and then open the topmost locker to get the M9. Work your way down and to the right, popping guards as you go.

Pliskin

Follow the hallway up and then down, then take a right. Open the locker just below to find the M9. To get to this point, remember your techniques for getting the guards' attention.

Level 08

07713
6300328420082
200200151937100214 05019

Mission Parameters

First Place Score	19000
Time Limit	2:40
Enemy Count	4
Difficulty	5

Raiden

Precision is the key to this mission, because one missed shot means losing precious time. Move to the right to pick up the M9, and then head back to your left and go up the stairs. Take aim through the window ahead and shoot the two guards. Move down the stairs above and turn to the right. Take out the final two guards you can see from here, and then head to the exit at the top of the level. Hug the walls to avoid cameras.

  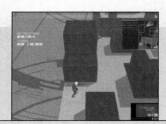 

Raiden (Ninja)

With no gun, you must modify your strategy considerably. Run to the right and up the center of the level, taking out the guard. Next, sneak up behind the guard located up and to the left and allow him to walk down a bit before eliminating him. Run up and to the right, going up the stairs and slicing up the guard. Finally, head for the top-center platform and wipe out the last guard.

Snake

Run all the way to the right to find the precious M9. Shoot the guards on the top level first, and then take out the ones below from high ground. Head for the goal at the top.

Pliskin

Toss a chaff grenade and then run up the center aisle to get the trusty M9.

Level 09

```
0200159801056700110400                    012033401
```

Mission Parameters	
First Place Score	35000
Time Limit	5:00
Enemy Count	3
Difficulty	1

Raiden

After the precision required on the last mission, this level should be a piece of cake. Pick up the M9 directly above and then eliminate the guard just ahead. Up a bit and to the right, you'll find another guard that you must eliminate. The final guard is at the top of the level. Just shoot him and wait for the exit to appear.

  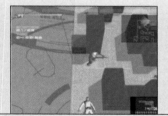 

Snake

The M9 is up and to the right. Take out the guard below first, and then work your way up. Head for the goal.

Pliskin

To find the M9, walk up from the starting point. It's sitting on top of a crate.

Level 10

Raiden

The last mission requires a steady hand, so be ready. Run to your right, pick up the M9, and step over the box beside it to save time. Follow the hallway up the stairs to the right, pausing at the end to hold up and shoot the guard. Stay in First-Person View, and shoot the guard patrolling the platform above. Run down the stairs to your left, and knock off the guard that comes around the corner. Go right and up until you're under a walkway, and then switch to First-Person View to shoot another guard ahead. Run up and to the left, taking out the last guard on your way to the exit.

   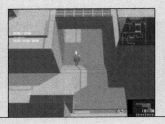

Raiden (Ninja)

Step over the box to your right and head up the stairs. Slice the waiting guard, and then knock to draw another guard. (This guard may have been alerted already if you messily killed the first guard.) Repeat this knock-draw strategy again, and then make your way down the stairs and up the level. Use the knock-draw method on the last two guards, and avoid the cameras on your way to the goal.

Snake

Run up and grab the M9 out of the topmost locker, being careful to stay out of the nearby guard's line of sight. Tranquilize the guards on the bottom half of the level first, and then head for the upper platforms and take the enemies down. Keep an eye out for the cameras posted all over the level as you move to the goal, and shoot each guard on patrol nearby.

Pliskin

Head to the right, go up the stairs, and duck into the opening to the right to get the M9.

HANDGUN MISSIONS

Level 01

Mission Parameters	
First Place Score	13000
Time Limit	1:00
Targets	10
Difficulty	1

To gain more points, shoot targets in rapid succession. This creates a combo that can be used to multiply your score.

Raiden

This level is just target practice. Targets pop up on your left side and work their way over to the right. When all 10 targets are gone, proceed to the goal directly behind you.

Snake

For all weapon missions, Snake has a few more targets per level. Otherwise, the levels are the same.

Pliskin

For all weapon missions, Pliskin has targets that disappear as they move. These levels are patterned after Raiden's missions.

Snake (Tuxedo)

For all weapon missions, Tuxedo Snake has more targets and they move and disappear.

Snake (MGS1)

For all weapon missions, MGS1 Snake has more targets and they move and disappear. With a few exceptions, his levels are the hardest to complete.

Level 02

Mission Parameters	
First Place Score	12000
Time Limit	1:00
Targets	10
Difficulty	2

Hitting a target in the right place can earn you more points. Always try to hit the center of a target for maximum effectiveness.

Raiden

More target practice ensues as you enter this level. Targets begin in the middle of the level and work their way to the left. Follow them through the center in the distance, and then go back up to your right to finish. The goal is behind you.

Level 03

Mission Parameters	
First Place Score	30000
Time Limit	1:30
Targets	29
Difficulty	3

Raiden

This level introduces explosive orange targets. Target them to destroy adjacent green targets with one shot. As the targets move together, time your shots to cause the most damage to maximize your accuracy. Remember, you can get more points by creating shot combos.

Level 04

Mission Parameters	
First Place Score	18000
Time Limit	1:30
Targets	13
Difficulty	2

Targets with red highlights will lower your score, so avoid shooting them.

Raiden

The quickest way to succeed on this level is to hold down the lock-on button and fire on each target while in Third-Person View. You can easily run and shoot through the first flight of stairs and the platform in the middle of the level. Once you reach the top level, watch out. The red targets will appear on the left side of the passageway. Avoid targeting them as you blast your way to victory.

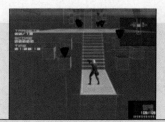

Level 05

Mission Parameters

First Place Score	37000
Time Limit	2:00
Targets	40
Difficulty	3

Raiden

The final handgun level will test your skills in both First and Third-Person Views. Shoot the first targets that pop up in First-Person View, and then switch to Third-Person View to advance. Work your way along the platform, shooting all targets that appear. Remember, when you need precise aiming, nothing beats First-Person View. Watch out for the red targets as you approach the final platform, and you'll finish with a record score.

  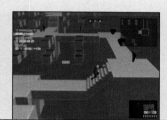 

ASSAULT RIFLE MISSIONS

Level 01

Mission Parameters

First Place Score	10500
Time Limit	1:00
Targets	12
Difficulty	1

Raiden

Another straightforward mission. Fire at the targets as they appear. Use the three sets of four targets to warm up for the trials ahead. Once the targets are gone, the exit will appear immediately to your left.

Level 02

Mission Parameters

First Place Score	9000
Time Limit	1:00
Targets	10
Difficulty	2

Raiden

This is also target practice, but this time you have some moving targets to blast. Do your best to make shot combos on each row of targets by using the assault rifle's rapid fire. When you're finished, the exit appears to your right.

Level 03

Mission Parameters

First Place Score	13000
Time Limit	1:30
Targets	15
Difficulty	4

Raiden

Be prepared for an even more difficult time with this level. The targets move around in a train-like fashion, following each other in a line. They circle around the structures in front of you, pausing only briefly. Add floating red targets to the mix and you have a difficult time ahead of you. When you complete the level, the exit appears to the left.

Level 04

Mission Parameters

First Place Score	40000
Time Limit	1:30
Targets	40
Difficulty	4

Use the orange boxes to create big explosions and even bigger point combos!

Raiden

This is your first Third-Person View assault rifle level, and it's a doozy. Use the lock-on button to target the boxes as they appear, and continue moving forward. Be warned, however, that you will encounter orange boxes that explode when fired upon. The explosions can knock you down, wasting valuable time so keep your distance. Work your way to the top of the level as quickly as possible to reach the exit.

  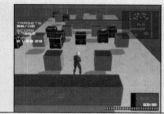 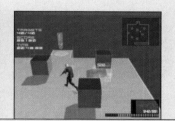

Level 05

Mission Parameters

First Place Score	42000
Time Limit	2:30
Targets	52
Difficulty	5

Raiden

The final assault rifle mission is the hardest you will face. You begin the mission in First-Person View with floating targets, and then you proceed up the center of the level in Third-Person View using the lock-on technique. Finally, you have another run of targeting in First-Person View, culminating in a strangely shaped target that has two red targets orbiting it. Shoot just the center target to complete the level. The exit appears right beside you.

C4-Claymore Missions

Level 01

071230154801010031200389

Raiden

Mission Parameters	
First Place Score	8200
Time Limit	1:00
Targets	2
Difficulty	1

It's time for a break from shooting everything. Pick up the C4 on the left, and then run up to the target on the left. Place the C4 next to this target, run to the exit marker, and detonate the explosives when the two boxes are next to one another. Easy!

Level 02

598010100

Raiden

Mission Parameters	
First Place Score	12000
Time Limit	1:00
Targets	9
Difficulty	1

This time you're dealing with orange explosive boxes. Run up to the center box and place the C4. When all of the boxes are close in together, blow up the C4. You may not be out of the way yet, but don't worry. The combo from the explosion will push you into high score territory. Get back up and run to the exit at the top of the level.

 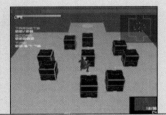 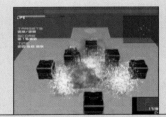 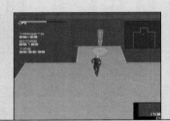

Level 03

2001598010010
1711002106810 010 101 111 20

Raiden

Mission Parameters	
First Place Score	16500
Time Limit	1:30
Targets	11
Difficulty	3

You can finish this level with one decisive explosion, if your timing is just right. Run around the left side, and grab the C4. Back up against the wall just below where the boxes drop, and place the C4 on the wall. Place two more charges on the sections where the boxes fall. Run around to the point were you started and detonate the charges sequentially, timing the blasts so that all the boxes are destroyed. Stand on the exit circle as you do this to leave the level rapidly.

Snake ▉▉[👤]▉▉

The boxes go the opposite direction from those on Raiden's level. You may have to place more C4 to take out the boxes, but use the same basic strategy.

Level 04

    100016502117   02020015560101002140016580001

Mission Parameters	
First Place Score	15000
Time Limit	1:30
Targets	10
Difficulty	3

Raiden [👤]▉▉▉▉▉▉▉·

To beat this level quickly, you need to place the C4 carefully. Try your best to bomb the orange boxes when the green boxes are nearby, and keep moving so you don't get caught in the blasts. The quickest path is up and to the right, and then proceed to the left to finish up. The exit appears next to the starting point.

Level 05

    01010021483387892   10320003037 ▉▉▉▉▉▉▉▉ 179105

Mission Parameters	
First Place Score	16000
Time Limit	1:30
Targets	12
Difficulty	3

Use the radar to find the boxes when you can't see them on-screen.

Raiden [👤]▉▉▉▉▉▉▉·

The last C4 level requires you to place the C4 in the center of a group of moving boxes and detonate it when all the boxes are close together. Place the C4 and run, using the radar to indicate when the boxes are aligned. Move through the area in a counter-clockwise pattern, and pick up any weapons along the way. With careful planning, you'll max out your score.

 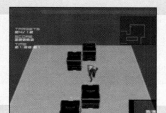  

Snake ▉▉[👤]▉▉

There are now more barriers to prevent you from easily moving between sections. Follow the same strategy, using your radar to achieve success.

GRENADE MISSIONS

Level 01

598010100

Raiden

Starting out with the grenade launcher is simple. Just pick up your weapon, shoot at the two boxes, and run for the goal. Not a problem.

Mission Parameters	
First Place Score	11000
Time Limit	1:00
Targets	2
Difficulty	1

Snake

On Snake's version of this level, the boxes move.

Level 02

900175034 08415 02006

Raiden

For the fastest time, use both First and Third-Person View. The boxes appear above you and to the right, and they're spread out a bit. Remember to aim higher to make your shots go farther. The exit appears behind the starting point.

Mission Parameters	
First Place Score	11000
Time Limit	1:00
Targets	4
Difficulty	1

   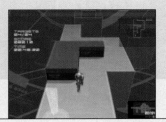

Level 03

069

Mission Parameters	
First Place Score	17000
Time Limit	2:00
Targets	6
Difficulty	2

Raiden

This time, the targets slide back and forth over open space. Time your shots to hit both boxes at once; to do this, you need to be in First-Person View. There are three sets of two targets at the base of each set of stairs, but you should be able to easily hit them from the top of each staircase. Your exit is at the topmost section of the platform.

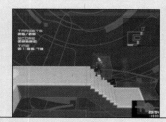 

Level 04

9700l236

Mission Parameters	
First Place Score	21000
Time Limit	2:30
Targets	6
Difficulty	3

Raiden

The key to this mission is timing your shots so that you eliminate all the targets with the fewest number of shots. Sounds familiar, doesn't it? To minimize the number of shots, fire into the middle openings on the structure in front of you. You should be able to clear each row with one shot when you get it down pat. The exit is right behind the starting point.

Level 05

Mission Parameters	
First Place Score	23500
Time Limit	3:00
Targets	10
Difficulty	4

Raiden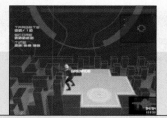

This is one of the most difficult weapon missions. The targets move around a maze beneath you, and you must time your shots almost perfectly to hit multiple targets in one try. Patience and practice are the only sure ways to beat this level with a high score.

 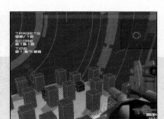

PSG-1 MISSIONS

Level 01

During the following missions, use Pentazemin to steady your hand for proper aiming. Remember that scoring a direct hit in the center of the targets knocks them out with a single shot and earns you the highest possible score.

Mission Parameters	
First Place Score	10000
Time Limit	1:00
Targets	6
Difficulty	1

Raiden

You now begin the sniper missions. Grab the PSG-1 and fire at the six targets spread out evenly in the distance. Destroy them all to proceed.

 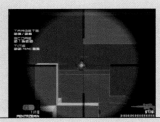 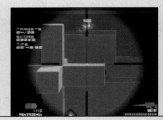 

Level 02

Mission Parameters	
First Place Score	10000
Time Limit	1:00
Targets	6
Difficulty	2

Raiden

This time the targets move, but slowly. Use the zoom feature of the PSG-1 to get an accurate aim on the targets. One target is turned to the side rather than facing you, so fire at the bright green area in the center to destroy it. You need to move around a bit to find all of the targets.

 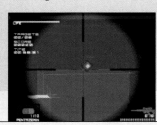  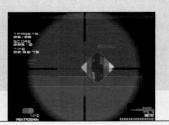

Level 03

Mission Parameters	
First Place Score	19000
Time Limit	2:00
Targets	13
Difficulty	2

Raiden

There are three platforms from which to aim on this level, plus an explosive orange target. You should be able to hit all targets from the topmost platform, but if you can't see them all, try the bottommost platform. As in previous missions, a little creative shooting at the orange target can eliminate multiple targets.

  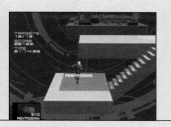

Level 04

Mission Parameters

First Place Score	19000
Time Limit	2:00
Targets	14
Difficulty	3

Raiden

This level has the same layout as the last one, but the target placement is drastically different. There's also a red target, so don't shoot it. Once the targets are gone, head out to the final level.

Level 05

Mission Parameters

First Place Score	33000
Time Limit	4:00
Targets	17
Difficulty	4

Raiden

This last level has targets that move through building structures. You must be as quick and accurate as possible to complete this level in time. Keep an eye out for red targets placed near the exploding orange targets. You can lose valuable points if you're not careful. This level also adds a new obstacle, black sheets of metal that block some windows. You must destroy these metal sheets to get to the targets behind them.

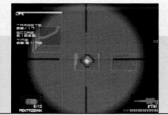 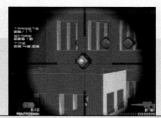 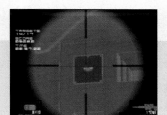 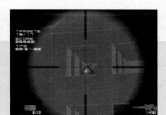

STINGER MISSIONS

Level 01

You can fire a rocket from the Stinger and then target something else. This lets you steer a rocket around corners.

Raiden

Equip the Stinger and aim upward slightly to pinpoint the target through the wall. Fire when the reticule is red, and then run for the exit. You're sure to get the first-place score.

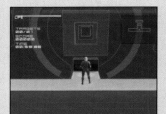 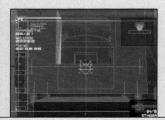 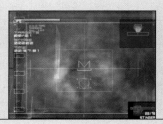 

Snake (MGS1)

This is one of the only levels that's totally different from the other weapon missions. MGS1 Snake has to fire a Stinger rocket through a small opening with multiple pieces of wall blocking its path. Your best bet is to fire the rocket and then lock onto the target after the rocket is inside the opening.

Level 02

Raiden

You should be able to stay in the center of the starting platform and aim upward slightly to find the targets. They're spread out on three sides. Try to hit multiple targets at once to increase your score.

   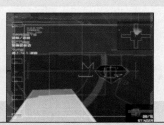

Snake

Snake has some orange targets to contend with on this level.

Level 03

Mission Parameters

First Place Score	19500
Time Limit	2:00
Targets	12
Difficulty	3

Raiden

Orange targets make their appearance on this level, and you can use them to your advantage. Make your way to the top of the staircase in front of you. Shoot the bottom target when each set of four targets is closest to one another. This destroys all four targets with one shot. After all the targets are clear, run for the exit.

   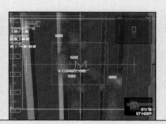

Level 04

Mission Parameters

First Place Score	21500
Time Limit	2:30
Targets	9
Difficulty	3

Raiden

In this mission, many more structures block the path to your targets. Make sure you have a good lock and enough clearance for the rockets to hit the targets. Oftentimes you must fire and make a rocket move behind an obstacle. Aim carefully!

   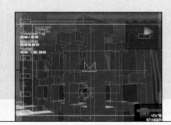

Level 05

1711002106B

Mission Parameters	
First Place Score	44000
Time Limit	3:00
Targets	37
Difficulty	4

Raiden

Your last mission requires some careful timing to hit the orange targets. Once more, you need to minimize the number of shots it takes to destroy the targets. After blasting through many waves of targets, you encounter a flying target made up of many smaller targets. Aim for the centermost target to finish off the entire "ship" with one shot! Not a bad way to finish off this weapons mission.

 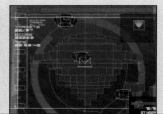 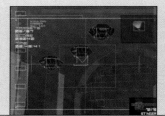 

Snake

Your final target on this level is shaped like a stealth bomber, rather than the UFO-shaped object from Raiden's mission.

NIKITA MISSIONS

Level 01

11370 02006

Mission Parameters	
First Place Score	7200
Time Limit	1:00
Targets	1
Difficulty	1

Raiden

These missions have a distinctly different feel to them because you're actually piloting the rockets. Fire the Nikita through the opening to your right, and then steer the rocket to the left a bit to find your target. That's all for this first level, so run for the exit.

Snake

Two more targets are added for Snake's level. The placement is different as well. Boxes are up, left, and right this time.

Level 02

071230154801010031200389

Mission Parameters

First Place Score	11500
Time Limit	1:30
Targets	4
Difficulty	2

Raiden

You face many more structural obstacles this time around. Move to the top, right, bottom, and left sections of the platform you're standing on to get the best shots for tracking your target. Remember, the rockets slow down when you turn. You can aim briefly and then let the rocket accelerate. Use this to your advantage here.

  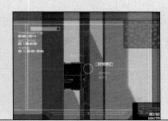 

Level 03

1024013295001002148601 87

Mission Parameters

First Place Score	13500
Time Limit	2:00
Targets	3
Difficulty	2

Raiden

This level uses a unique mechanism that you must master before you can continue. The rockets follow any section of ground they fly over, even slopes. Fire each rocket at the base of a slope, and then guide the rocket up to hit the three targets. If you aim carefully, this level shouldn't be too tough at all.

Level 04

Mission Parameters

First Place Score	11750
Time Limit	2:00
Targets	1
Difficulty	3

8 7 0 2 0 0 1 5 9 8 0 1 0 1 0 0 2 1 4 0 0 3 8 7

Raiden

Did you get the hang of guiding rockets up a slope? I hope so, because this entire level is based on that skill. Fire a rocket into the opening in front of you, and then veer off to the right. Dodge the red boxes placed along the path as you follow the corridor to the top. When you see open sky, your target should be just in front of you. Once it's destroyed, you can leave the mission.

 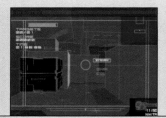  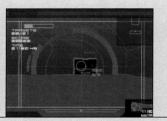

Snake

You encounter more red boxes on this level.

Level 05

Mission Parameters

First Place Score	14500
Time Limit	2:30
Targets	1
Difficulty	4

0 0 3 2 0 0 2 0 0 6 9

Raiden

This last level can be very trying, but have patience. Red targets move back and forth as you attempt to steer the rocket. Try to get into the opening ahead and to the left, dodge the moving red boxes, and go for the center opening in the middle of the area. After making it that far, follow a corridor up until you reach a section of slopes with more red targets on them. Use the slopes to make your way up until you see your destination—the final target. Take it out to finish this section.

  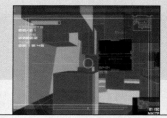 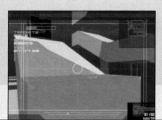

HF BLADE/NO WEAPON MISSIONS

Level 01

07713
6 3 0 0 3 2 8 4 2 0 0 8 2 2002001519

Mission Parameters	
First Place Score	12000
Time Limit	1:00
Targets	13
Difficulty	1

Raiden

Armed only with a sword, you must chop down all targets as they appear. Slice carefully and you can take out multiple targets with one attempt. Make your way up the level, destroying all targets you encounter.

Snake

Snake faces these levels with only his bare hands. It takes four punches to destroy each target. However, when you follow the punches with a kick, you can send the target flying and use it to knock down other targets nearby. Snake's target placement is just about identical to Raiden's for all levels.

Level 02

069
1 0 0 0 1 6 5 0 2 1 1 7

Mission Parameters	
First Place Score	14000
Time Limit	1:00
Targets	16
Difficulty	1

Raiden

This time, the targets move around. The layout of this level is very similar to the previous one, so keep moving to complete the level quickly. The exit is in the same place as before, at the top of the level.

   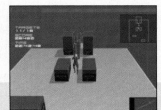

Level 03

Mission Parameters

First Place Score	26000
Time Limit	1:30
Targets	30
Difficulty	2

Raiden

You must kick some of the targets to make this level easier. Make your way up the level, and kick targets into one another across gaps in the floor. This saves a lot of time as you proceed to the exit at the top.

Level 04

Mission Parameters

First Place Score	14000
Time Limit	1:30
Targets	12
Difficulty	3

Raiden

Red targets rear their ugly heads on this level. Almost every set of targets here has a red counterpart nearby, so make your moves deliberately. Again, move up and avoid the red targets to complete the level.

   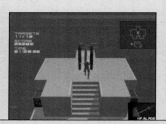

Level 05

Mission Parameters

First Place Score	41000
Time Limit	2:00
Targets	50
Difficulty	3

Raiden

Begin this level by kicking the first target into the targets behind it, and then make your way up once more. There are even more red targets this time, and more moving green targets as well. Use the same strategy of kicking targets across gaps to save time. You need careful precision to get the high score here.

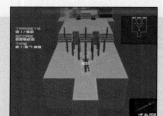   

FIRST-PERSON MODE MISSIONS

Level 01

Mission Parameters

First Place Score	19000
Time Limit	2:00
Targets	25
Difficulty	2

002001519371002140501.9 0151937100

Raiden

It's time for a complete change of pace. You're totally in First-Person View, with no option to switch to Third-Person View. As the level begins, shoot the targets to your left and right with a USP. Head up the stairs in front of you, grab the RGB-6, and take out the box targets that pop up from the floor. If you time it properly, you can combo the explosions and get major extra points. From here, continue up the stairs, taking out the targets to your left and right once more. Get out an automatic weapon, such as the M4, and blow away the targets that pop out on the right side. Then finish up by facing the left side and strafing down the corridor. Shoot all the targets in the openings along the wall as you move. The exit is at the end of this corridor.

Snake

For missions 1-4, Snake has more targets and slightly different item placement.

Level 02

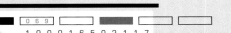

Mission Parameters

First Place Score	37000
Time Limit	5:00
Targets	N/A
Difficulty	2

069 100016502117

Raiden

This level is a bit different from the last one. You must avoid detection as you run through a maze of corridors. Head forward, and then follow the leftmost corridor. When this corridor veers to the left, slow down and peek around the corner heading up. The guard at the end of the hall should have his back to you. Run up the hall toward him, and then duck into a passage on the right. Climb up slowly, because another guard waits near the top. Knock him out, and then continue moving up on the map. Take the next left turn and follow the corridor to the exit.

Level 03

Mission Parameters

First Place Score	38000
Time Limit	6:00
Targets	6
Difficulty	3

Raiden

Here you must hunt down six enemy soldiers, but it doesn't matter if you're spotted or not. Take an immediate right from the starting position, and follow an enemy soldier. Stay behind him until he hangs a left, and then stay back. There's another guard facing you, so don't get spotted. When you see the guard you were following move forward, tranquilize the guard who was facing you. Once again, follow the original guard, and then take him down. Just ahead is the third guard. Take him down, turn back around, and head toward the beginning of the level while moving to your right. You should encounter another guard along the way. Turn around and head back to the top of the map, keeping your eyes open for the remaining guards patrolling the top of the area. The exit is at the topmost point of the map.

Level 04

Mission Parameters

First Place Score	51000
Time Limit	8:00
Targets	3
Difficulty	4

Watch out for the clear floor panels on this level. They dissolve if you stand on them for too long, dropping you to your doom.

Raiden

You must find three targets, shrouded in darkness, and destroy them. You have no radar on this level, but there's really only one path through it. The key here is to keep your bearings and don't get turned around in the darkness. The first target is on ground level, protected by a single guard. An automatic weapon will destroy the target quickly. The next target is further along, at the top of the first staircase. Be wary because two guards are awaiting you here. Take out this target, and look to the left to find the final one on ground level. Dispose of this guard, and then you're on your way out the exit a bit further up.

Level 05

Mission Parameters

First Place Score	90000
Time Limit	25:00
Targets	4
Difficulty	5

Gather up the abundant extra weapons on this level to earn more points.

Raiden

As the level opens, you see a box of Pentazemin. Grab it and head for the ledge to your right and pick up the PSG1-T. From here, snipe all of the guards you find on patrol. Check the roofs of the buildings in front of you as well. Drop down when the way is clear, and turn around to see a doorway in front of you. Walk through it, being wary of the guard who patrols here. You should see a staircase dead ahead. Run up and check your radar for the bomb cloud attached to a wall at the top level. Retrace your steps and take the first left you see. The next bomb cloud should now be visible. Go down the stairs, step over the box in front of you, and then check the post to your right. Defuse it, and then head west on your map. Another cloud should appear at the westmost point. Once you disarm this one, the final bomb waits for you to the north. Make your way up a series of staircases until you reach the roof. On the roof, hang an immediate right and go up one more flight of stairs. Your quarry sits alone on a post to your left. This is a bit tricky. You must do a somersault over the gap and land on the platform in front of the bomb. After a few tries, you should have it. Defuse the bomb to complete this mission.

Snake

After sniping enemies from the starting point, follow the stairs down and look up to find the first bomb. Go to the building on the left and look in the top-left corner. The second bomb is attached to a box. Go up to the third floor and look for a vent at ground level. Crawl inside and down to find the third bomb. Continue through the vent and come out on the other side. Make your way over to the roof of the building on the right, and then go down one level and look out the windows on the left. There should be a bomb in the second one. To reach it, turn 180 degrees, look down at the floor, and crawl through the vent. Retrace your steps and head for the center of the building's roof from which you started. You should find a large stack of crates here. Climb to the top of the pile and look under the ledge above you for the final bomb.

VARIETY MODE MISSIONS

Level 01

9700123 6

Raiden

Mission Parameters
First Place Score 10000
Time Limit   2:00
Difficulty   2

This mission is more like an obstacle course, requiring you to use almost every skill you've learned so far. Follow the corridor, being careful to dodge the floating mines. You also face disappearing floors, so don't stop running until you reach solid ground. When you come to a dead end, crawl through the opening at the base of the wall. Climb over the structures in front of you. When you get the chance, jump over to the platform on your right. Climb up to the top, and jump again to another platform on the right. Hop onto the winding pathway above and continue to the right. Finally, drop over the ledge just below and run for the goal, being mindful of the floating mines.

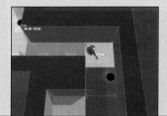  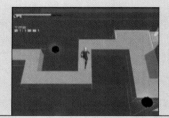 

Raiden (Ninja)

This level is actually based on Raiden's Variety level 5. Skip ahead to read the map description. The only differences are that you only have the sword and there are two more enemies. This is the only Variety mission for the ninja.

Snake

Rather than being able to leap across openings, Snake must follow the pathway to the left. Be careful as you wind along the walkway to your goal.

Pliskin

Pliskin must protect a plate of curry in the middle of the floor from seven enemies who are hiding behind boxes nearby. Equip the PSG-1 and snipe away. Use Pentazemin to steady your hand.

Snake (Tuxedo)

Tuxedo Snake also has a variant of the sniper mission, with a few changes for variety. First, he has no Pentazemin to help keep his aim true. Alleviate this problem by lying down and then taking aim. Second, there are now 20 enemies that walk out onto the field in two single-file lines. Target the men when they're coming toward you and unload on them.

Snake (MGS1)

Surprise! Another variant of the sniper mission. Protect the cardboard box. This time, the enemies will not only walk up the center of the level, but will also spread out and to the left.

Level 02

020200155601010002140016580001

Raiden

The layout for this level is identical to the last level, but the objective is different. In addition to contending with the terrain, you must destroy all of the targets in the area. To start out, let the first two targets come to you. After you destroy them, be prepared to run and shoot two more targets on the disappearing tiles. Make your way to the centermost platform with the staircase, and get your weapon out. You should be able to shoot the remaining targets from here. When they're history, head for the goal. You're blocked by a set of four walls, but with the newly acquired AKS-74U, you should have no trouble getting rid of them.

 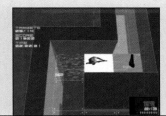  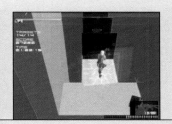

Snake

Charge out and use the lock-on button to fire on targets as you run across the trap floors. Go into First-Person View and shoot the floating targets in the middle of the room. Then run to the left and shoot the remaining targets. If you run out of ammo, there's more just ahead on the walkway. The remaining level is identical to Raiden's.

Pliskin

This level is a variant of Raiden's and Snake's mission 5. You must hunt down seven enemies in a dark level with no radar. The enemies are distributed just as they are in mission 5, so take them down and move out.

Snake (Tuxedo)

Just like Pliskin, Tuxedo Snake has his own variant of mission 5. You have limited ammo as a handicap, so keep your eyes open for more bullets to help you out.

Snake (MGS1)

Again, MGS1 Snake has his variant of mission 5. You have to contend with insanely alert enemies, as well as shotgun-toting guards. As is the norm for MGS1 Snake, this level is incredibly difficult.

0.69
000165021117

020200155601010002140

020200155601010002114

Level 03

Mission Parameters

First Place Score	9500
Time Limit	2:30
Difficulty	3

To build up your grip for the last section of this level, make sure you catch every ledge as possible during your initial vertical drop.

Raiden

You face a drastically different challenge on this level. You must drop from the top of a building and catch ledges on the way down. When you reach the bottom ledge, line up so you can grab the pole beneath you. Drop down, and pray that you catch it. Once you successfully grab the pole, work up until you can drop off onto the goal platform.

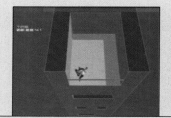

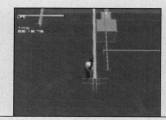
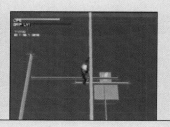

Snake (MGS1)

MGS1 Snake is the only character with more than one variety mission. You face another Zako Survival level similar to Raiden's and Snake's Level 07. This time, however, the difficulty is ramped up extremely high. Good luck on this one.

Level 04

Mission Parameters

First Place Score	42000
Time Limit	3:00
Targets	8
Difficulty	2

Raiden

You must protect the person on the floor from the oncoming horde of enemy soldiers. Say, she looks a lot like Meryl from Metal Gear Solid! Perhaps it's just a strange coincidence. Anyhow, simply get out the sniper rifle and eliminate everyone who appears in the area. If anyone makes it to the person on the floor, you fail the mission.

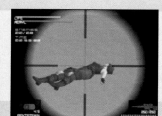
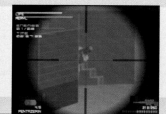
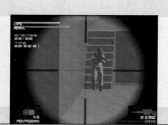

Snake

Snake's level is identical to Raiden's, except for one minor detail. There are many more guards this time.

Level 05

`020200155601010021400165 8001`

Raiden

You have no radar on this level and no light, so you must proceed with caution. The area moves up and then to the right. The first three targets are located in the up-and-down section, and the last two are in the left-to-right section. Watch out for disappearing floor tiles in the left-to-right area as well. Keep your eyes open for Thermal Goggles against a wall near the starting position. There's also a PSG1 nearby. With these tools, you can pick off enemies from a distance even in the darkness.

Mission Parameters

First Place Score	40000
Time Limit	6:00
Targets	5
Difficulty	3

Level 06

`100016502117`   `020200155601010021400165 8001`

Raiden

The world has been invaded by giant, monster-like soldiers! You must avoid their gaze at all costs! Use the columns above for cover as you head to the right. Climb the stairs, and then carefully make your way up. Climb the stairs next to the building, being careful to avoid any monsters that may be looking into the windows. When you reach the roof, jump to the next building to your right to reach the goal.

Mission Parameters

First Place Score	40000
Time Limit	3:00
Difficulty	3

Snake

When Snake faces the giant soldiers, he must be very cautious. The soldiers watch much more closely, so take your time in making your way up to the top of the building to the right.

Level 07

Mission Parameters

First Place Score	50000
Time Limit	20:00
Targets	1, 6, 14, 1
Difficulty	Varies from 1 to 4

You've reached the Zako Survival missions! There are four parts to this mission, and you will carry any items, any damage you incur, and any remaining time from section to section. Get ready!

Raiden

You face a single soldier in round one. Gather up all items on the level (especially any Rations) and shoot the soldier when you're ready.

In round two, you face six soldiers. Again, collect all of the items on this level in-between shooting the oncoming enemies. Don't waste a lot of time here, because you'll need it later.

Round three introduces the vicious Tengus ninja soldiers, in addition to the standard-issue grunts. Unsheathe your blade and attack the Tengus who land near the starting point. When they're all eliminated, start hunting down the remaining enemies scattered throughout the level. Don't forget to pick up the items!

The Monster from Another Dimension Gurlugon

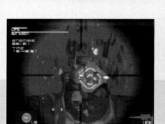

As you complete round three, a totally unexpected beast appears. It's Gurlugon, the Monster from Another Dimension! To defeat Gurlugon, you must first target a body part with the Stinger and blow it up. Next, shoot the exposed target within the body part with a sniper rifle. As you may have guessed, this isn't terribly easy to do. Not all body parts contain a target, so target his head, chest, right and left arms, the foot on your left, and the thigh on your right. Be warned that when Gurlugon roars, he often shoots rings that can stop you where you stand. Then he fires explosives at you while you can't move. Do your best to dodge and shoot and you'll succeed.

Snake

Snake's first three challenges are very similar to Raiden's, but his third one is very different. His enemy is a giant version of the snow soldiers from MGS1. You must use the Stinger to knock off the giant's head. Once it lands on the ground, use the Stinger again to bump the head into the opening in the back of the level. You must do this three times to defeat this massive enemy, each time going more quickly than the last.

STREAKING MODE MISSIONS

Level 01

00200151937100214050190151937100

Mission Parameters	
First Place Score	11000
Time Limit	2:30
Difficulty	1

X Raiden

To spice things up a bit, Raiden has ditched his uniform and is now streaking through VR training. His challenge is to make it through four consecutive levels of VR missions without being detected. Luckily for you, you've already completed all four missions with Raiden. The only difference is the single time limit you have to complete all four levels. Simply use the strategies laid out in the Raiden Sneaking missions and you'll be successful.

10240132950010021486018
014787370 5011   017

BOMB DISPOSAL MISSIONS

Level 01

Mission Parameters	
First Place Score	36000
Time Limit	7:00
Targets	2
Difficulty	1

Raiden

Find and dispose of all bombs in this section of the Big Shell. Luckily, there are only two bombs here, so you shouldn't have much trouble. From the starting point, follow the hall west, north, and then west again. Once you're inside the room, head for the top-left corner of the room and look up slightly. You should see the bomb here. To find the second bomb, head back out the door and follow the corridor as it winds south and west. Go down a set of stairs and then back up another, taking out the guards as you go. You should see a stack of boxes just above your position and to the left. The second bomb awaits you here.

Raiden (Ninja)

The first bomb is located up and to the left, inside the vent on the far-left wall. You can't see the bomb or get too close to the wall, but spray the coolant into the vent to hear it click once it's frozen. The second bomb is located down and to the left. Once you go down a flight of stairs, step up onto the lower box and look at the wall. The bomb is inside the vent.

Snake

Walk down the hall and head left, climbing on top of the boxes stacked at the base of the stairs. Look up at the ceiling to find a bomb. Keep walking left, and then head up and duck into the room with the gun sentries mounted on the walls. Toss in a chaff grenade, and then walk over to the right wall. Spray coolant into the vent there to defuse the second bomb. Head back out into the hall and follow it to the top-right corner. Look at the bottom-right corner of the electrical boxes to find the final bomb.

Pliskin

Go down the hall, head down the stairs, and look to the right to find the first bomb. The second bomb is attached to the drink machine in the break room.

Snake (Tuxedo)

Go to the room at the top of the hall at the starting location. Check out the right side of the lockers in the top-right corner of the room to find the first bomb. Head out and down the hall. Check the vent at the base of the stairs, the one at floor level. The second bomb is there.

Snake (MGS1)

Go to the room at the top of the hall and crawl into the vent on the bottom wall of the room. The first bomb is here. Go over to the snack room. There is another bomb attached to a guard's back, and one under the table.

Level 02

031200389

Raiden

This time, you're back on the ship from the beginning of MGS2. The first bomb is a piece of cake to find. Just walk down the corridor in front of you and look on top of the locker on the left. Once the target is disarmed, head out of the door to your left. Make your way through the catwalks over to the bottom-left platform in the engine room. (Use the screenshots for reference.) When you arrive on the platform, walk over to the railing on the right and look down slightly. The bomb is attached to some equipment across from your position.

Raiden (Ninja)

From the starting point, take the door on your left and head to the bottom platform in the engine room. Walk onto the walkway connecting the two sides and look to your right. The first bomb is attached to the outside of a crate at eye level. Continue to the left, and go over to the bottom-left platform on the opposite side. Look out over the railing to find the last bomb.

Snake

Step out of the door on the left and go to the second floor from the top. As you descend the stairs to the third level, get out the coolant. You'll find a bomb attached to the railing on the right. Head for the exit at the top-right side across from the entrance, and follow the hallway as it veers left and then up once more. When you reach a locked door, look to your left to locate the final bomb.

Pliskin

Walk ahead and take a right. Climb up on top of a crate and face right. You should see a bomb on top of the lockers. Head into the main engine room and go to the far left side. Go up the first flight of stairs and run to the end of the walkway, looking to the outside left wall. The last bomb is here.

Snake (MGS1)

Go into the engine room, going down to the bottom platform. Walk down the middle walkway and follow it back up to the top of the room. Look to your right between the pipes to find a bomb. Go to the walkway directly above where you were standing, and then look out and to the right over the railing to find the next bomb. Finally, head over to the second-level staircase on the left side of the room and look behind it. The last bomb is here.

Snake (Tuxedo)

Walk out the door to your left and drop off the ledge. You'll fall a good distance. Look down and to the right underneath the walkway to find a bomb. Go to the far-left side of the room to the lower platform. Look under the staircase leading up to find the last bomb.

Level 03

Raiden

You're taking care of bombs inside of Arsenal Gear, and this time there are three of them. Start out by going through the door to your left and moving down and to the right. The bomb is inside a sink in front of you. Retrace your steps to the starting point and take the door to the right this time. Knock out the guards in the area, and then go up to the right side of the top level. Walk onto the second catwalk from the bottom and face the right side of the screen. With your coolant out, look down and to the left a bit. You should see the bomb just outside of the catwalk railing. Continue left on the catwalk, and then head up and right on the next catwalk you come to. There should be a doorway on the right wall. Go through the door and turn around. The final bomb is attached to the frame of the door.

Raiden (Ninja)

Take the door to your left and look under the torture device to find the first bomb. Head back out the way you came and continue out the next door to the right. Go to the top level and stay on the right side. The second bomb is under the nose of the second Metal Gear from the bottom. Go to the left side and up to the stairs leading down. Go down the first flight of stairs, and then inch slowly about halfway down the second flight. Get out your coolant and look over the right edge of the stair railing to find the last bomb.

Snake

Go through the door on your left and defuse the bomb under the cart with two computers on it. Head into the Jejunum area and take the stairs to the top floor. Walk to the top of the level and look down at the large box pile to find the second bomb. Leave this area and head for the exit on the right. Move downward and look under the pipes on the left side of the hall for the final bomb.

Pliskin

Walk through the left door and look up at the light over the torture device to find a bomb. Head back to your right into the Jejunum area. Go all the way to the top of the lower level and take the stairs up. Walk down the upper level to reach the stairs in the bottom-right corner. A bomb sits on the floor. Go back up and exit the door on the top right and proceed into the colon. Stop just short of the Ration on the floor. The final bomb is behind it.

Snake (Tuxedo)

Walk through the door on your left and look at the ceiling to find the first bomb. Head back into the Jejunum area and stay on the bottom level. Go to the third Metal Gear Ray on the left and look at the legs to find another bomb. Finally, go to the giant crate at the top of the bottom level and crawl underneath for the final bomb.

Snake (MGS1)

Go through the door to your left and make a wide path around the computer to your left. This is where the first bomb is located. Walk into the Jejunum area and stay on the bottom level. Go up to the last Metal Gear Ray on the right side and look up and to the right. Lastly, head for the colon area and walk down the hall a bit. The final bomb is on the left wall.

Level 04

Raiden

Mission Parameters

First Place Score	79000
Time Limit	20:00
Targets	5
Difficulty	4

Back on the tanker, you must now defuse five bombs. Start out by going through the door south of your position and follow the corridor to the locker room. The first target is inside the locker next to a sink on the leftmost wall. Head back out into the corridor and continue left. Take the door at the bottom of the hall. You'll go out onto the deck of the ship, but only for a moment. Find a staircase leading up to the next level of the ship.

Walk to the right and head south down the hallway. Take the first door on your right. You come out at the top of the stairs just above two guards. Look closely–they both have bombs attached to them! Sneak up behind the guards and spray the bombs with coolant, and then run back out the way you came. Head down the hall again, following it as it winds left and then up. Just past the corner where the hall turns up is a bomb planted on the left wall. Go back to the door where you entered from the outer deck. Go up the stairs here, head to the right down the hall, and then take the next set of stairs up. Hang a left into the kitchen and go over to the pans hanging near the stove. The last bomb is attached to a pan.

Raiden (Ninja)

Go down through the door just below the starting point. Follow the hallway down and to the left, and take the door on the bottom side of the hallway out to the ship's outer deck. Switch to Sensor A. Go up the first set of stairs to your left, and then go up another flight of stairs just ahead. Walk to the front of this platform. Look out toward the mast over the railing to find a bomb. Switch back to Sensor B and go back down that last flight of stairs and through the door on the right.

Go up and to the right, and then go down and through the first door on your right. You should see a bomb attached to the ceiling on the left. Head back out the door you came in, and move up and to the left around the loop here. At the bottom of the loop is another bomb attached to the ceiling. Walk back to the stairs next to the entrance to the outer decks and go up. On this floor, walk to the right side and look behind the crates stacked at the top of the staircase. You should see another bomb here. Backtrack to the staircase in the middle of the hallway and walk up. Head left into the kitchen and look above the stoves to the left to find the final bomb.

Snake

The first bomb is behind the liquor bottles at the bar. Go back to the starting point and take the south door. Walk through the corridor until you come to the first door on the bottom wall. Go outside and then walk up and to the left until you reach a dead end. Walk to the outside edge and look up. Another bomb awaits you here. Go up a level and take the first door on the right. Walk to the opposite side of the deck to find another bomb at the blocked-off staircase leading up. Climb up the stairs and turn around to locate it. Head back to where you entered the ship and take the stairs up. Walk down the hall and look up at the first doorway you come to. A bomb is attached to the doorframe. Take the stairs to your right to go up a level. Run to the food storage area to the right and disarm the bomb on the floor.

Pliskin

The first bomb is planted at the base of the large glass window in the center of the bar area. For more bomb-defusing fun, go next to the locker room and look at the top of the lockers in the middle of the room. Head for Deck C, crew's quarters, port side. Go to the far-right end of the hallway and look in the vent at floor level for another bomb. Head up to the kitchen and circle around the table on the left to find the last bomb.

Snake (Tuxedo)

Head over to the couches at the far-left side of the lounge to find the first bomb. Go up the stairs in the middle of the room and out the door to the left. Walk to the right side of this floor and go outside onto the ship's deck. Crawl under the lifeboat hanging here to find another bomb. Go back inside and run left across the level into a room with a staircase. Look underneath the gas tanks beneath the stairs for another bomb. Head upstairs two levels to the floor with the kitchen. Head right, crawl under the explosives set in the hallway, and look on the inside wall for the final bomb.

Snake (MGS1)

Go behind the bar near the starting point and face outward. Look up and to the right to find a bomb. Walk up the stairs in the center of the room and go out the door to the left. Walk up and around the loop to the right. The bomb is located just above the door leading back to the lounge area. The third bomb is located in the food storage area on Deck D. Just spray the box on the top shelf with coolant. Go back outside on the main deck and circle around to the right side of the ship. The last bomb is strapped to the back of a crate on a raised platform. You must be in First-Person View to see it.

Level 05

Mission Parameters	
First Place Score	90000
Time Limit	25:00
Targets	5
Difficulty	4

4 2 3 0 1 0 3 0 0 5 5

Raiden

Your final mission has you back on the Big Shell. Follow the hallway to the left and take the first door to your right. Go up to the top-left corner of the room and look at the ceiling. Freeze the bomb and move out of the room and onto the walkway between shell buildings. The next bomb is positioned to the right of the doorway across the walk. Head into the dining hall and look in the bathroom on the right. Look to your immediate right to see the bomb nestled in the wall. Walk back out and run up through the area to the next walkway. Take the lower walkway and run all the way across. Some panels will drop as you run. When you reach the other side, slowly go back. You'll see the bomb attached to the outside of the walkway railing near the middle. Go up and into the final shell building, making your way around the top walk to the doorway at the top of the room. Go down a level and look at the ceiling to find the last bomb.

Raiden (Ninja)

Switch to sensor A. Go to the left and up the hall, avoiding the mounted cameras. When you reach a locked door on the left, duck and then look down and slightly to the left into the pipes to find a bomb. Switch back to Sensor B and move up the hall to the exit. Once you're on the walkway between shell buildings, walk to the section of the bridge that's blown out on the right. Look down to find a bomb. Continue up to the next building and go up to the kitchen. When you enter, spray the first box on the counter to your left. You should hear the click of the bomb being disarmed. Head to the exit to the right of this area to reach the next connecting bridge. Switch back to Sensor A. Run across the lower-level walkway, being careful not to stop. Panels fall out as you cross. When you reach the other side, flip back across the first gap and look down and to the right. You'll see a bomb attached to the bottom part of the bridge. Keep moving to the next shell building. The final bomb is located on the staircase heading down at the top of the room.

Snake

Walk left and then go through the door on your right. Run to the top of the room and take the stairs down to the right. Look into the cage just below you to find a bomb just inside the grating. Head for the exit that leads outside. Once you're on the walkway, turn around and look above the door you came through to find another bomb. Continue to the next shell building and go into the bathroom on the left. Walk to the leftmost urinal and look up and to the right for yet another bomb. Move to the next connecting bridge and check the outside of the railing to your left for more defusing fun. Go down the stairs to the immediate right and walk under the bridge. Examine the bottom of the platform above you for another bomb. Go into the sediment pool room and go down to the last walkway. Head for the bottom-left corner and look over the railing. Then defuse the bomb on the floor. Staying on the bottom level, walk over to the right side of the room opposite your location. Look up to find the last bomb attached to the railing above your head.

Pliskin

Walk up the hallway you started in, steering clear of the cameras. Step back a bit from the lockers in the top-right section of the hall, and fire at the center locker to blow off the door. Inside the locker is a bomb. Walk out the top door, and look to your left once you're on the walkway to find another bomb. Proceed to the kitchen and look in the chairs around the top table for another bomb. Head back out to the CD connecting bridge and take the lower walkway. Pause and look at the steps heading up to find a bomb. The last bomb waits in the sediment pool area. Look under the walkway at the top center door to find it.

Snake (Tuxedo)

Follow the hall you start in, ducking into the second opening on your left. Facing the locked door, look to your left to find the first bomb. Proceed up to the connecting bridge. Walk almost to the far end and look to the right just in front of the door. A bomb is attached to a large canister there. Go inside and spray coolant in the far-right end of the planter to defuse another bomb. On the next connecting bridge, go outside and look to the left. There are six bombs attached to the wall, in the shape of the number 4. Continue to the sediment pool and find the last two bombs on the caged area in the center. You'll need to duck to see one of them, but they're both there.

Snake (MGS1)

Follow the hallway up and to the right, and then check behind the stack of boxes in the upper-right corner of the room. You must lie down to reach this bomb with your coolant. Walk out onto the connecting bridge and turn around once you pass the broken section to your right. Look under the walkway to find another bomb. Go over to the kitchen and defuse the bomb on the back of the guard, and then walk into the food preparation area and look inside the bucket under the center table for another. When you arrive at the next connecting bridge, look to your left to find the bomb attached to the cipher patrolling the area. Get as close as you can to it so you can spray the bomb with coolant. The remaining bombs are located in the sediment pool room ahead. Sneak out to the middle section of the room to grab a much-needed M9. Continue to the far side of the room and go to the lower level. There's a bomb on the ground across the railing, and another one attached to the guardrail above. The final bomb is fastened to a guard patrolling the area. Track him down to defuse the final bomb.

ELIMINATE MODE MISSIONS

Level 01

On these missions, accidentally raising the alarm does not cause swarms of troops to pour in. You only have to contend with a fixed number of enemies per level.

Raiden

Once again, you must wipe out all soldiers in the area. You'll find two guards on the top walkway and two on the bottom. When they're all eliminated, head for the exit at the top of the bottom walkways.

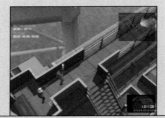   

Snake

This level is identical to Raiden's, with the addition of two more guards to take out

Pliskin

Pliskin's levels are a mix of Snake's and Raiden's, but he always starts with an M4. It's much easier to take out the guards with automatic fire!

Snake (MGS1)

MGS1 Snake starts with an absurdly low amount of ammunition and no radar, in addition to having the highly alert guards.

Level 02

10001650 2117

Raiden

This level is actually easier than the first one. Make your way down a single corridor, and dispose of the three guards you encounter. No problem at all. The exit is at the end of the corridor.

Snake

There are now four guards, with one inside the locker room in the center of the corridor. It's still a piece of cake, though!

Level 03

Mission Parameters

First Place Score	19500
Time Limit	2:30
Targets	4
Difficulty	3

Raiden

Back on the Big Shell, you must snipe four targets from a distance. Step out onto the walkway, pop a Pentazemin, and zoom in with the PSG1. There's a guard at the opposite end of your walkway and another one above him on the higher walkways. Swing back down to where you shot the first guard to catch another one, and finish up with a soldier on the roof once again. You must be quick and accurate to take them out without raising an alarm. Run across the walkway to find the exit.

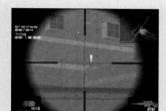
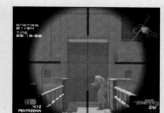

Snake

There are still two soldiers on the roof, but now there are also two soldiers who stay on the bottom walkway and one who walks up and down the stairs. You need to move around a bit to snipe the soldiers on the bottom level

---

Level 04

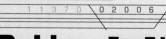

Mission Parameters

First Place Score	18000
Time Limit	2:30
Targets	4
Difficulty	2

Raiden

The targets are scattered around the room in which you start, so quietly eliminate them for the best score. You should be able to take them out with minimal effort. The exit is in the bottom-right corner of this area.

Level 05

Raiden

Mission Parameters	
First Place Score	21000
Time Limit	3:00
Targets	4
Difficulty	3

The quickest way to wipe out these guards is with the liberal use of stun grenades. There are three guards in the hallway, and one in the central control room. Try to take out multiple guards with a single grenade to minimize your effort. The exit is in the top-left corner of the control room.

Level 06

Raiden

Mission Parameters	
First Place Score	35000
Time Limit	5:00
Targets	6
Difficulty	3

Take a slow approach to this level to minimize your effort. Go up from the starting point, follow the hallway to the left, and then go down. The guards are more or less evenly spaced out as you go. The exit is a door to your left in the last corridor.

Level 07

Raiden

Mission Parameters	
First Place Score	32000
Time Limit	5:00
Targets	7
Difficulty	3

More guards to be eliminated? Good thing you brought extra ammo. Make a sweeping path up and to the left, and then head back down and left. The difficulty of this mission revolves around how closely the guards patrol near one another. Follow the corridor around the perimeter of the level until you reach the exit at the top right.

Level 08

Raiden

1 0 3 2 0 0 3 0 3 7 1

Mission Parameters	
First Place Score	35000
Time Limit	5:00
Targets	5
Difficulty	3

This area has two levels. The top floor has two guards, and the bottom floor has three. Just take it a floor at time, quietly picking off each guard. Walk downstairs, take out the guards, and head for the exit in the center of the room

Level 09

Raiden

9 8 0 1 0 1 0 0

0 0 3 2 0 0 2 0 0 6 9

Mission Parameters	
First Place Score	30000
Time Limit	5:00
Targets	7
Difficulty	3

This is another two-level area, so use caution when moving about. There are four guards on the bottom level and three on the top. After disposing of all the guards, the exit appears at the top right of the level.

Level 10

Raiden

Mission Parameters	
First Place Score	29000
Time Limit	5:00
Targets	7
Difficulty	4

The final challenge adds stealth soldiers to the mix. There are two invisible soldiers, one on each side of the level. You must look carefully to spot them. Take out three soldiers on the right side of the level, and the remaining four on the left. The exit appears on the top-left platform.

HOLD UP MODE MISSIONS

Level 01

Raiden

Mission Parameters	
First Place Score	21000
Time Limit	3:00
Targets	1
Difficulty	1

The objective for these missions is to sneak up behind each enemy and hold him up. As soon as his hands are in the air, you can move on. To start with, you only have one guard on this level. Run straight ahead, hold him up, and step into the goal.

Snake

As a general rule, Snake usually has one more guard added to his levels. This doesn't significantly increase the difficulty, so don't worry. Stick with the Raiden strategy in most cases, allowing for the extra guard.

Pliskin

Fire off a shot beside the guard to make him turn away from you. Run up behind him and hold him up at gunpoint.

Level 02

Raiden

Mission Parameters	
First Place Score	20000
Time Limit	3:00
Targets	2
Difficulty	2

Stand at the starting point for a moment until the topmost guard on your radar turns away from you. As soon as he does, run out to the left and hold him up. Immediately run down, and stay to the left of the boxes below. Hold up the last target, and then run for the goal in the middle of the area.

Pliskin

Wait a moment for the left guard to look away from you, and then run down and hold up the right guard. Loop back up to hold up the remaining guard.

Level 03

Mission Parameters

First Place Score	18000
Time Limit	3:00
Targets	4
Difficulty	2

607 201 208 68

Raiden

Head to your right and down a flight of stairs, and then pause at the base of the second flight of stairs. Wait for the guard there to turn his back before you charge out and hold him up at gunpoint. Continue to the left and hold up the next guard ahead, and follow the corridor that leads to the control room. Once you reach the control room, wait for the guards to face away from you and then run in. Take out the one on the right first, and then the one on the left. The goal appears in the top-left corner of the room.

Pliskin

Take the left entrance down and pause at the bottom of the stairs, and wait for the guard to turn his back on you. Run down the hall to the right, and hold up the two guards there. Go to the control room and hold up the two guards patrolling the area.

Level 04

Mission Parameters

First Place Score	19000
Time Limit	3:00
Targets	2
Difficulty	2

11010

Raiden

Go out through the starting corridor and head outdoors, holding up the guard walking to the left as you go. Continue up the left walkway, and somersault over the grating on the floor so as not to make noise. Follow the walkway around to the right and down, still being careful not to walk on the grating. Hold up the final guard, and then walk back up and into the door-way above your position to find the goal.

Pliskin

Wait for the guard on the left walkway to come around the corner at the bottom and hold him up, and then run around the loop clockwise. Roll across the grating to remain quiet. Hold up the other guard at the other side.

Level 05

Raiden

071230154801010031200389

Mission Parameters	
First Place Score	19000
Time Limit	3:00
Targets	4
Difficulty	2

With a little careful timing, you can clear this mission in record time. Walk to your left and duck into the first doorway ahead on your right. Walk slowly up and wait for the guard to walk into your range. Then, run back and somersault down the stairs just below. You should land right beside another guard. Take care of him, and then run back up the stairs and out the door. Two guards should be just below your position, so hold up both of them at once. The goal is at the end of the hallway above.

Pliskin

Run around the corner and hold up the first guard you reach. This alerts another guard to check him out, so duck back behind the corner and wait for him to come into range. Go into the center room and hold up the guards there, and then run for the goal.

Level 06

Raiden

Mission Parameters	
First Place Score	18000
Time Limit	3:00
Targets	5
Difficulty	3

Run to your right and up, then duck behind the small crate against the left wall. The guard nearest you should walk past your position, giving you a chance to point your gun at him. Wait just a bit longer here in the hallway and wait for another guard to walk by. You know the drill by now. Go up around the walkway and find the third guard, and then back up against the top section of railing in the middle of the room and flip down. You should land behind another guard, and there's yet another nearby. Hold them both up and the exit appears in the center of the bottom floor.

Pliskin

Use Raiden's strategy, except you should pause at the beginning of the level and wait for the guards to turn around before charging forward.

Level 07
Raiden

Mission Parameters	
First Place Score	18000
Time Limit	3:00
Targets	4
Difficulty	2

This level is pretty straightforward, so if you keep moving you'll reach the high score. Head to your left, following the hallway as it completes a circular loop. The four guards are evenly spaced throughout the hallway. Just make sure they're not facing you as you approach. The exit is next to the starting point.

Level 08
Raiden

Mission Parameters	
First Place Score	15000
Time Limit	3:00
Targets	8
Difficulty	3

The targets for this area are spread over two levels. Take out all five guards on the lower level, and then go down to the bottom-right staircase. Wind back and forth across the catwalks as you take out the remaining three guards, using the crates stacked around the level for cover as needed. The goal appears in the top-right corner of the top level.

Level 09
Raiden

Mission Parameters	
First Place Score	19000
Time Limit	3:00
Targets	5
Difficulty	3

Fatman's area is the background for this mission. Swing around to the right of the giant boxes in the middle of the area, and cut to the left between them to hold up the first enemy. Continue to the left slightly, and you should be able to hold up two guards at once. Quickly run up and wait for the next guard to round the corner into your view, and then move down and to the left to find the last one. Head for your exit as it appears just below the harrier jet.

Level 10

Raiden

0200159801056730011 0400

Mission Parameters

First Place Score	18000
Time Limit	3:00
Targets	7
Difficulty	4

The final hold-up mission includes four soldiers using stealth outfits, so keep your eyes open for them. Start out by heading up the first hallway to take out the first guard. Go into the room on the left and hold up the invisible guard, and then retrace your steps and continue down the hallway. You encounter another invisible soldier standing next to the stacked crates. Keep going left, taking down another guard as you go. When you go up the stairs, duck into the door on the right and hold up the invisible guard here. Run across the hall, hide in the doorway opposite your current position, and wait for your next target to approach. After eliminating him, advance slowly because the final target is using stealth. The exit is at the top-right corner of this hallway.

Snake

Snake doesn't have the luxury of radar on this level, making it all the more challenging. Guard placement is very similar to Raiden's level.

Pliskin

Pliskin doesn't have radar on this level, but otherwise it's very similar to Raiden's level.

0200159801056730011 0400

012033401

0 00110010067

PHOTOGRAPH MISSIONS

Level 01

Mission Parameters

First Place Score	50000
Time Limit	5:00
Difficulty	1

Raiden

Each one of these missions requires you to take a specific photograph as quickly as possible. On this level, walk over to the lockers on the far-right wall. Look on top of the lockers to see a little tiki statue. Center it in your camera's viewfinder and snap the shot.

Snake ▮▮▯[▯]▯▮▮

Being more of a ladies' man, Snake prefers to take pictures of women. You'll have to take one of four possible pictures in one of four lockers: top left, bottom second row, bottom third row, or bottom fourth row.

Level 02

Mission Parameters	
First Place Score	48000
Time Limit	5:00
Difficulty	3

Raiden ▯▮▯▮▮▮▮▮▮▯

To complete this mission, you must get a shot of a guard jumping with his hands raised in the air. Walk down the hall a bit and place a magazine on the floor. Knock on the wall and run back to the starting point. As the guard rounds the corner, he sees the magazine. Zoom in with your camera as he jumps down to read it to get your shot.

Snake ▮▮▯[▯]▯▮▮

Again, Snake gets to take pictures of women. There are two variants of this level, but the strategy for getting the snapshots is the same. Sneak up behind the lone guard on this level and wait for him to type on a computer. When the screen on the computer changes, break the guard's neck and take a photo of the girl on the computer desktop.

Level 03

Raiden

Another unusual assignment. This time you must get a shot of an exclamation point over a guard's head! Sneak into the lounge area and stand at the entrance to the bar, facing the magazine racks at the other end of the room. Zoom in with your camera and wait. The guard patrolling the room walks into your path and sees you. This triggers his exclamation point. Make sure you're zoomed in on it, and quickly snap the picture.

Snake

This time, Snake must find a girl whose pose matches a silhouette. Go down to the bottom of the room and walk to the second locker from the right. Open the door and snap a picture.

Level 04

Raiden

This level is a bit sneaky. The objective states that you need a picture of the stars. However, a quick glance to the sky reveals a heavy layer of clouds. It's up to you to make your *own* stars. Equip the empty Nikita and head up the stairs to the top deck. Take a swing at the guard standing there to knock him out, and then snap a picture of the stars circling his head.

Snake

Similar to the last level, you must find a girl to match the pose presented in a silhouette. This time, however, you have a real moving girl to photograph. Go through the door on the left and look to the left across the level. You should see Meryl walking around on a platform. Wait until her hands are behind her head and snap away.

Level 05

11010
071230154801010031200389

Mission Parameters

First Place Score	48000
Time Limit	5:00
Difficulty	1

Raiden

Here you must find a ghost soldier who wanders the decks. Flip over the ledge behind the starting point and turn around when you land. See the guard patrolling here? He has no vision cone on your radar. He must be the ghost! Just take any old shot of him to complete this mission.

Snake

This level is a bit different from the others, but it's very easy nonetheless. You must snap a shot of the person who killed Raiden. Just walk to the bottom of the room and zoom in. You should see Fatman skating around. Get any shot of him and you're set.

Level 06

Mission Parameters

First Place Score	48000
Time Limit	5:00
Difficulty	2

Raiden

Walk up the hall until you find the dead crewman lying on the floor. Get out the USP and shoot out the light above him. Then equip your camera and take a shot of the ghost that appears.

Snake

Another whodunit photo, just as easy as the last one. Walk up to the top of the room and look into the glass. You'll see an older man standing in the room. Give him a second or two and he'll suddenly do some backflips! When he lands, grab a shot of him.

Level 07

97001236

Snake

Snake must now photograph close-ups of body parts of the women from Level One. There are also five variations, using the same lockers from the first level, with the addition of a locker on the leftmost row. You now must open the bottom locker to find one of your objectives.

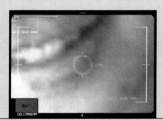

07713
6 3 0 0 3 2 8 4 2 0 0 8 2   2 0 0 2 0 0 1 5 1 9 3 7 1 0 0 2 1 4 0 5 0 1 9   0 1 5 1 9 3 7 1 0 0

SNAKE TALES

The Snake Tales are a group of missions that take elements of the Sons of Liberty scenario and change them to add Snake. Each one has a self-contained story to read, but keep in mind that they aren't strictly tied to the actual main storyline. This will quickly become apparent when you duel Meryl or challenge Solidus in a duel with your bare hands...

A Wrongdoing

Snake has been sent to infiltrate Big Shell and save the President. Unfortunately, you don't have use of your radar. You start out on top of Strut A. Go downstairs and out the door on the right side of the middle area. Go across the walkway here to reach Strut F.

Once you're inside Strut F, clear out all of the enemy guards on the top floor. Head for the door in the top-left section of the center area. You meet Ames here. Listen to his story, and then move out.

You can choose which route to take, so head to the Shell One core. Make a loop around the first floor to reach a locker room at the end of the hall. Look inside one of the lockers at the bottom of the room to find the Directional Mic, and then go to the elevator at the top of the level. Head for B1 and go left and down, then take the first door on your right.

Inside the auditorium, you must now locate Jennifer, the agent who was captured when the Big Shell was taken by terrorists. You must completely avoid the guard here. If you harm him, the terrorists will kill the hostages. Using the D. Mic, you must find Jennifer by pinpointing the sound of a cell phone dialing. Jennifer's location is random, so keep looking. When you find her, she gives you a key card to get into B2.

Head back to the elevator and go to B2. Go to the central control room and look beneath the computer console in the middle of the room. There's a bomb here. Defuse it and then head back upstairs toward Strut A. To cross the walkway with the missing tiles, simply press your back up against the railing and walk slowly across. Head for the helipad on top of Strut A to face Fatman. This battle is exactly like the one in the main game story, so follow the strategy from the main walkthrough. The mission ends when Fatman is down.

Big Shell Evil

Otacon wants Snake to help locate his long-lost sister Emma, so it's back to Big Shell for another mission. You land on Strut E, and you must go to Strut C to find Emma. She's in the kitchen, and when you find her there, you must defend her from an onslaught of guards.

Once you've cleared out the guards, head for Strut B. Go through the door to the right and walk to the bottom of the lower level. A computer terminal is waiting for you here. After you grab the data, you learn that Emma has been captured and taken to Strut F! You must fight back there because the door from B to A is locked.

Once you reach Strut F, you must avoid detection until you find Emma. She's in the room below and to the right of the center area. She cannot move quickly, so grab her hand and lead her outside. When you reach the F-E connecting bridge, toss a chaff grenade so you can walk across easily. Inside Strut E, you're ambushed by an endless stream of guards. While protecting Emma, go to the left exit in the room. When you finally make it out, you face a Harrier jet! Once again, this fight is the same as the Harrier battle in the full game, so follow the strategy presented in the full walkthrough. When the Harrier is destroyed, this mission ends.

Confidential Legacy

In search of Meryl, Snake decides to go to the tanker and check around for her. You start on the main deck of the ship. Run up and take the unlocked door on the left. Once you're inside, follow the hallway to the right and up. You come out on the right side of the lounge. Continue upstairs until you reach the ship's main control room. You run into Meryl here. After you speak to her, proceed down to the engine room.

When you arrive in the engine room, go over to the left side and out the door. Head up the hall to a door laden with C4. You must shoot out the bomb detonators to continue. Climb onto a turbine and look to the right of the doorway to find the first detonator. Walk down the hall a bit and look to the right side for the second detonator, then look further down on the left behind the last C4 for the third one. Go through this door and follow the hallway down and to the right.

You then get ambushed by a group of guards. Take out an automatic weapon and mow them all down. When you're done, Snake receives some disturbing news about Meryl. You must now run through lots of enemies as you try to escape. Again, run and fire with an automatic weapon to plow out of this trap. After you make it out of the hallway, head back up to the control room to confront Meryl. This battle is just like the Olga fight from the main game. When she goes down, the mission ends.

Deadman Whispers

This time, Snake is in his Pliskin persona. It's up to you to save some marines from Vamp. Pliskin starts out in the bottom of Strut F with no ammunition, so you'll need to be sneaky to make it through successfully.

Go to Strut B. Once you've been briefed on the situation, walk around the level to collect ammunition. Proceed to Strut D, and then to the B1 level of Strut E. Climb down across an oil fence and go to Strut L. Take the KL Bridge and head to the left into the Shell Two core.

Inside, collect the weapons and ammo, then climb on top of the boxes at the bottom of the first set of stairs you came down. Fire the Nikita into the vent at eye level, and guide it through the vent system. When the rocket reaches an open area, cut to the right and reenter another vent. Continue guiding the missile until it reaches an open room, and then steer for the lockers in the top-right corner. Blowing up these boxes disables the electric flooring that blocked your path earlier. Go down the hall and to the left to read more of the story, then proceed to the elevator at the top of the floor when you're done.

Go to B1 and face Vamp! The Vamp battle is exactly like the later battle Raiden faces in the main game. After defeating Vamp, the mission ends.

External Gazer

Run out on the walkway to the right and pause. You can see the water churning, and Snake has a flashback to what he was doing up to this point. Suddenly, you're in a bomb disposal mission! See the section on Level 02 in the "Bomb Disposal Missions" chapter for the strategy to find all of the bombs. Next, you face Level 06 of the "Eliminate Mode" scenario. Just shoot all of the enemies and run for the goal on the left side of the level.

You're finally back on Big Shell on the CD connecting bridge. Walk toward C, read the story, and head for the AB bridge. When you arrive, get your camera out! You must catch some shots of Gurlugon, the giant monster from another dimension. The monster pokes its head out of the water on occasion, so you must be zoomed in and ready to shoot when it appears. You need to get a clear shot of its head and face, with no railing in the shot. When you get a good shot, a stream of enemies pours onto the walkway. Run to a doorway for cover, and then take them all out. Finally, you square off against Gurlugon in a VR mission just like Snake's Level 07 in the "Variety Mode Missions" chapter. Use that strategy to defeat this boss.

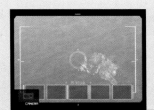

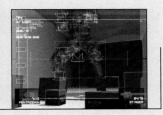

When you're done reading, you must face Snake's Level 03 of the Sneaking mission, and then Level 03 of the Handgun VR mission. Next, you must complete Level 05 of the Eliminate All mission and Level 08 of the Sneaking mission. Then it's on to Level 01 of Raiden's Bomb Disposal mission. Luckily, you can just exit the mission to regain control as Snake and continue on. You must now face a squad of Metal Gear Ray units, and employ the strategy you learned from the main game.

The final battle is against Solidus, but you have no weapons! Dodge his attacks, and punch and kick him when there's an opening. You can usually hit him before or after he swings his swords at you. Grab the pair of Rations in the corners as well. Defeat Solidus to complete this lengthy and challenging mission.

SECRETS AND BONUSES

Conquering *Metal Gear Solid 2* is only the beginning. There are several dozen secrets in the game, which serve as interesting and amusing nuances that encourage playing through the game multiple times. There are also secret items and hidden modes of play that you can open by completing the game. Following are just a few of the game's many secrets. How many more can you find?

GAME NUANCES

This section lists a lot of the little things you might have missed while playing *Metal Gear Solid 2* the first time through. They are all available to see during your first game if you have a keen eye.

Title Screen Titillation

While you're staring at the title screen and Snake's red mug, you can manipulate the background's position and color by moving the Right Stick. Press the White button and a gunshot will sound.

Codec Craziness

While watching any Codec conversation, move the Right and Left Sticks and the characters' faces will move. Press on the sticks, and the faces will zoom in close. Press the Right trigger button while Snake or Raiden is listening to someone, and you can hear their thoughts. Some of the guys' secret attitudes toward the other characters are quite funny!

Camera Surveillance

Equip the Scope, the Camera, or the Digital Camera and watch soldiers from a distance. Press the Action button and something strange but useful happens; if you have collected that soldier's Dog Tags, his name will be displayed. This helps you determine which guards remain to be captured.

Different Olga Cinemas

Depending on which side of the Port Navigational Deck you defeat Olga Gurlukovich during the "Tanker" episode, the cinema afterward changes slightly. If you defeat her on the left side of the area, she is seen hanging over the rail in the cinema. Defeat her on the right side, and she is slumped against an open crate. All of the camera angles are changed accordingly.

Cinema Control

During any of the cinemas depicting real-time events in the game, press the Right trigger button to zoom in on the scene. Then move the Right Stick to move the camera. This is a great way to examine the fantastic amount of detail in the character modeling and background textures.

Calisthenics and Stunts

Either character can improve the level of his Grip Gauge by doing pull-ups from a rail. Hang over any rail and press the two trigger buttons simultaneously to exercise. Do 100 pull-ups, and the Grip Gauge will increase in level. After an indeterminate number of additional pull-ups, the Grip Gauge will max out at Level 3.

This will be sufficient to level up the Grip Gauge in your first game. However, in your second game, the Grip Gauge can only be leveled up through "rail drops." A rail drop can be performed when two platforms are directly on top of one another, so that the character can drop from one railing and grab the next one down before falling to his death. To do this, jump over the top rail and hang. Then press ⊗ to drop down to the next level. As you're falling, press ① again with just the right timing to grab the rail. Perform this a couple of times, and the Grip Gauge will go up. Continue repeating this maneuver and the character will reach Level 3. Raiden can perform this move anywhere in Strut E, and Snake can perform it on the starboard side of the Engine Room, using the top two levels. There is also a place at the top of Hold No.1 where he can do rail drops. A high Grip Gauge is essential to collecting every Dog Tag in the Tanker episode, since Snake must shimmy across the top of Hold No.1 to reach the marines on the upper level.

In subsequent games, you'll need to perform a combination of pull-ups and rail drops to level up your Grip Gauge. Good luck!

Tanker Shortcuts

Use First Person Mode at the top of the Engine Room, and you'll notice a wire that extends from one side of the room to the other. Leap over the back rail and shimmy onto the wire. It helps if you have a leveled-up Grip Gauge!

When sneaking into the cargo holds, look for hatches at the back of each room. There is a hatch that Snake can climb into at the back of Hold No.1. Crawl through the vent into Hold No.2, and look for another hatch on the other side of the projectors. Crawl through this vent, and you'll reach Hold No.3 with no problems! Also, look for wires that span the upper levels of the holds...

Photo Evidence

During the "Tanker" episode, use the Camera to take pictures of things like the pinups in the lockers, Olga sleeping, the muscular chest on the outside of the locker, and the Vulcan Raven action figure. You know you have a worthy shot when Snake makes a sound or says something. Play through the "Tanker" chapter without restarting the game, and when you reach Hold No.3, transmit your photos to Otacon. His reactions to these kinds of photos are very amusing.

Mei Ling's Cameo Appearance

Each time you call Otacon and save your game in the Tanker episode, he will try to reassure Snake with philosophical quotes, but he's horrible at it. If you call him and save your game enough times, Mei Ling from Metal Gear Solid will come on the line to gripe out Otacon. Save your game five times before the Olga boss fight, four times afterward and four more times after entering Deck-2, Port.

Seagull Splatter

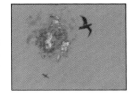

If you look up in the sky in First Person View and a bird flies over-head, droppings will land right on the camera!

Parcel Travel

Hop onto the conveyor on the east side of the Strut E Parcel Room and equip any Cardboard Box. You can ride the conveyor belt around the Big Shell. The box you equip determines where you are transported. The box marked "The Orange" takes you to Strut C, and the *Zone of the Enders* box takes you to the small room below where the Digital Camera is located. This is a good way to get the camera earlier in the game. Try using the other boxes and see where you end up!

Flashback Photos

In one of the flashback cinemas during the "Plant" episode, you will see the photos *you* took during the "Tanker" episode. Also, if you threw any guards overboard or knocked them over the railing, photos of this will be shown as well.

Hidden Books

There are five Books hidden above a locker on the west side of the Shell 1 Core's B2 level. Punch the locker until the door falls off, and the Books will fall from atop the lockers!

Nature Calls

Move around the Strut L Perimeter undetected, and a guard will start to pee off the side of the building. If you look up in First Person View, you can see Raiden is getting sprinkled. If you fire a warning shot upward at him, the guard will stop for a moment. When he decides the coast is clear, he goes right back to business.

Perverted Troopers

Leave open one of the lockers with a pinup on Deck-A of the Tanker. If soldiers come into the room on a "clearing" mission, they will stop and gawk at the pretty lady. We don't want to repeat the noises they make…

Very Easy . . . Too Easy!

In Very Easy Difficulty, you only have to access the Node once. All areas will appear on the Soliton Radar automatically for the rest of the game.

Steaming Stillman

When Stillman hides in the pantry, knock on the door or try to open the door. He responds each time. If you do this eight times, his reactions become quite amusing.

Fatman Fun

During the Fatman boss fight, watch for him to become stationary. Stop and watch him in First Person View. When Fatman is having fun with the seagulls, if one of them lands on his collar, it will peck at his head. Also, when Fatman is skating, it only takes one shot at his inline skates to knock him down.

Birdie Talk

The parrot in the Shell 1 Core's B2 Computer Room is fun to mess around with. If you fire bullets at it or spray the Coolant at the bird, it will imitate one of the guard's voices. If any of them are nearby, they will be instantly alerted! If two enemy soldiers stop and have a conversation in the upper portion of the room, wait until they are finished. Then go back to the parrot and view it in First Person. It will repeat their conversation, which reveals clues about where to find some hidden dirty books!

Easter Island Statues

There are four Easter Island MOAI statues that decorate various areas in the game. Use First Person View in every area to search for them.

Floating Debris

In the underwater areas of the Shell 2 Core, Filtration Chamber 1, swim to the last skylight at the south end of the west corridor and surface. There's a rubber ducky floating on the water, which represents a little inside humor.

In the corridor leading to the last area of Chamber 1, there is a second Vulcan Raven Action Figure floating near the doorway.

More Arsenal Gibberish

If you are killed in Arsenal Gear and use a Continue, when Raiden reenters the area the name will be displayed in gibberish.

Imprinted Dog Tags

At the end of the game, the information that you entered during the first login to the Node will appear on Raiden's Dog Tags, nicely imprinted into the metal.

Ghost of Kojima

In Hold No. 2, take a picture of the right screen with the camera that Snake uses to photograph RAY. A face flashes on the screen when you take the picture. If you upload the photo for Otacon's viewing, he will be seriously creeped out. The face is Mr. Hideo Kojima, creator of the *Metal Gear* series!

Hidden Konami Eyes Girls

There are two more photos of Konami Eyes Girls hidden in the Engine Room. Stand near the M9 Bullets at the top of the starboard side, and search the port wall under the platform. Also, the central guard is using his binoculars to stare at another shapely lass.

Radar Weather Girl

When Raiden is waiting for Snake in the Arsenal Gear corridor, a short video featuring a Konami Eyes model will suddenly overtake the Soliton Radar display. Don't answer a Codec call while the video is playing, or it will disappear.

Pantless!

In Hold No. 1, descend the first ladder and use the camera to look over the rail. Zoom in on the soldiers below. One man isn't wearing any trousers. Take a photo of this and show it to Otacon, and he will really crack up!

Ocelot Spotted!

Use the floor hatch in Hold No. 2, and enter Hold No. 3 by crawling through the underground vents. In Hold No. 3, climb the ladder and stand on the platform. Equip the camera, and look down at the leg of RAY. Hidden just behind the leg is the menacing figure of Ocelot, planning his attack! If you look away, move, or do anything else, he disappears. If you manage to take a photo of Ocelot and show it to Otacon, he will be really creeped out!

REPLAY VALUES

Following are things you'll notice about *Metal Gear Solid 2* in a replay game.

Clear Code

Jot down the code at the end of any episode. Then go to the *Metal Gear Solid 2* website and input the code. Your code contains information about your ranking, which will be displayed for you.

To receive a better clear code, replay the entire game and move with better stealth. Complete the harder difficulty levels, finish the entire game quickly, don't kill anyone you don't have to, don't use a Continue, and don't save your game. Your ranking is a summary of everything you see on the Result screen after the credits.

Standing at Attention

During your second game, all the Marines in the last Hold of the Tanker will be missing their trousers.

Different Title Screen

Clear the game once, and the title screen will feature a blue image of Raiden. Clear the game again, and it goes back to Snake's red face. Metal Gear RAY can be seen in the background of the next screen.

Skip the Dialogue

Certain scenes that you couldn't skip in your first game can be skipped in replay games. Press START or ● to skip a scene.

Plant Chapter: Big Shell Facility

DIFFICULTY SETTING: VERY EASY

✓	DOG TAG	LOCATION
	000	Arsenal Gear – Ascending Colon
	001	Strut A Deep Sea Dock
	002	
	003	Strut A Roof
	004	Strut A Pump Room
	005	
	006	AB Connecting Bridge
	007	
	008	Strut B Transformer Room
	009	
	010	BC Connecting Bridge
	011	Strut C Dining Hall
	012	
	013	CD Connecting Bridge
	014	
	015	Strut D Sediment Pool
	016	
	017	DE Connecting Bridge
	018	
	019	Strut E Parcel Room
	020	
	021	Strut E Heliport
	022	
	023	Strut F warehouse
	024	
	025	FA Connecting Bridge
	026	Shell 1 Core, 1F
	027	
	028	
	029	Shell 1 Core, B1
	030	
	031	
	032	Shell 1 Core, B2 Computer Room
	033	
	034	
	035	
	036	KL Connecting Bridge
	037	Strut L Sewage Treatment Facility
	038	
	039	Shell 2 Core, 1F Air Purification Room
	040	
	041	
	042	Strut E Heliport

DIFFICULTY SETTING: EASY

✓	DOG TAG	LOCATION
	000	Arsenal Gear – Ascending Colon
	001	Strut A Deep Sea Dock
	002	
	003	Strut A Roof
	004	Strut A Pump Room
	005	
	006	AB Connecting Bridge
	007	
	008	Strut B Transformer Room
	009	
	010	BC Connecting Bridge
	011	Strut C Dining Hall
	012	
	013	CD Connecting Bridge
	014	
	015	Strut D Sediment Pool
	016	
	017	DE Connecting Bridge
	018	
	019	Strut E Parcel Room
	020	
	021	Strut E Heliport
	022	
	023	Strut F Warehouse
	024	
	025	
	026	FA Connecting Bridge
	027	Shell 1 Core, 1F
	028	
	029	
	030	Shell 1 Core, B1
	031	
	032	
	033	Shell 1 Core, B2 Computer Room
	034	
	035	
	036	
	037	KL Connecting Bridge
	038	Strut L Sewage Treatment Facility
	039	
	040	Shell 2 Core, 1F Air Purification Room
	041	
	042	
	043	Strut E Heliport

DIFFICULTY SETTING: NORMAL

✓	DOG TAG	LOCATION
	000	Arsenal Gear – Ascending Colon
	001	Strut A Roof
	002	Strut A Pump Room
	003	
	004	AB Connecting Bridge
	005	
	006	Strut B Transformer Room
	007	
	008	BC Connecting Bridge
	009	Strut C Dining Hall
	010	
	011	CD Connecting Bridge
	012	
	013	Strut D Sediment Pool
	014	
	015	
	016	DE Connecting Bridge
	017	

✓	DOG TAG	LOCATION
	018	Strut E Parcel Room
	019	
	020	
	021	Strut E Heliport
	022	
	023	
	024	Strut F Warehouse
	025	
	026	
	027	FA Connecting Bridge
	028	Shell 1 Core, 1F
	029	
	030	
	031	

DIFFICULTY SETTING: NORMAL

✓	DOG TAG	LOCATION
	032	Shell 1 Core, B1
	033	
	034	
	035	Shell 1 Core, B2 Computer Room
	036	
	037	
	038	
	039	KL Connecting Bridge
	040	Strut L Sewage Treatment Facility
	041	
	042	Shell 2 Core, 1F Air Purification Room
	043	
	044	
	045	
	046	
	047	
	048	Strut E Heliport

DIFFICULTY SETTING: HARD

✓	DOG TAG	LOCATION
	000	Arsenal Gear – Ascending Colon
	001	Strut A Roof
	002	Strut A Pump Room
	003	
	004	AB Connecting Bridge
	005	
	006	Strut B Transformer Room
	007	
	008	BC Connecting Bridge
	009	Strut C Dining Hall
	010	
	011	CD Connecting Bridge
	012	
	013	Strut D Sediment Pool
	014	
	015	
	016	
	017	DE Connecting Bridge
	018	
	019	Strut E Parcel Room
	020	
	021	
	022	
	023	Strut E Heliport
	024	
	025	
	026	Strut F Warehouse
	027	
	028	
	029	
	030	FA Connecting Bridge
	031	Shell 1 Core, 1F
	032	
	033	
	034	
	035	Shell 1 Core, B1
	036	
	037	
	038	Shell 1 Core, B2 Computer Room
	039	
	040	
	041	
	042	KL Connecting Bridge
	043	Strut L Sewage Treatment Facility
	044	
	045	Shell 2 Core, 1F Air Purification Room
	046	
	047	
	048	
	049	
	050	
	051	Strut E Heliport

DIFFICULTY SETTING: EXTREME & EUROPEAN EXTREME

✓	DOG TAG	LOCATION
	000	Arsenal Gear – Ascending Colon
	001	Strut A Roof
	002	Strut A Pump Room
	003	
	004	AB Connecting Bridge
	005	
	006	Strut B Transformer Room
	007	
	008	BC Connecting Bridge
	009	Strut C Dining Hall
	010	
	011	CD Connecting Bridge
	012	
	013	Strut D Sediment Pool
	014	
	015	
	016	
	017	DE Connecting Bridge
	018	
	019	Strut E Parcel Room
	020	
	021	
	022	
	023	
	024	Strut E Heliport
	025	
	026	
	027	Strut F Warehouse
	028	
	029	
	030	
	031	
	032	FA Connecting Bridge
	033	Shell 1 Core, 1F
	034	
	035	
	036	
	037	Shell 1 Core, B1
	038	
	039	
	040	Shell 1 Core, B2 Computer Room
	041	
	042	
	043	
	044	KL Connecting Bridge
	045	Strut L Sewage Treatment Facility
	046	
	047	Shell 2 Core, 1F Air Purification Room
	048	
	049	
	050	
	051	
	052	
	053	Strut E Heliport

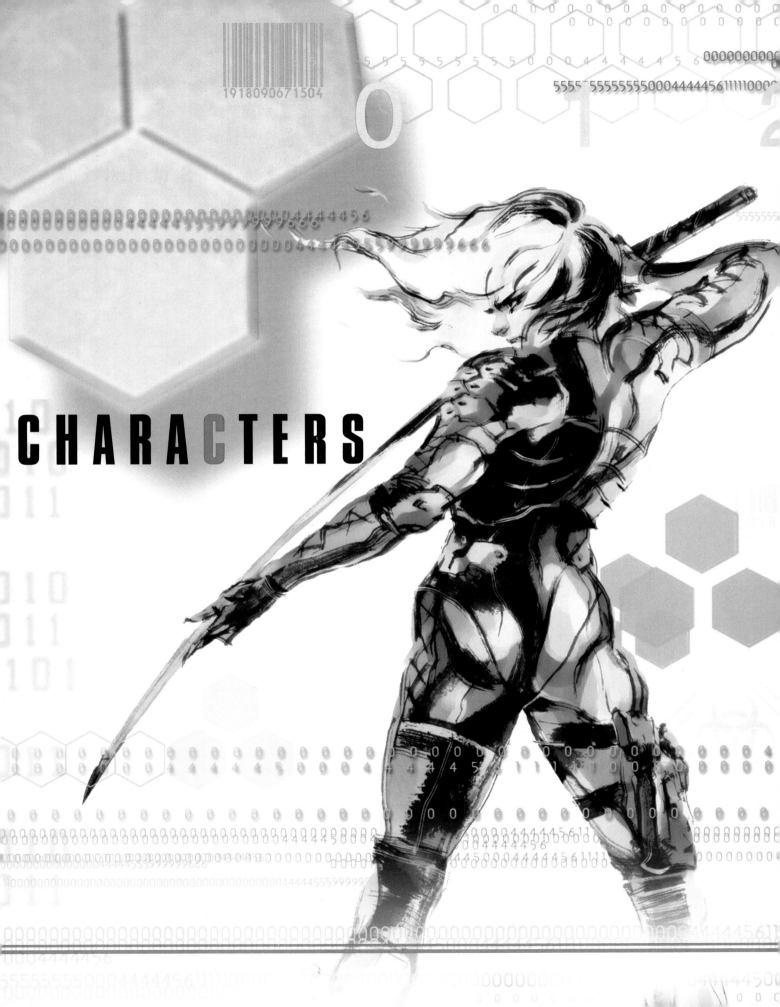

CHARACTERS

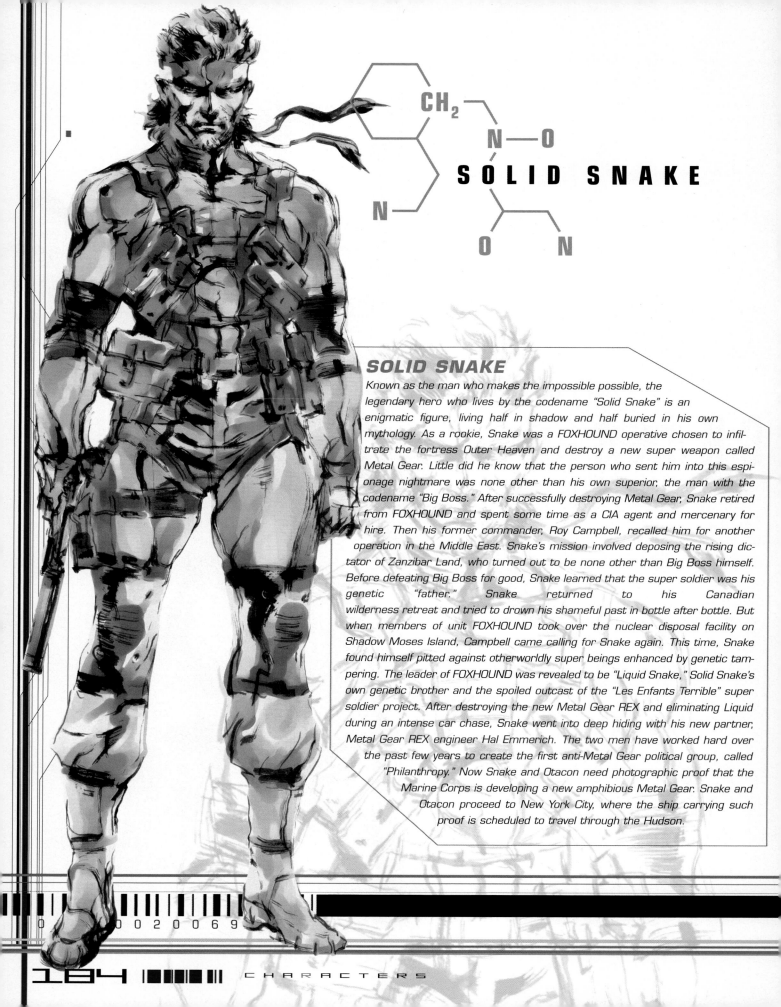

SOLID SNAKE

$$CH_2$$

SOLID SNAKE

Known as the man who makes the impossible possible, the legendary hero who lives by the codename "Solid Snake" is an enigmatic figure, living half in shadow and half buried in his own mythology. As a rookie, Snake was a FOXHOUND operative chosen to infiltrate the fortress Outer Heaven and destroy a new super weapon called Metal Gear. Little did he know that the person who sent him into this espionage nightmare was none other than his own superior, the man with the codename "Big Boss." After successfully destroying Metal Gear, Snake retired from FOXHOUND and spent some time as a CIA agent and mercenary for hire. Then his former commander, Roy Campbell, recalled him for another operation in the Middle East. Snake's mission involved deposing the rising dictator of Zanzibar Land, who turned out to be none other than Big Boss himself. Before defeating Big Boss for good, Snake learned that the super soldier was his genetic "father." Snake returned to his Canadian wilderness retreat and tried to drown his shameful past in bottle after bottle. But when members of unit FOXHOUND took over the nuclear disposal facility on Shadow Moses Island, Campbell came calling for Snake again. This time, Snake found himself pitted against otherworldly super beings enhanced by genetic tampering. The leader of FOXHOUND was revealed to be "Liquid Snake," Solid Snake's own genetic brother and the spoiled outcast of the "Les Enfants Terrible" super soldier project. After destroying the new Metal Gear REX and eliminating Liquid during an intense car chase, Snake went into deep hiding with his new partner, Metal Gear REX engineer Hal Emmerich. The two men have worked hard over the past few years to create the first anti-Metal Gear political group, called "Philanthropy." Now Snake and Otacon need photographic proof that the Marine Corps is developing a new amphibious Metal Gear. Snake and Otacon proceed to New York City, where the ship carrying such proof is scheduled to travel through the Hudson.

6 0 7 2 0 1 2 0 8 6 8

HAL EMMERICH,
a.k.a. "OTACON"

During the events on Shadow Moses Island, Solid Snake saved Hal Emmerich from the mysterious Cyborg Ninja. The two men could not be less alike. While Snake had the cold and detached attitude of a heartless mercenary, Emmerich was an upbeat and optimistic scientist. Another difference was Hal's somewhat childish love of Japanese Anime. Emmerich adopted the nickname "Otacon," taken from the Otaku Anime Convention, which occurs in Japan every year. Snake now refers to him solely by this name. Snake revealed to Otacon that he had been deceived by Armstech president Kenneth Baker into creating a prototype weapon of nightmarish proportions, the nuclear-equipped walking battle tank named Metal Gear REX. Emmerich's family has a dark history in science; his ancestors were responsible for the atomic bomb, among other twentieth century weapons of mass destruction. The news wounded Otacon deeply, and he resolved to help Snake destroy REX. After a tense battle with FOXHOUND leader Liquid Snake, they escaped Shadow Moses together. Since then, Otacon has worked with Snake to create the anti-Metal Gear coalition called "Philanthropy." Recently, Otacon was able to convince the United Nations to recognize "Philanthropy" as a legitimate political organization. But further proof of covert Metal Gear development is required to make the dream of "Philanthropy" into a reality. Snake and Otacon infiltrate the military installations and facilities of the world, delving into their compounds through stealth and cyber hacking. In a sense, Snake is the brawn and Otacon is the brains behind "Philanthropy."

O
OH_4
H — OTACON

OLGA GURLUKOVICH

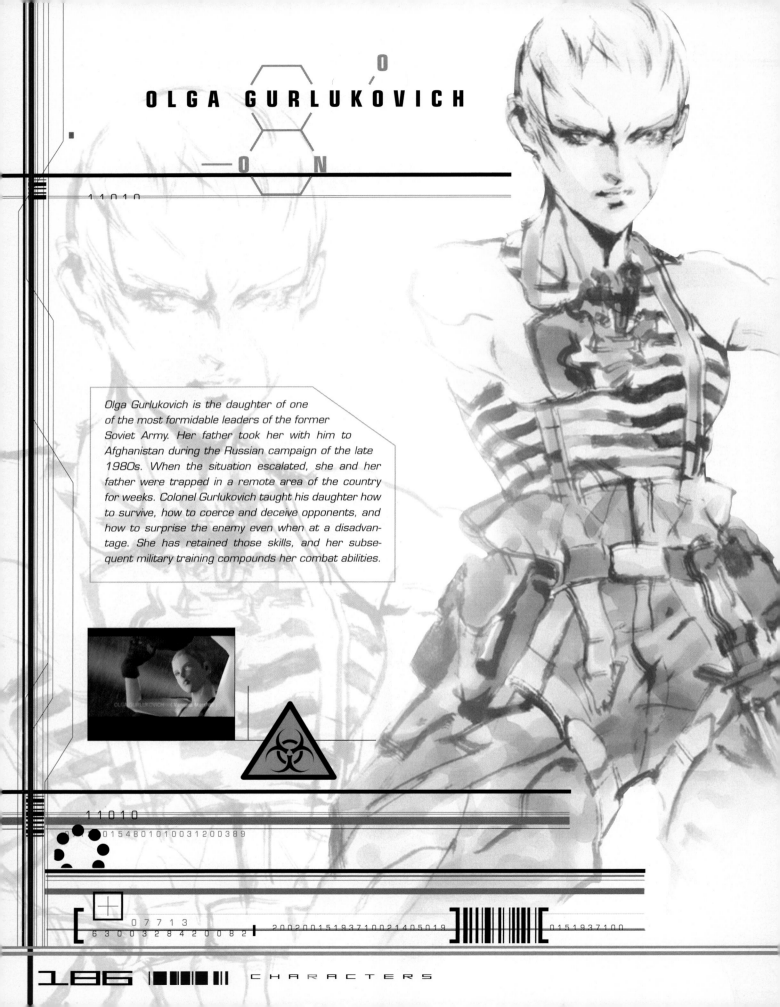

Olga Gurlukovich is the daughter of one of the most formidable leaders of the former Soviet Army. Her father took her with him to Afghanistan during the Russian campaign of the late 1980s. When the situation escalated, she and her father were trapped in a remote area of the country for weeks. Colonel Gurlukovich taught his daughter how to survive, how to coerce and deceive opponents, and how to surprise the enemy even when at a disadvantage. She has retained those skills, and her subsequent military training compounds her combat abilities.

REVOLVER OCELOT

G   O
H₃

11010

11010

Shalashaska, a.k.a. "Revolver" Ocelot

A well known terrorist from the Shadow Moses Incident two years ago, "Revolver" is the Russian double agent who stole the exercise data of the Metal Gear REX combat test, and sold the specifications for the weapon on the international black market. His two names indicate more than just the duplicity of his nature, each also represents a different aspect of his personality. "Revolver" is an expert marksman with superhuman quick-draw skills and a love of old-time American cowboy films. There is no man who handles a pair of six shooters better. As for "Shalashaska," the prisoners of Russia bestowed this name upon him while he was working as an interrogation methods consultant to the Soviet Spetsnaz during the Cold War. A brutal and highly intelligent former FOXHOUND agent, Ocelot's cunning is a perfect match for Solid Snake's razor sharp survival skills. But as we soon witness, there seems to be another factor currently affecting Ocelot's behavior...

SOLIDUS SNAKE

VAMP

"Dead Cell"

P—H
H
O
FORTUNE
C₄
O

Dead Cell is a highly skilled anti-terrorist training squad developed under the Navy SEALS with the guidance of former U.S. President George Sears. Their purpose was to stage random terrorist simulations to test the countermeasures of the SEALS and other military branches. Six months ago, all of that changed when former Dead Cell leader Colonel Jackson was arrested on charges of corruption and misappropriation of funds. It was a devastating event for the group, and apparently they snapped. They began attacking various military installations as well as federal office buildings. They are as ruthless as the terrorists they were trained to emulate, and their knowedge of military anti-terrorist respons measures makes Dead Cell a formidable enemy.

The name was originally intended to reflect its anti-terrorist functions.

N
C
C
FATMAN
CH₄
C

CHARACTERS

RAIDEN

$$N \!-\! O \quad H \!-\! OH$$
$$O \quad CH_3$$

The rookie operative codenamed "Raiden" is an unseasoned veteran of over 300 VR missions, plus the full simulations of Shadow Moses, Zanzibar, and Outer Heaven. While fully trained in the required abilities of a FOXHOUND agent, he has never tasted true battle. However, the comfort he displays in the field indicates that this young man has a bright future in the shadow services, and he may one day even fill the gigantic shoes of the legendary Solid Snake. Under the guidance of Snake's former ally and personal friend, Colonel Roy Campbell, Raiden is sure to liberate the Big Shell from the evil clutches of Dead Cell. He just needs to settle things with his girlfriend, Rose, who acts as mission analyst and can't seem to get the hang of referring to him by his designated codename.

9 0 0 1 7 5 0 3 4   0 8 4 1 5
0 1 3 9 8 0 1 0 1 0 0 2 1 7 0 0 3 9 7

1   0   0 2 0 0 6

Emma is the younger sister of the brilliant Armstech engineer, Hal Emmerich, also known as "Otacon." Hal was the lead designer on the Metal Gear REX project and developer of the PAN Card Security system in the Shadow Moses facility and in Big Shell. Living in a family of great scientists and inventors, Emma feels that she has a great deal to live up to. Pushing her mind and computer skills past their limits, she has created an Artificial Intelligence (AI) and programmed it into the computer system of the massive new Metal Gear project named Arsenal Gear. The sibling rivalry that has always existed between Emma and Otacon has never abated, and even a crisis situation such as this is not enough to curb Emma's need to prove herself to her famous older brother.

EMMA EMMERICH

TACTICAL ESPIONAGE ACTION

METAL GEAR SOLID 2
SUBSTANCE

BY DAN BIRLEW & PHILLIP MARCUS

BradyGAMES Publishing

An Imprint of Pearson Education
201 West 103rd Street
Indianapolis, Indiana 46290

ISBN: 0-7440-0226-5

Library of Congress Catalog No.: 2002114326

Printing Code: The rightmost double-digit number is the year of the book's printing; the rightmost single-digit number is the number of the book's printing. For example, 02-1 shows that the first printing of the book occurred in 2002.

04 03 02   4 3 2 1

Manufactured in the United States of America.

BradyGAMES Staff

PUBLISHER
DAVID WAYBRIGHT

EDITOR-IN-CHIEF
H. LEIGH DAVIS

MARKETING MANAGER
JANET ESHENOUR

CREATIVE DIRECTOR
ROBIN LASEK

ASSISTANT LICENSING MANAGER
MIKE DEGLER

ASSISTANT MARKETING MANAGER
SUSIE NIEMAN

Credits

TITLE MANAGERS
TIM FITZPATRICK
TIM COX

SCREENSHOT EDITOR
MICHAEL OWEN

LEAD BOOK DESIGNER
CAROL STAMILE

BOOK DESIGNER
CHRIS LUCKENBILL

PRODUCTION DESIGNER
BOB KLUNDER

MAPS BY
IDEA + DESIGN WORKS, LLC
WWW.IDEAANDDESIGNWORKS.COM

Acknowledgments

BradyGAMES would like to thank the entire Konami team. Many thanks to Hideo Kojima and the KCEJ Team for producing a Metal Gear title that upholds the tradition of redefining the state of the art. Many thanks to Ken Ogasawara, Tim Vogt, Jason Enos, Wilson Cheng, Monique Catley, and JoJo The Wonder Dog for their gracious assistance and expert game knowledge—this guide would not have been possible without you.

About the Author

Dan Birlew was born in St. Louis, Missouri, and lives in Las Vegas. Dan is the author of 20 official strategy guides, all published by BradyGAMES, including the *Zone of the Enders* and *Silent Hill 2* official strategy guides. The author would like to acknowledge the contributions of many folks to this guide. Thanks to Ken Ogasawara at Konami for his guidance and support on this text. Special thanks to my wife Laura for working so hard to get the best screenshots possible. And special thanks to my family for checking up on us and showing us how much we are loved.